Social Work Practice

4th Edition

Social Work Practice

Jonathan Parker & Greta Bradley

Los Angeles | London | New Delhi
Singapore | Washington DC

Learning Matters
An imprint of SAGE Publications Ltd
1 Oliver's Yard
55 City Road
London EC1Y 1SP

SAGE Publications Inc.
2455 Teller Road
Thousand Oaks, California 91320

SAGE Publications India Pvt Ltd
B 1/I 1 Mohan Cooperative Industrial Area
Mathura Road
New Delhi 110 044

SAGE Publications Asia-Pacific Pte Ltd
3 Church Street
#10-04 Samsung Hub
Singapore 049483

First published in 2003 by Learning Matters Ltd. Reprinted in 2003, 2004 (twice), 2005 (twice) and 2006.

Second edition published in 2007. Reprinted in 2008 (twice), 2009. Third edition published in 2010. Reprinted in 2011. Fourth edition published in 2014.

Editor: Luke Block
Production controller: Chris Marke
Project management: Deer Park Productions, Tavistock, Devon
Marketing manager: Tamara Navaratnam
Cover design: Wendy Scott
Typeset by: C&M Digitals (P) Ltd, Chennai, India
Printed by Henry Ling Limited at The Dorset Press, Dorchester, DT1 1HD

Library of Congress Control Number: 2014930437

British Library Cataloguing in Publication Data

A catalogue record for this book is available from the British Library.

ISBN 978-1-4462-9504-5(pbk)
ISBN 978-1-4462-9503-8

Contents

Acknowledgements

We offer our continued gratitude to those friends, colleagues and loved ones who have supported us during the preparation of the fourth edition of this book. We are also grateful to our students, past and present, and to colleagues who have offered criticism and made suggestions that have helped reframe our thinking year on year, although, of course, responsibility for the changes must remain with us. Finally, we would like to thank the staff at Learning Matters/SAGE, especially the unstinting work and passion of Luke Block, for their ongoing support for the *Transforming Social Work Practice* series.

Dedication

For Sara (JP)

Series Editors' Preface

The Western world, including England and the rest of the UK, faces numerous challenges over forthcoming years. These include dealing with the impact of an increasingly ageing population with its attendant social care needs and working with the financial implications that such a changing demography brings. At the other end of the lifespan the need for high quality childcare, welfare and safeguarding services has been highlighted as society develops and responds to the changing complexion.

Migration has developed as a global phenomenon and we now live and work with the implications of international issues in our everyday and local lives. Often these issues influence how we construct our social services and determine what services we need to offer. It is likely that as a social worker you will work with a diverse range of people throughout your career, many of whom have experienced significant, even traumatic, events that require a professional and caring response. As well as working with individuals, however, you may be required to respond to the needs of a particular community disadvantaged by world events or excluded within local communities because of assumptions made about them.

The importance of social work education came to the fore again following the inquiry into the death of baby Peter and the subsequent report from the Social Work Task Force set up in its aftermath. However, it is timely to reconsider elements of social work education – indeed, we should view this as a continual striving for excellence – as this allows us to focus clearly on what knowledge it is useful to engage with when learning to be a social worker.

The books in this series respond to the agendas driven by changes brought about by professional body, government and disciplinary review. They aim to build on and offer introductory texts based on up-to-date knowledge and to help communicate this in an accessible way, so preparing the ground for future study as you develop your social work career. The books are written by people passionate about social work and social services and aim to instil that passion in others. The current text introduces you to the processes involved in social work, setting the scene for exploring more specialised areas of practice.

Professor Jonathan Parker

Greta Bradley

Introduction

During the first decade of this century, social work education underwent a major transformation to ensure that qualified social workers were educated at least to honours degree level and developed knowledge, skills and values which are common and shared. At the time the third edition was published social work education and practice in England was under scrutiny once again following the report of the Social Work Task Force (2009) and a range of reviews into its being 'fit for purpose' (GSCC, 2009; House of Commons Children, Schools and Families Committee, 2009; 2010; Laming, 2009). Scotland underwent a major review of its social services in the last decade (Scottish Executive, 2006). Concerns at the time suggested that student social workers were not able to work at the required level and did not have the requisite knowledge, skills and qualities for qualified practice. Capacity for critical and reflective thinking was highlighted as central alongside the ability to apply knowledge to practice. The Social Work Reform Board developed the recommendations of the Task Force into an action plan for social work practice and education. An element of this will concern consolidation of learning in key areas. However, change being the only constant, and driven by political change in 2010, attacks on the 'soft target' of social work offered an opportunity to deflect attention from grave structural and welfare problems arising from ongoing austerity, while requirements for change continued unabated. These demands, supposedly concerned to improve social work quality, drew cross-party support and fuelled the agenda for separating social work into children and families services and adult social work. Support for such changes appears to be more reliant on ideology and securing popular political capital than robust evidence, presenting an anti-intellectual polemic and unfounded criticisms of social work in England and the rest of the UK (Professional Social Work, 2010; Parker and Doel, 2013). This book addresses some of the central elements of the process of social work.

A common vision for social work operating in complex human situations has been adopted. This is reflected in the following definition from the International Association of Schools of Social Work and International Federation of Social Workers, 2001:

> *The social work profession promotes social change, problem solving in human relationships and the empowerment and liberation of people to enhance well-being. Utilising theories of human behaviour and social systems, social work intervenes at the points where people interact with their environments. Principles of human rights and social justice are fundamental to social work.*

While there is a great deal packed into this short and pithy definition, and not everyone subscribes to it, it encapsulates the notion that social work concerns individual people and wider society. Social workers work with people who are vulnerable, who are struggling in some way to participate fully in society. Social workers walk that tightrope between individuals excluded from taking a place within society and the social and political environment that may have contributed to their marginalisation (Parker, 2007c). Because of the difficulties and disagreements resulting from this definition, the International Federation of Social Workers (IFSW) has consulted on and reformulated it with a view to gaining endorsement in Melbourne in July 2014. It is perhaps better to consider common principles and visions and, globally, to talk about many different types of social work. The important aspects are the concern for humanitarian actions and social justice.

Social workers need to be highly skilled and knowledgeable to work effectively in this context and successive government ministers have been keen for social work education and practice to improve, as seen in the recent review (Social Work Task Force, 2009). In order to improve your knowledge and skills, it is crucial that you, as a student social worker, develop a rigorous grounding in and understanding of theories and models for social work. Such knowledge helps social workers to know what to do, when to do it and how to do it, while recognising that social work is a complex human activity with no absolute 'rights' and 'wrongs' of practice for each situation. We agree with Jacqui Smith, the former Minister of Health responsible for developing the initial degree level qualifying award, in championing the practical focus of social work and of being able to apply our knowledge to help others, although not with the somewhat naïve and anti-intellectual stance implied in her foreword to the *Requirements for Social Work Training* (Department of Health, 2002a).

> *Social work is a very practical job. It is about protecting people and changing their lives, not about being able to give a fluent and theoretical explanation of why they got into difficulties in the first place. New degree courses must ensure that theory and research directly informs and supports practice.*
>
> *The Requirements for Social Work Training set out the minimum standards for entry to social work degree courses and for the teaching and assessment that social work students must receive. The new degree will require social workers to demonstrate their practical application of skills and knowledge and their ability to solve problems and provide hope for people relying on social services for support.*
>
> (Department of Health, 2002a)

This book aims to meet the learning requirements for social work that are outlined in the Department of Health's prescribed curriculum for competence in assessment, planning, intervention and review, and that incorporate the necessary professional knowledge, skills and the development of values through meeting the Professional Capabilities Framework (PCF) and Standards of Proficiency (SoPS) of the professional body, the Health and Care Professions Council (HCPC).

The book will also help you to attain the academic subject skills identified in the Quality Assurance Agency (2008) academic benchmark criteria for social work. These include subject knowledge and understanding comprising the following areas:

- social work services, service users and carers;
- the service delivery context;
- values and ethics;
- social work theory;
- the nature of social work practice.

The benchmark statement also refers to subject specific problem-solving skills which include managing problem-solving activity (something common to many interventive approaches), gathering and researching information, analysing and synthesising information, and intervening and evaluating what is done.

This approach will draw and rely on you to acquire high quality communication skills, skills in working with others, and reflective skills in personal and professional development.

In essence, the book will concentrate on the social work process as well as models that are current in contemporary practice and are transferable across settings. The models described in this book are active and practical and are open to evaluation. This choice is deliberate and open to critique. It is designed to develop practical approaches of relevance to contemporary learning and practice. Case studies, which focus predominantly on work with children and families and older people, will be used throughout to enhance this process and to illustrate key points. In doing this we will necessarily omit several areas of social work practice. We have deliberately limited our focus in the main to two service user groups, those of children and families, and older people, recognising that this omits central knowledge. However, much of what we discuss in terms of process can be applied and transferred to other areas of practice. We refer readers with different subject interests to other texts in the series, such as Golightley's (2014) *Social Work and Mental Health* (fifth edition) or Williams and Evans' (2013) *Social Work with People with Learning Difficulties* (third edition).

This book is written for student social workers following a qualifying degree or master's programme who are beginning to develop their skills and understanding of the knowledge and value requirements for practice. While it is primarily an introductory text, it will be useful for student social workers throughout their study, depending on how their programme is designed and what they are studying, and especially as they move into practice learning in an agency setting. It is an entry level text designed to lead students to deeper critical and analytical study. It will also appeal to people considering a career in social work or social care, but not yet studying for a social work degree, as it will introduce them to some of the ways in which social workers practise. Perhaps you are studying for a health and social care foundation degree, an Access to Higher Education programme or similar. It will assist students undertaking a range of social and health care courses in further education by providing a glimpse of the social work role and some of the methods used. Nurses, occupational therapists (OTs) and other health and social care professionals will be able to gain an insight into what is demanded of social workers. Experienced and qualified social workers, especially those contributing to practice education, will also be able to use this book for consultation, teaching, revision and to gain an insight into the expectations raised by qualifying programmes in social work, whether at degree or master's level.

Book structure

Research indicates that social workers vary considerably in the extent to which they make and test hypotheses in practice (Sheppard et al., 2001). A shift towards understanding 'knowledge as process' as opposed to 'knowledge as product' is suggested as a way of integrating theory and practice (Fook, 2002). This means seeing knowledge as something that develops by your active involvement in using it rather than being given a set of instructions and understanding developed by others. It is a practical and pragmatic approach to learning (see Parker, 2010). Changes to social work education and the implementation of degree and master's courses mean that there is a need for new, practical learning support material to help you achieve the qualification. This book is designed to help you gain knowledge concerning the social work process of assessment, planning, intervention and review, to reflect on that knowledge and apply it in practice. The emphasis in this book is on you achieving the requirements of the curriculum and developing knowledge that will assist you in meeting the occupational standards for social work. The intention is, however, to ensure this is not an instrumental activity but one in which you will actively and critically engage.

The book has five main chapters covering assessment, assessment tools, planning, intervention, and review and evaluation of practice. In the first chapter you will be introduced to assessment in social work and will explore what an assessment means for social workers and the people with whom they work. Key issues in respect of ethics, power, professionalism in social work and anti-oppressive practice will also be discussed. You will examine different models and types of assessment and look in detail at two aspects of contemporary practice that demand good assessment skills: working with children and families, and community care, and care management with older people.

Chapter 2 continues the theme of assessment. Here you will learn about and develop an understanding of a range of practical tools designed to help in making assessments. While assessments are not simply information gathering exercises but are jointly constructed ventures undertaken with service users, a certain amount of information is crucial. By gaining an understanding of family stories and histories (genograms), people, organisations and agencies important to service users (ecomaps), cultural issues (culturagrams), and the individual's perceptions of important life events (life road maps and flow charts), you will begin to develop useful techniques for undertaking assessments.

In Chapter 3 you will consider how an assessment leads social workers to develop and write clear plans for work with service users and carers. This chapter will provide an introduction to the construction of plans and some key issues to be taken into account when formulating them. When making plans, you will be asked to consider the effects of working with other professions and with informal carers and service users. Contemporary guidance and advice on care planning will be provided and activities will help you to forge links between knowledge and practice. A particular focus will concern the writing of care plans and the importance of accessibility and involvement to make plans effective. How plans can be person focused and proactive in achieving agreed aims and in charting a course for intervention will link to Chapter 4.

In Chapter 4 you will explore ways of intervening in social work to implement plans made and to achieve agreed goals. The chapter will introduce a number of important and commonly used models for social work practice. These will be applied to case study material. Current guidance, research and advice on intervening effectively will be provided and the activities will help you to make links between knowledge and practice. You will be asked to question the purpose and use of intervention, especially in respect of care and control issues. You will explore and reflect on the use of power and authority to protect or when working with people who do not want to see you.

The fifth chapter is concerned with the final stage of the social work process: reviewing what has been achieved. Student social workers, and experienced practitioners, often have many anxieties about reviewing and evaluating their work in a systematic way. In an effective review and evaluation of work undertaken, practice is subject to scrutiny and outcomes and objectives are measured. While this can be a somewhat daunting process, it emphasises accountability and allows practitioners to develop knowledge and skills in determining what works in which circumstances. In these days of increased accountability and audit it is essential that social workers evaluate their practice. This can have the added bonus of ensuring that your practice is refined to achieve agreed goals and that social work is promoted as effective to other professions and the wider public. In this chapter you will explore the importance of formal reviews and a number of ways of evaluating social work practice.

Concluding remarks and signposts will be offered at the end of the book. At this stage you will be invited to review the learning outcomes set for the chapters. You will be encouraged to chart and monitor your learning, taking developmental needs and reflections forward to other books within the series.

Learning features

The book is interactive. You are encouraged to work through the book as an active participant, taking responsibility for your learning, in order to increase your knowledge, understanding and ability to apply this learning to practice. You will be expected to reflect creatively on how immediate learning needs can be met in the area of assessment, planning, intervention and review and on how your professional learning can be developed in your future career.

What do we mean by reflection? While it is a much used term it is often left undefined, which can lead to confusion (Parker, 2010). What we mean follows. There are a number of case studies throughout the book that will help you to examine theories and models for social work practice. We have devised activities that require you to reflect on experiences, situations and events and help you to review and summarise learning undertaken. In this way your knowledge will become deeply embedded as part of your development. When you come to practice learning in an agency, the work and reflection undertaken here will help you to improve and hone your skills and knowledge.

This book will introduce knowledge and learning activities for you as a student social worker concerning some of the central processes relating to issues of daily practice in all areas of the discipline. Suggestions for further reading will be made at the end of each chapter.

Professional development and reflective practice

Great emphasis is placed on developing skills of reflection about, in and on practice. This has developed over many years in social work. It is important also that you reflect prior to practice, as this emphasis on a thoughtful and planned approach will help you make your work clear to service users and also more open to review, so you can improve your practice in the future. This book will assist you in developing a questioning approach that looks in a critical way at your thoughts, experiences and practice and seeks to heighten your skills in refining your practice as a result. Reflection is central to good social work practice, but only if action results from that reflection.

Reflecting about, in and on your practice is not only important during your education to become a social worker, it is considered key to continuing professional development. As we move to a profession that acknowledges lifelong learning as a way of keeping up to date, ensuring that research informs practice and striving continually to improve skills and values for practice, it is important to begin the process at the outset of your development. The first four levels of the Professional Capabilities Framework relate to the 'level' of capability a social work student should be demonstrating at different points in his or her social work training, whether that be entry, assessment of readiness for practice learning, after the first placement or by completion of the programme (www.tcsw.org.uk/levels-within-the-pcf/). Towards the end of the programme these are mapped against the HCPC SoPS, which must be met for you to meet registration requirements (see www.tcsw.org.uk/standard-2col-rhm.aspx?id=6442451337). This book will help you to meet the domains of the PCF appropriate to your level of study. While it is an entry level text, it will prepare you in knowledge and understanding at the required level for capabilities as a beginning social worker and will therefore address some of the SoPS.

The PCF nine domains used throughout this book are as follows.

1. **Professionalism**: Representing and being accountable to the profession.
2. **Values and ethics**: Apply social work ethical principles and values to guide professional practice.
3. **Diversity**: Recognise diversity and apply anti-discriminatory and anti-oppressive principles in practice.

4. **Rights, justice and economic well-being**: Advance human rights and promote social justice and economic well-being.
5. **Knowledge**: Apply knowledge of social sciences, law and social work practice theory.
6. **Critical reflection and analysis**: Apply critical reflection and analysis to inform and provide a rationale for professional decision-making.
7. **Intervention and skills**: Use judgement and authority to intervene with individuals, families and communities to promote independence, provide support and prevent harm, neglect and abuse.
8. **Contexts and organisations**: Engage with, inform and adapt to changing practice contexts and operate effectively within own organisational frameworks and within multi-agency and inter-professional settings.
9. **Professional leadership**: Take responsibility for the professional learning and development of others through supervision, mentoring, assessing, research, teaching, leadership and management.

References to these standards will be made throughout the text and you will find a diagram of the PCF in the Appendix on page 183.

Chapter 1
Understanding assessment in social work practice

ACHIEVING A SOCIAL WORK DEGREE

This chapter will help you to develop the following capabilities, to the appropriate level, from the PCF.

- **Diversity**
  Recognise diversity and apply anti-discriminatory and anti-oppressive principles in practice.
- **Knowledge**
  Apply knowledge of social sciences, law and social work practice theory.
- **Critical reflection and analysis**
  Apply critical reflection and analysis to inform and provide a rationale for professional decision-making.
- **Intervention and skills**
  Use judgement and authority to intervene with individuals, families and communities to promote independence, provide support and prevent harm, neglect and abuse.
- **Contexts and organisations**
  Engage with, inform and adapt to changing practice contexts and operate effectively within own organisational frameworks and within multi-agency and inter-professional settings.

It will also introduce you to the following academic standards as set out in the social work subject benchmark statement.

5.1.4 Social work theory.
5.1.5 The nature of social work practice.
5.5 Problem-solving skills.
5.5.2 Gathering information.
5.5.3 Analysis and synthesis.

Introduction

It has long been acknowledged that assessment is a key task in social work practice (Parker, 2013; Bartlett, 1970). Government policy acknowledges this and has developed frameworks for assessment that emphasise its centrality for effective planning, intervention and positive outcomes (see later below). As beginning social workers you will be asked to complete, contribute to and present assessments during your practice learning for the degree and once qualified. It is important that you have a thorough knowledge of what makes a good assessment, how they are conducted and some of the difficulties that might arise when making an assessment. The centrality of good social work assessment was emphasised by the inquiry into the death of Victoria Climbié (Laming, 2003), is further reinforced in Lord Laming's updated report (Laming, 2009), and forms an important plank within Eileen Munro's final report (Munro, 2011) in calling for higher quality assessment to improve the child protection process throughout its duration.

The Climbié inquiry puts centre stage some of the actions and responsibilities social workers need to take into account when making an assessment. For instance, when a referral is made concerning children they must be seen within 24 hours or the reasons why this cannot be achieved must be clearly recorded (recommendation 35). Where there are allegations of deliberate harm the social worker must:

- speak alone to the child;
- see and speak with carers;
- visit the child's accommodation;
- seek and consider the views of other professionals;
- agree a plan to provide for the child's welfare (recommendation 40).

In making these assessments, social workers should have the confidence to question other agencies and their involvement or conclusions (recommendation 37). This is not always easy and developing confidence demands that we as social workers know what it is we do and why we are doing it. This, again, is something that the Climbié inquiry focuses on. For instance, recommendation 34 states that social workers should not undertake home visits without being clear about the purpose of the visit, what information is being sought and what will happen if there is no one at home. It is also important that social workers check any prior information they have, if at all possible, and pay strict attention to recording visits and information gained in a case file. It is recognised that these responsibilities are demanding and the Climbié inquiry, again, states that social workers should receive regular supervision that considers case recording (recommendation 45).

Social workers, albeit not exclusively, undertake a wide range of assessments that are not solely confined to children in need and child protection, including the following:

- community care assessments (National Health Service and Community Care Act 1990, s.47);
- specific assessment for carers (Carers [Recognition and Services] Act 1995);
- mental health assessments for admission to hospital or guardianship (Mental Health Act 1983, ss.2, 3, 4, 7);
- 'best interests' assessment (Mental Capacity Act 2005, s.4).

In this chapter, you will be introduced to some definitions of assessment, types of assessment and key influences affecting social work assessments such as ethics, power, professionalism and anti-oppressive practice. You will be invited to consider how an assessment is made with service user groups common to social work – in child and family work, and work with adults. As mentioned in the introduction, we will not cover all groups of people who use social services but cover a selection to illustrate key points. Contemporary guidance and advice on assessment in childcare and on the assessment process for older people will be provided and activities will help you to make links between knowledge and practice throughout this chapter. To illustrate some of the processes involved we will introduce our developing case studies later in the chapter. The importance of a multidisciplinary focus in assessments will be emphasised in terms of sharing information with other professionals, and from the perspective of service users who are unlikely to want to be assessed again and again for the same service by a number of agencies and professions (see Quinney and Hafford-Letchfield, 2013). You will be asked to question the purpose and use of assessments, and how they can be person-focused and proactive in achieving agreed aims. This will provide you with knowledge that you can use when considering the five key tools for use in assessment that will be introduced in Chapter 2.

The centrality of assessment work is recognised also in social work education. Indeed, being skilled in conducting assessments is a key requirement for social workers and is recognised in the government's drive to improve social work education. It is reflected in the Teaching, Learning and Assessment Requirements for the qualifying degree at its inception:

> *... providers will have to demonstrate that all students undertake specific learning and assessment in the following key areas*
>
> *assessment, planning, intervention and review.*
>
> (Department of Health, 2002a, pp3–4)

Learning about assessment during university-based and practice-based education was confirmed as important by newly qualified social workers in a study on newly qualified social workers by Bates et al. (2010). The importance has also been confirmed by the professional body's SoPS and the PCF in England:

> *1.3 be able to undertake assessments of risk, need and capacity and respond appropriately*
>
> *14.2 be able to select and use appropriate assessment tools*
>
> (HCPC, 2012, pp7, 13)

So, learning about assessment, how to assess and how to develop skilled competence in making assessments is central to your development as a social worker. Before you can begin learning these skills, however, it is important to have some idea of what an assessment is and how one might be defined.

What is assessment? Definitional perspectives

This section introduces ways in which assessment might be understood. It is important to have an awareness of different understandings of assessment because the ways in which it is understood can affect what is done, how the assessment takes place, how information is used and interpreted, and what plans are made as a result. This will affect the ways in which you work, but also how service users, carers and other professionals involved in the assessment perceive the process and work with you.

It is often useful to start with a dictionary definition. The *Oxford English Dictionary* sees assessment in terms of judging or valuing the worth of something. This is an indication of a skilled activity by someone who is competent to judge between things of different value. It implies the use of standards against which something can be appraised. This certainly appears to be the case in many social work assessments. However, it leaves out the interactive and human contexts which also feature in social work assessments. The definition suggests that there are right and wrong situations or good and bad values – a suggestion that, in social work, demands critical appraisal. The dictionary definition offers an economic understanding that underpins much of contemporary social welfare practice. However, it is important for social workers that it is not the worth of the person that is being assessed but the potential for growth and change.

Assessment: art or science?

The perceived conflict between social work as 'art' or as 'science' is central to the debate about definitions. The debate is well rehearsed in the literature (see Richmond, 1917; England, 1986; Reamer, 1993; Munro, 1998) and links to contemporary discussions concerning evidence-based practice (Webb, 2001; 2006; Sheldon and Macdonald, 2009). If assessment is an art it cannot be limited by definitions, structured questionnaires or checklists, or even be fully described; rather it would rely on the wisdom and skill of the assessor as refined through experience. This may leave people open to the whims of individual social workers and their particular views and beliefs. It would not provide a systematic approach or one that service users could expect to receive regardless of practitioner, team or region. If, on the other hand, it is a science, then assessments should be open to precise measurement and be practised effectively by following steps outlined in a 'technical manual' of social work. This could be seen as reducing human relations and situations to a common set of standards and criteria and would not allow for diversity in setting, culture and interpretation of situations. Consider the following example.

CASE STUDY

John has contacted the local community mental health team. For some time he has felt depressed, lethargic and unable to cope with his job. The team leader has asked that an assessment be undertaken.

a) Tim, a social worker using an arts-based approach, talks with John about his situat in a free-flowing and broad way. He decides on the basis of his assessment and his prior experience that John is particularly vulnerable and would benefit from intensive support from the team.

b) Janice takes a systematic and 'scientific' approach to assessment. Her assessment of John takes into account a range of risk and vulnerability indices that are validated by their use on groups of similar people. Her assessment scores John below the threshold of risk that would guarantee him eligibility to a service from the team.

A balanced approach would suggest that social work assessment is both an art and a science since it involves wisdom, skills, appreciation of diversity and systematically applied knowledge in practice (Parker, 2007a; 2008). Clifford (1998) puts this well when describing the interconnected elements in assessment:

> *... assessment has to partake of scientific, theoretical, artistic, ethical and practical elements – something which has long been recognised by practitioners, and regarded as traditional in social work and all the helping professions.*
>
> (p233)

Let us return to the case of John.

CASE STUDY

A third social worker, Jeannette, would use her prior experience of social work with people in John's position, weighing that knowledge against the eligibility criteria of the agency and the structured assessment tools that are designed to assist decision-making. The difference between Jeannette and Janice is that Jeannette would see the assessment instruments as 'tools' for a job and not prescriptions.

The approach taken by Jeannette is echoed by Milner and O'Byrne (2009) who describe assessment in terms of its practical application although also an art form. For them assessment is identified as follows:

> ... analysis *is about making sense of events and statements, arriving at an overall picture and an understanding of what is happening and perhaps giving some thought as to how the situation has come about ...* Judgement *is about what is good enough and what is not, what is dangerous and what is reasonably safe, what is of reasonable standard and what is not.* Decision making *is about future action or inaction and aspects of that action, with a plan for carrying it out and reviewing it.*
>
> (Milner and O'Byrne, 2009, p4, emphasis in original)

Values, diversity and service user involvement

Middleton (1997) locates the process of assessment firmly in the context of social work values and states that respect for individual differences is central if the process is not going to disempower the individual but enhance their strengths and coping abilities. The emphasis on values is important because assessments are about making judgements but not about being judgemental. Milner and O'Byrne (2009) identify several potential pitfalls in making judgements that we need to avoid. These include paying attention selectively, stereotyping and labelling people (attributing certain characteristics to people because we think that is how they are likely to behave) and sensory distortions. Groups, agencies and teams, as well as individuals, can also be affected by developing collective assumptions and perspectives on situations (see the following case study).

CASE STUDY

Chris is well known in the social work office. Since having his first child removed from his care and subsequently freed and placed for adoption, he has been to the office on several occasions, becoming angry and shouting and swearing at the social work staff. Once he threatened violence to the social worker involved in the initial assessment.

Three years after this incident he has again come into contact with the social work team as he has become involved in a relationship with a woman who has two young children. Jeremy, a social worker new to the team, has been asked to assess the new situation. His colleagues have warned him about Chris's 'dangerousness'. Chris is a big man, sporting several tattoos on each arm and a 'skinhead' haircut. On first meeting Chris, Jeremy was quite nervous, and a little on edge when Chris became loud. Jeremy realised that Chris was wearing a hearing aid, and was being open and detailed about the past and present situation. He appeared to want to engage with him.

COMMENT

You may have experienced something like this yourself, or perhaps you have been on the receiving end of such misunderstandings.

Starting from strengths, respect for service users and keeping clear records can assist in offsetting some of these difficulties. Milner and O'Byrne (2009) present a model of assessment that acknowledges that knowledge is developed through interactions with other people and does not necessarily proceed in a straight line between point A and point B. This is important if we are going to avoid labelling people like Chris in the case study above, and if we are to undertake comprehensive and valid assessments.

The reduction of individual situations to a set of problems and causes may suggest that there are clear 'right and wrong' actions and situations that can be observed and assessed. The constraint of resources and the setting of eligibility criteria to restrict access to services compound this view, according to Milner and O'Byrne.

Assessments are rarely, if ever, 'value-free' and the particular perspectives of social workers influence the way they are conducted and their analysis (Ney et al., 2013; Parker, forthcoming). It is imperative, therefore, that workers should be aware of and check their individual bias and how this may well affect the assessment undertaken (Clifford, 1998).

Milner and O'Byrne (2009) suggest social workers acknowledge the power they have in making assessments and that multiple interpretations of situations are considered. Negotiation between service users and social workers and the construction of a joint narrative form the basis of their assessment approach. Assessment concerns the development of a social narrative that takes into account diversity. Writing from a childcare perspective, Cooper (2000) argues that when social workers are reflexive – identifying, questioning their own biases and ensuring assessments are interactive and collaborative – it is possible to create effective interpersonal relationships and offset potential bias. The importance of reflection and reflexivity in assessment has been shown by the analysis of critical incident accounts (see Parker, 2010), many of which mirror the situations described by people who use social work services. Social workers need, in their assessments, to listen to people, validate their experiences and work collaboratively to promote service users' strengths. This is something with which Fook (2012) also agrees. She considers that the traditional and accepted approach to assessment involves sorting into categories and creating eligible and ineligible types, the common element being to frame situations in terms of 'problems' which fit those holding the power and resources. The alternative approach allows for multiple and diverse understandings developed in the particular context of the individuals involved. The models developed by Milner and O'Byrne (2009) and Fook (2012) use a narrative approach that is constructed with the service user and is open to change and development. Assessment becomes a process of dialogue rather than fact-finding. It is also important not to be bound by restrictive assessment proformas but to question what information is needed, why it is needed and to what uses it might be put, something that Munro (2011) emphasised in raising the quality of practice. Let us return briefly to the case study of Chris.

CASE STUDY

In developing a working relationship with Chris, Jeremy was able to allow him time to rehearse his past experiences with social workers, the hurt he had felt and the anger that it had aroused in him. Jeremy was also able to put forward the reasons why the actions had been taken and the responsibilities that social workers have. While this was painful for Chris, it allowed him to work with Jeremy in a more open and collaborative way. They were able to discuss together ways in which progress might be made.

Theory and assessment

One problem in defining and understanding assessment is that there have been very few attempts to construct a systematic theory of assessment in social work (Lloyd and Taylor, 1995). Coulshed and Orme (2006) describe how assessment may be understood by its core processes, its purposes or its theoretical base. What is clear is that the theoretical approach taken by social workers and the agencies in which they work influences the assessment process in a similar way to personal values and belief systems. Social workers need to acknowledge not only their personal beliefs, values and biases, but also the impact their approaches might have on the way an assessment proceeds. Social workers should be open, honest and explicit with service users (Coulshed and Orme, 2006). For instance, Howe (1992) identifies a range of broad theoretical categories that can be adopted in social work that take one of the following approaches:

- a problem-solving perspective, starting from the position that there is something wrong that needs to be fixed, whether in the present (cognitive behavioural) or in the past (psychoanalytic);
- a perspective that is concerned with the construction of subjective experiences or how people understand their experiences within society, how labels are applied to people on the basis of their actions;
- a political model that considers social problems in relation to social inequalities and the dominant political system.

Each of these approaches to social work affects the way an assessment proceeds. Consider the following case study and the different responses that might be made depending on the perspective or approach of the social worker.

CASE STUDY

Jane, mother of Tony, separated from Eddie, Tony's father, after two years of domestic violence. Tony received an injury to his arm during one of these incidents. Eddie is now requesting greater contact with Tony.

A social worker taking a problem-solving approach would look to examine the risks that Eddie might pose to Tony and seek and test alternatives or ways of reducing any risks. This social worker might assess the capacities for change, development and protection of those involved.

A social worker from the second school of thought might assess the impact the situation might have on Tony, whether or not he wished for contact and the meanings that a lack of contact might have for both Tony and Eddie, and indeed Jane. This social worker might also explore how being seen as violent might impact on Eddie's capacity for change.

A social worker taking a more overt political approach may look to the problems that male domination has led to in creating a context in which violence towards women is seen as acceptable and where women are seen as victims. This social worker may also make a class-based analysis looking at education, employment and environmental factors that may have contributed to the previous situation.

COMMENT

Social work assessments, therefore, combine the judgement or weighing up of something with the explicit acknowledgement of the importance of values, diversity and the views of others. One further way of looking at assessment in social work is to separate the 'types' of assessment used.

Assessment types in social work

In this section, we will examine the different types of assessment in terms of their focus and duration. Before we look at different types of assessment it is important to take a little time to consider the question, 'Why is assessment so important?' We have seen the stress put on assessment in the Climbié inquiry. It is, however, not a discrete entity that can be undertaken in isolation from other aspects of social work and social care practice. Assessment is an integral part of the social work process and, certainly in practice, assessment and intervention cannot be clearly separated. Assessment is part of a continuous process which links with planning, intervening and reviewing social work with service users. This is exemplified well in the ASPIRE model:

> *AS – Assessment*
>
> *P – Planning*
>
> *I – Intervention*
>
> *RE – Review and Evaluation*
>
> (Sutton, 1999)

If assessment is effective then it makes it more likely that intervention will succeed (Milner and O'Byrne, 2009). Assessment is the key to effective social work practice in whichever area you are working and also a central task in contemporary social work (McDonald, 2006). Watson and West state:

> *Assessment is at the heart of all good social work practice. It covers a spectrum of activities, from observation and judgements made within the context of an initial encounter through to more formal and complex frameworks of assessment. Its purpose is to enhance understanding of the service user's situation, helping workers to identify areas for potential change that will assist the development of a rationale for future intervention.*
>
> (2006, p30)

Unfortunately, the converse can also be true. When assessments are undertaken without adequate preparation and without a clear sense of purpose and direction, they are unlikely to produce good quality material that will help in planning to improve the lot of service users and could even be dangerous if failing adequately to identify risks (Munro, 2011). The following case study illustrates some reasons for paying attention to planning for assessment and specifying purpose.

CASE STUDY

As a student on her first practice learning placement, Margaret was allocated a case concerning a mother, Carol, and her two young children. The referral from the health visitor had requested help with parenting and behaviour management.

Margaret was eager to begin practice. She telephoned Carol and organised a convenient time and date to visit. The day of the visit arrived. Margaret made her way to the house, rang the bell and introduced herself when Carol answered. It was at this point that she realised she had no plan, did not know what information to collect, how to collect it and to what ends she was making an assessment. Carol asked Margaret what she was going to do to help her with her children. Margaret did not know how to answer. The visit became tense and after 15 minutes ended with no further plans. Carol telephoned her health visitor the following day to say the social worker was 'useless'.

Fortunately, you are not likely to be placed in such a position because you will have a practice assessor who will help you to plan and prepare for visits. However, this case study illustrates some of the difficulties that can arise when planning is inadequate or when the social worker has not clarified their role and the reasons for and expected outcomes of the assessment visit.

In social work, assessments can be separated into two basic types – ongoing and fluid, or time limited and issues specific. Superficially, these two types may be seen as corresponding to the debate about social work as an art or as a science. In practice, they are more complex and often assessments comprise elements of both. Coulshed and Orme (2006) are clear, for instance, that assessment does not simply represent a singular event, but continues after the production of a specific piece of work or report.

Assessment as an ongoing, fluid and dynamic process

Assessment is increasingly acknowledged to be a continuous process (Hepworth et al., 2009; Coulshed and Orme, 2006; Department of Health, Department for Education and Employment, Home Office, 2000). This is emphasised in the new *Working Together to Safeguard Children* guidance (HM Government, 2013a). This develops the *what* and *how* that need to be done but acknowledges that changes and developments occur in a person's life that may have a significant impact on how a situation is seen or responded to. It is something that continues over time. The benefits of this approach lie in seeing social work as a process in which assessment and intervention are interconnected and that social work is a dynamic activity that changes throughout its course (see Chapter 4). It also clearly associates assessment and evaluation in the social work process. Pincus and Minahan (1973) develop this 'process' model of assessment in their systemic approach to social work practice:

> *The process of assessment ... continues throughout the planned change process. While the initial assessment serves as a blueprint, it will be modified as ideas are tested out and new data and information are gathered. The worker continually reassesses the nature of the problem, the need for supporting data and the effectiveness of the approaches chosen to cope with it.*
>
> (p116)

Single event/time-specific formulations

In practice, however, social workers sometimes do not continue the assessment throughout a planned piece of work (Sheldon and Macdonald, 2009). In fact, community care law and practice may preclude such a continuous process because of the artificial separation of assessment from the social work process as a discrete activity (McDonald, 2006) and the development of a split between assessing and commissioning or purchasing functions and the provision of services.

A second way of categorising assessment in social work is as a *time-specific formulation* (Hepworth et al., 2009). This means the production of a report after a time-limited period of assessment has taken place. For instance, a court report, a report for a case conference or an initial community care assessment report may represent such a type of assessment.

It is this kind of assessment that may suggest there are clear norms and standards. The assessment judges aspects of the service user's life against expected or accepted ways of seeing similar situations. It offers a way of examining a situation, event or individual within a specific timescale or period in a person's life. This focused approach lends itself to making predictions or identifying needs, goals and ways of achieving these. It also offers, at times, a baseline from which change can be continually monitored. It does not, however, necessarily tell you anything about the individuals or events except at this particular point in time. It may not present a full or accurate picture that holds over time or in different circumstances and it may reflect the values of those making the assessment rather than those being assessed. This is where the development of practice wisdom becomes important. Sheldon and Macdonald (2009) offer a valuable way forward in understanding the distinction between assessment types, suggesting that an assessment can be seen as finite but that continued monitoring and final evaluation add to the initial formulation arrived at through the assessment.

The debate is extended by the increasing recognition that spirituality forms an important part of comprehensive assessments that focus on potential service user strengths (Hodge, 2001; Gotterer, 2001). However, concern with spirituality is more widespread in health care practice than social work (Puchalski, 2006). Social workers need to acknowledge their own belief systems while respecting those of others but not shy away from spirituality or religious faith when making assessments (Ashencaen Crabtree et al., 2008). Often spirituality, which concerns matters of existential importance to individuals that may not include religious belief, can be confused with religion and, again, social workers need to take care not to make assumptions that can skew assessments. Equally important when working with people who have a strong religious faith is not to 'essentialise' that faith by imposing a prescriptive and rigid interpretation on it. Using good assessment skills will assist social workers in learning of the centrality or otherwise of belief systems from those people with whom they work.

ACTIVITY **1.1**

Write down as many reasons as you can think of for social workers undertaking an assessment. Place these in three lists:

- *those that focus on producing reports or specific products;*
- *those that see assessment as a continuous process;*
- *those that fall into both categories.*

COMMENT

The activity above may not have been as easy as it may have seemed at first sight. Indeed, you may have hesitated when placing each assessment in one of the three columns. Don't worry if this was the case. Assessments are, as we are beginning to see, complex and do not fit neatly into categories. Even an assessment that resulted in a court report, or case conference report, might be seen as a stepping stone to further assessment work, and an open assessment may have produced a summary and 'measuring point' from which progress or changes can be determined.

Risk assessment

The concept of risk has assumed increasing importance within our daily lives and activities (Webb, 2006). This is also the case in respect of social work practice and assessment. Risk can be understood in actuarial terms as the likelihood of certain outcomes, whether positive or negative, occurring under certain circumstances or dependent on decisions made. Whether or not it is believed that such calculations can be made accurately in social work, the regulation of risk has become central to contemporary practice.

RESEARCH SUMMARY

One of our (Parker) recent PhD students studied the utility of formalised risk assessment. She employed a risk assessment instrument used in the USA. Her study aimed to assess the feasibility of using a formal actuarial risk assessment tool to identify those children who are most at risk of abuse, significant harm or neglect. She adapted the Michigan

Structured Decision Making System's Family Risk Assessment of Abuse and Neglect (FRAAN), a research-based tool constructed during a study of 2,000 Michigan families and recently revalidated with a cohort of 1,000 families, and applied this to Serious Case Review (SCR) files.

Wood (2011) recognised that actuarial risk assessment tools cannot be perfect predictors in any of the areas of decision-making where they are used, but she argued that they could identify high-risk situations and aid professional practice.

The use of the FRAAN correctly identified cases as high or intensive risk but could not distinguish between fatal and non-fatal outcomes in the SCRs. To support her findings of the risk assessments for this single group, external studies of comparable size and using data derived from similar review reports were sought.

Wood concluded that FRAAN risk assessments could be useful for UK child protection assessment, demonstrating adequate sensitivity to identify high-risk cases. However, caution was needed, as the instrument could not identify the small and special high-risk group of adults who may kill or inflict life-threatening injuries on a child where perhaps the need is greatest.

Webb sees the assessment of risk as a potential problem, however, in social work, suggesting that:

> *Its methods are based on strong notions of predictability and calculation that a future event is likely to occur... These partly rely on existing scientific knowledge, which is often provided by experts. In social work the assessment of risk often lacks scientific rigour and may not be modelled in a satisfactory way... Risk assessment is pervaded by value-laden assumptions and is often used as a rationing device that excludes some from service provision.*
>
> (2006, p19)

However, despite the caution raised, it is important to mention risk assessment here as you will be required to complete such assessments in your work, and understanding some of the complicating factors, as pointed out above, can be helpful. Such instruments are also promoted often by hard-stretched organisations who want to make efficiencies, and as a social worker you will need to have the knowledge and capability to make arguments for and against their use. The assessment of risk is uncertain and accurate predictions are not always possible but it can provide a framework for honest discussions which allows those using services to make informed choices (Watson and West, 2006). Coulshed and Orme (2006) promote Corby's earlier work on risk assessment in child protection identifying three elements of risk assessment, and suggest this can be adapted for different settings. The three elements are associated with the stage in the process at which they are undertaken (see Table 1.1).

Table 1.1 Types of risk assessment (after Coulshed and Orme, 2006)

	Preventive risk assessment	Investigative risk assessment	Continuation risk assessment
Process stage	Prior to intervention	Initial contact and assessment stage	Continuing involvement
Key questions	Should anything be done?	What is happening here?	Has the risk reduced?
Comment	Relies on research evidence which is often equivocal	Procedures, guidelines and checklists may be interpreted too prescriptively	Balances risks of intervening against not intervening

All these forms of risk assessment have their own inherent 'risks' and it is important to remember that an individualised, reflective approach needs to be maintained when conducting such assessments.

Levels of assessment in social work

As well as looking at assessment by type, we can distinguish between the levels of assessment. By this we mean whether the assessment is broad based, fluid and holistic (taking into account all aspects of the service user's life and situation), or whether it is focused on a particular issue or serves to inform a particular intervention. These levels do not necessarily preclude one another. It may be appropriate in many circumstances to undertake a broad social assessment prior to focusing on an agreed goal and target for intervention which may demand a much more specific focus and activity. In practice, social work assessments often not only reflect different levels throughout the intervention but also contain elements of both types identified in the previous section. Doel and Marsh (1992) use a helpful illustration to show the importance of levels in an assessment for task-centred social work. They employ the example of a newspaper which can be scanned by its headlines to give an indication of what topics are covered. If there are articles of particular interest you might read the first paragraph or indeed the whole article depending on your focus at the time. Another way of considering the refinement of an assessment is to think of a funnel tapering towards the bottom. As you 'pour in' your information it will gradually be refined until the key elements remain. An example of this funnel approach is shown in Figure 1.1.

Being explicit about the type of assessment used and the implications this may have for service users is important. The type and level of assessment used will have implications for the service received and the approach employed. If service users are to be fully involved in the assessment, an understanding of what will take place, how it will proceed and for what reasons the information is being gathered is crucial. The example below presents a way of conceptualising social work assessments by type and level.

The issues or interventions given as examples in the diagram above change and shift between points on the matrix. However, the diagram provides a helpful visual way of identifying some of the key features of an assessment.

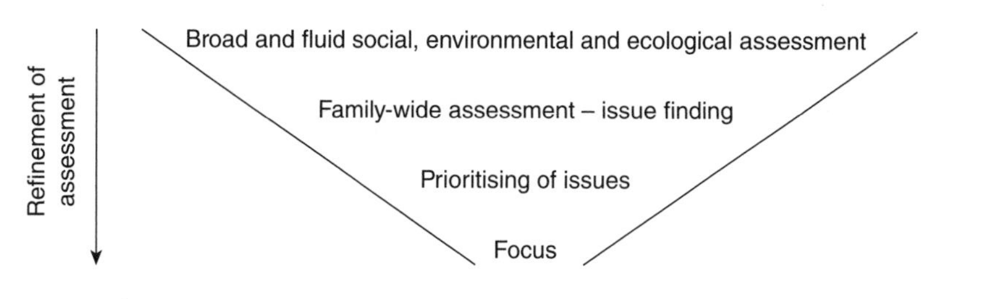

Figure 1.1 A funnel approach to levels of assessment (adapted from Parker and Penhale, 1998)

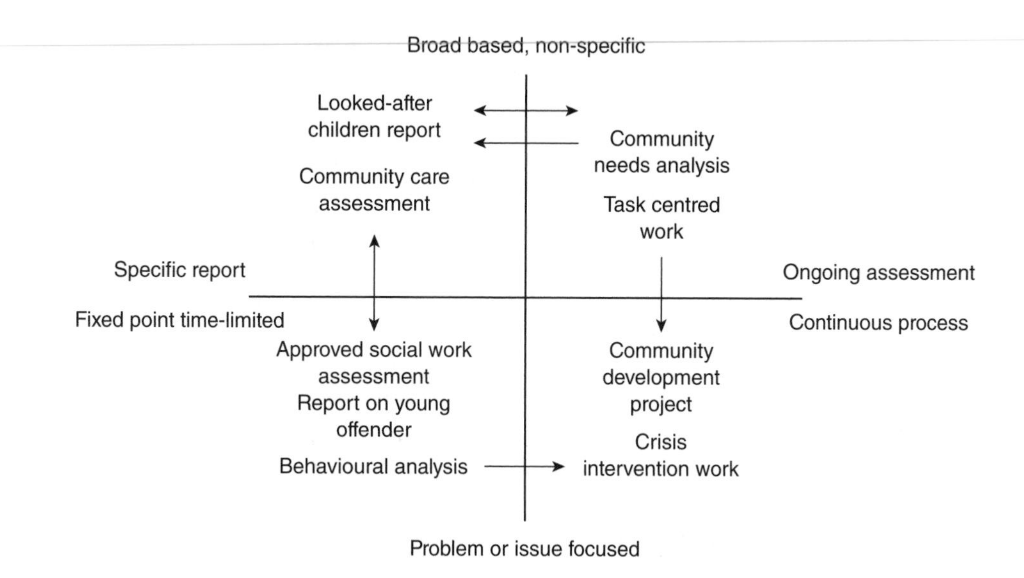

Figure 1.2 Assessment types and levels (with some examples)

The purpose of assessment in social work

The purposes of assessment are as many and varied as the methods designed for undertaking them. The assessment itself serves to reach initial conclusions that describe, explain, predict, evaluate and prescribe or suggest interventive methods. Thus it has a purposive element and to achieve its purpose assessment should be focused, factual and explicit. Assessments have often followed resource-led pathways (those dependent on what services are available at the time) rather than the broader needs-led approach (looking not at what is available but what is needed to make a difference) which has been in vogue for some time although seems to skirt over the perpetual realities of resource limitations. The needs-led approach separates out ends and means and is not dependent upon the resources available. It is hoped that by taking this view the larger picture will help clarify and identify service gaps and therefore allow for ways of filling these. However, Coulshed and Orme (2006) relate this to the 'real world' and state that needs-led principles cannot work unless there are plenty of resources and that in social work there will always be a situation where demand exceeds supply and a judgement must be made between competing needs.

This returns us to the definition that takes into account the economic and fiscal realities of human situations. Indeed, it could be argued that it would be unethical to present an assessment that could not result in the services it identifies.

For writers who consider social work as a purposeful activity, there has long been an association between assessment and a problem-solving approach to working with service users.

> *The problem solving model ... demands that the client's purposes and expectations in joining the worker in interaction be explored and understood and kept in the centre of concern. It is our firm conviction that lack of initial exploration of expectations and goals and lack of careful selection of the starting place in the contact phase ... account for a large percentage of the failures in the helping process.*
>
> (Compton and Galaway, 1975, p285)

Because of the contexts in which social work assessments are undertaken and the many purposes to which they are put, all forms of assessment practice run the risk of inducing normative behaviour: following the rules prescriptively and as though they represent unquestionable givens. Social work assessments, therefore, need to be 'troubled' or questioned closely. It is important that assessment is not seen simply as an activity, skill or practice that can be undertaken in a linear fashion, moving from 'A' to 'B' without recognition of theoretical and philosophical underpinnings or ideologies, and the importance of working together with people who use social work services (Hepworth et al., 2009). One approach that can help you critically to evaluate the ways in which assessment can be understood, to appreciate the meanings constructed in the acts of assessment and to identify possible impacts that assessment can have on individuals, is to group social work assessment around its purposes. The model in Figure 1.3 clusters assessment around the following types: prescribed and

Normative

Frameworks and regulatory frameworks – **(political assessment)**, for example: Common Assessment Frameworks, the Single Shared Assessment process (see Turney et al., 2011) *Theoretical*	Procedural assessment – (**ritual – liturgical or prescriptive)** Understanding and critiquing the assessments employed by agencies and organisations and the ways in which these are conducted (Smale and Tuson, 1993; Preston-Shoot, 2012) *Relational*
Theoretically influenced assessment – **(tribal assessments)**, for example (Payne, 2005; Milner and O'Byrne, 2009): • evidence-based practice • psychodynamic assessments • cognitive-behavioural assessments • person-centred assessments • community assessments	Interpersonal assessment – **(ritual – relational)** Critical reflection on the interpersonal processes involved in assessment (Ruch, 2013) – data choice and gathering; data analysis and interpretation; the impacts of relationship

Adaptive

Figure 1.3 Purposes of assessment

political approaches, 'tribal' allegiances fostered by theoretical ideologies, and processes or rituals involved in the 'dance' or inter-relational conduct of assessment (see Parker, forthcoming).

While social work assessments are, to a greater or lesser extent, politically determined, prescribed and driven, it is possible for individual social workers to engage with individuals, to recognise theoretical and personal biases and to engage with others rather than 'apply' an assessment. Fostering a critically reflective approach to your assessment will help here.

In essence, we can state that a social work assessment is a focused collation, analysis and synthesis of relevant collected data pertaining to the presenting problem and identified needs. Assessments are often confused with evaluation but are, in fact, *more akin to an exploratory study which forms the basis for decision-making and action* (Coulshed and Orme, 2006, p26). This problem-solving model may suggest that a focused and scientific approach is being advocated. However, it must be remembered that the model is intended to be collaborative and works effectively if service users work together with the social worker in an active exploration of the issues. Perhaps this purposeful approach would benefit from being balanced with a strengths-based model which takes into account the capacities and resources of the service user.

Strengths and social exclusion

Hepworth et al. (2009) stress the importance of including service users' strengths in assessments. Past social work practices focused upon pathology and appeared to ignore strengths for change. This created dependency and was seen as damaging to a service user's self-esteem. An individual's needs do not occur in isolation, however. Problems are often complex, involve other people and agencies and occur in a variety of social situations. Therefore, an assessment requires extensive knowledge of the service user's environmental and living system and the wider systems impinging upon it.

Working with service user strengths helps ensure that an anti-oppressive focus is maintained, that the values of social work are promoted and that individual and self-responsibility are emphasised. The strengths perspective focuses on positives with the intention of increasing motivation, capacity and potential for making real and informed life choices, as Saleebey (1996) states:

> *The strengths perspective honors two things: the power of the self to heal and right itself with the help of the environment, and the need for an alliance with the hope that life might really be otherwise. Helpers must hear the individual, family, or community stories, but people can write the story of their near and far failures only if they know everything they need to know about their condition and circumstances. The job is to help individuals and groups develop the language, summon the resources, devise the plot, and manage the subjectivity of life in their world.*
>
> (p303)

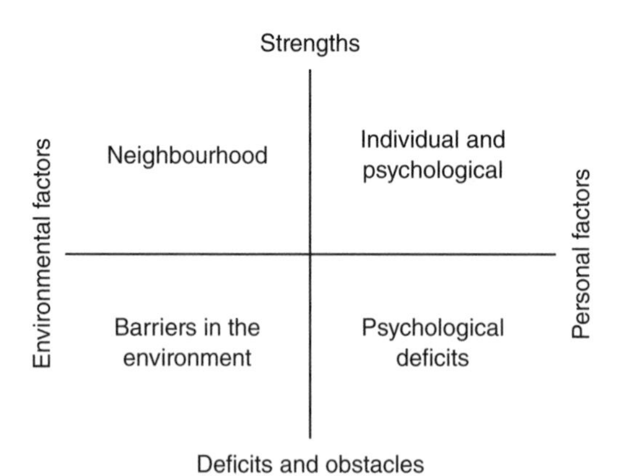

Figure 1.4 Saleebey's strengths and barriers model (see Pierson, 2002)

Pierson (2002) understands the assessment of children in need as being similar to the central concept of social exclusion in social work. Both draw attention to the wider environment and ecological factors (those relating to the individual's living situation) in the lives of children, young people and families, and the structural barriers people face. Where he differs is in promoting the strengths-based approach as opposed to a deficit model. The strengths perspective focuses on resilience, survival in the face of significant hardship or threat to well-being. There is room within the assessment framework to focus on the cognitive skills, coping mechanisms, temperamental and dispositional factors, interpersonal skills and social supports that can be built on as strengths. He uses Saleebey's model to examine barriers and strengths as shown in Figure 1.4.

Taking a strengths-based or solution-focused approach demands a change in emphasis for social workers. No longer can they be seen as expert but as collaborators, facilitating service users to identify their needs and explore alternative ways of acting or conceptualising their experiences. This can be achieved by adopting Smale et al.'s (2000) perspective on assessment in which social workers do not act as 'experts' questioning service users, or simply follow agency procedures. Rather, social workers develop an exchange model, similar to Fook's (2012) notion of the joint construction of a narrative. The exchange model acknowledges that service users are the experts on their situations. It sees service users and social workers exchanging ideas, information and ways forward to make a difference and find alternative ways of approaching the situation being considered.

A strengths-based approach aims to reduce some of the imbalance in power between social workers and service users. It must be acknowledged, however, that the power will never be fully balanced and there are times when social workers are empowered by law to undertake assessments and legitimately to use their authority. It is central in these cases for social workers to be honest and open with service users as indicated by Parker:

> *While social workers necessarily employ procedures, they can still use an exchange model in their work. Indeed, the spirit underlying many procedures demands that social workers advance collaborative exchanges that put users centre stage.*
>
> (2007a, p116)

Skills in assessment

Watson and West (2006) suggest that effective assessment depends on the deployment of key skills, especially communication, negotiation and decision-making. While these interpersonal skills are certainly important, it must be remembered that administrative skills are also central to accurate and purposeful assessment (see Coulshed and Orme, 2006).

RESEARCH SUMMARY

Platt (2011) describes a model of analysis in social work assessments, focusing on children and families building on earlier hypothesis testing work designed to improve and enhance social workers' analysis in assessment. He draws his model from approaches designed to facilitate study skills training in post-qualifying childcare education run at the University of Bristol.

Platt's model is based on three key principles:

- *conceptual clarity in the assessment process;*
- *developing and practising analytical and practical skills such as making hypotheses and formulating and expressing written conclusions;*
- *encouraging reflection and the transfer of learning to different areas of practice.*

Platt used a quantitative method to evaluate the model, using a self-efficacy scale to measure how confident social workers were in making such analyses. He also used independent examination of social workers' assessment reports and marking of assignments. The findings suggested a degree of statistical support for the model and made suggestions about the centrality of adequate support and supervision when making detailed analyses of children and families in social work practice.

Assessment demands an ability to *organise, systematise and rationalise* knowledge gathered. Concurrently, the social worker has to be sensitive and demonstrate an ability to be able to value *the uniqueness of each individual* assessed.

As well as administrative, communication and written skills in undertaking assessments, social workers need to develop and use listening and hearing skills when working with children, observing them and especially when engaging with and talking to them. This may involve using a range of activities to facilitate communication. In research that the Department of Health, Department for Education and Employment, and the Home Office (2000) cite, children prefer:

- to be listened to;
- professionals to be available and accessible;
- professionals to be non-judgemental and non-directive;
- professionals to have a sense of humour;
- straight talking;
- to be able to trust professionals and, where appropriate, to have confidentiality respected (see also Forrester et al., 2008).

It is, of course, not always possible for information to be kept confidential. Social workers must inform service users of the times at which information cannot be kept confidential and will need to be shared with others. To ensure practice is of the highest ethical standards, this should be done at the outset of the assessment process and not left until the matter arises in the course of an assessment.

ACTIVITY 1.2

List the administrative and interpersonal skills that you think are needed to conduct an effective assessment. Identify which skills you already have and which you need to develop, and outline ways in which you may increase these skills. Refer back to the standards and benchmarks detailed at the outset of this chapter and match these against your answers.

COMMENT

You may have included your ability to write clearly, to organise a system, to store and file information. Or perhaps you have considered the importance you attach to matters of confidentiality, ensuring that privacy procedures are carried out to the letter. Some of the interpersonal skills you might have identified concern communication in written reports and letters, face-to-face or on the telephone, and indeed use of information and communication technologies. Try to think of the skills that you have not added to your list and think of how you might develop these in your practice.

Hepworth et al. (2009) emphasise that assessment is critical to social work intervention and its effectiveness. This leads to the identification of goals for change, the means of achieving these and alternatives. Since assessments can be construed as fluid and dynamic, the assessment changes as the change process proceeds. Bartlett (1970) states that it is only after understanding and identifying relevant factors in any situation that plans to act may be formulated (Coulshed and Orme, 2006; Parker, 2008; 2013). Thus, we can say that the purpose of assessment in social work is to acquire and study information about people in their environment to decide upon an identified problem and to plan effective options to resolve that problem. It must also be remembered that assessments are not simply fact-finding exercises but represent a joint construction of a narrative or story between social workers and service users. Remembering this helps to locate the assessment in context and draws attention to issues of power when undertaking assessment work.

Characteristics and features of assessments

Most writers agree on the features comprising an assessment although models differ slightly, as shown in Table 1.1. Also the ways in which different teams collect and organise their information will differ depending on the purpose of the assessment,

Table 1.1 Characteristics of assessments

	Cournoyer (1991)	Hepworth, Rooney and Larsen (1997)	Middleton (1997)	Milner and O'Byrne (2009)
Preparation, planning and engagement		**Clarification of ecological factors** including a configuration of the systems involved	Establishing a working relationship Timing Ground rules Acknowledging feelings	**Preparation** Identify key people Create a schedule for data collection Determine the interview schedule Produce a statement of intent and include purpose and systems of accountability Note tentative explanations
Data collection and creating a problem profile	**Description** A. Client identification information B. Description of person system, family/household/ primary social system and ecological system C. Presenting problems and goals D. Strengths and resources E. Referral source and process; collateral information F. Social history	**Identification of the problem** This should be person centred although, of course, this is recognised to be difficult in the case of involuntary users of social work services. (This comes first in Hepworth, Rooney and Larsen's model.)	Data collection Individual wants Barriers, problems, stresses, resources and supports Coping mechanisms Evidence from professional/expert sources	**Data collection** Create a contents page for the case file Store data Check verbal data by summarising and reporting Check written data and mark opinion clearly Consider other sources of information Note inconsistencies but keep an open mind
Preliminary analysis of data	Tentative assessment A. Person B. Family/household/ primary social systems C. Ecology/environment D. Summary assessment	**Assessment of developmental wants and needs** Stresses associated with life transitions		**Weighing the data and applying professional knowledge** Consider seriousness of situation or how well service user is functioning

(Continued)

Table 1.1 (Continued)

	Cournoyer (1991)	Hepworth, Rooney and Larsen (1997)	Middleton (1997)	Milner and O'Byrne (2009)
				Identify persistent themes or patterns and list them Cluster themes and begin to rank in order of importance Identify gaps Identify people to help Develop a reflexive approach List people to be consulted
Testing the data, deep analysis		**Assessment of developmental wants and needs** Stresses associated with life transitions	**Analysis** Individual wants Changes required Risks Opportunities Roles Costs Alternatives and options	**Making judgements** Identify and use theories to gain a depth of analysis Develop hypotheses around goals Develop tentative explanations Test explanations for theoretical fit Check with key people involved Check data again Consult with reflexive group Develop further explanations and list ways they can be tested
Use of data, creating an action plan	Contract A. Problems B. Final goals C. Plans		Planning Draft proposals Negotiation Recommendations Reviews Quality assurance	**Deciding** What help is needed and by whom? List outcomes to be achieved and consequences to avoid Explain how outcomes can be measured Prepare intervention plan Develop independent mechanism to monitor outcomes – supervision, service user, multi-agency group Prepare draft report listing sources of information, analysis, initial judgement Obtain feedback on report and revise it accordingly

the focus of the team and the particular approaches taken. These have beco
constrained over recent years as instrumental approaches towards standar
and commonality have channelled questions and processes into inflexible
forms. It is generally helpful, however, to have a framework in mind when ga
information. This can help you to engage with service users who will want to know what information you want to collect and why you might want to do so. Having a clear understanding of what you are doing and why can also help you create an atmosphere that is more participative and negotiated.

Specific uses of assessment with children and families and in care management

We will now consider how your developing knowledge of assessment applies to two key areas of social work practice. We will look first at assessments in social work with children and families, considering Department of Health guidance and the Climbié inquiry. We will follow this by looking at changing assessment practice in care management – social work with adults – and in particular with older people. To illustrate how an assessment might be undertaken we will introduce case study material in each situation. The current version of the *Working Together to Safeguard Children* guidelines (2013) sets out its understanding of the purpose of assessment as gathering information, analysing needs, and the nature and levels of risk of harm in order to plan to address those needs and ensure children's safety (see chapters 3 and 4). Thus, the understanding mirrors that which we have illustrated in this chapter as dynamic and continuing and also presents social work as a process that cannot fully disaggregate assessment from the other elements of practice. Assessment is delineated, however, as a guide for the professionals to make evidence-based decisions, but this does not mean you cannot jointly construct an assessment narrative and, indeed, should do so as a means of developing a fruitful working relationship with service users.

There has been a change to reflect greater flexibility and local development that has resulted from the Munro review (2011). Following the Climbié inquiry (Laming, 2003) and the introduction of the Children Act 2004 there was a focus on sharing robust information. An IT solution known as the Integrated Children's System was proposed, but this created a prescribed, generally inflexible assessment culture that failed many who needed social work support. Munro (2011) recommended a simplification in case recording indicating that systems should be adaptive, flexible and humane while building a systemic family-focused narrative. Recording systems should follow the social work process: basic information, assessment, planning, intervention and review. Systems for recording will differ, however, according to agency and/or local authority. The information included in this part of the book concerns good practice and follows related research and guidance. While the forms and IT systems used will differ on your placements and in employment, so the kind of information included in the following case studies is likely to be that which you will be gathering.

Framework for Assessment of Children in Need and their Families

The *Framework for Assessment of Children in Need and their Families* (Department of Health, Department for Education and Employment, Home Office, 2000) *provides a systematic way of analysing, understanding and recording what is happening to children and young people within their families and the wider context of the community in which they live* (pviii). If you are planning to work in childcare social work you will need a thorough understanding of the *Framework*. Whereas assessment in the Children Act 2004 relates to inspection, review or investigation of children's services – a type of assessment we will not cover here – the *Framework* builds on the duties of assessment of needs set out in section 17 and Schedule 2 para 3 of the Children Act 1989:

> *Where it appears to a local authority that a child within their area is in need, the authority may assess his needs for the purposes of this Act ...*

It also builds on responsibilities under section 47 of the Children Act which obliges local authorities to consider making inquiries if concerns have been expressed about a child's well-being or possible maltreatment. An assessment in this case would be made to determine whether a child is suffering or likely to suffer significant harm. Social workers carry a great deal of responsibility for this process and it is important that the assessment is comprehensive and effective. However, it must be remembered that assessments under section 47 involve a shared responsibility and any plans or action taken will be in consultation with supervisors, managers and other professionals.

The *Framework* stresses the need for inter-agency co-operation and maintaining clarity about the following areas:

- the purpose of the assessment and anticipated outputs;
- the legislative basis for the assessment;
- the protocols and procedures used;
- which agency, team and professional has lead responsibility;
- how the child and family members will be involved;
- which professional has the lead responsibility for analysing the assessment findings and developing a plan;
- the respective roles of the professionals involved;
- the ways in which the information will be shared;
- the professional responsible for taking the plan forward.

The principles on which the assessment is based consist of:

- being child centred;
- being informed by child development theories;

- being ecological in approach;
- ensuring equality of opportunity;
- involving children and families in the process;
- building on strengths as well as identifying difficulties;
- an inter-agency approach;
- seeing assessment as a continuous process and not a single event;
- assessments being carried out in tandem with other actions and services;
- being grounded in evidence-based knowledge.

The *Framework* provides a systematic approach that can be individually tailored. In this way it seeks to be both an art and a science that can apply threshold criteria of need to each individual, taking into account diverse circumstances and situations. Each assessment covers three key areas relating to: the development of the child; the capacities of parents and caregivers to respond to needs; and the impact of wider family and environmental factors. Figure 1.5 shows the 'assessment triangle'. These three domains interact and the analysis of the child's needs is used to develop a clear plan of action to secure the best outcomes for the child. A range of useful tools and methods for undertaking assessments using the *Framework* are detailed by Fowler (2003), and a useful introduction is provided by Horwath (2009).

The stress on systematic and evidence-based assessment is clear. The social worker's role when conducting an assessment is to plan for the assessment and, in

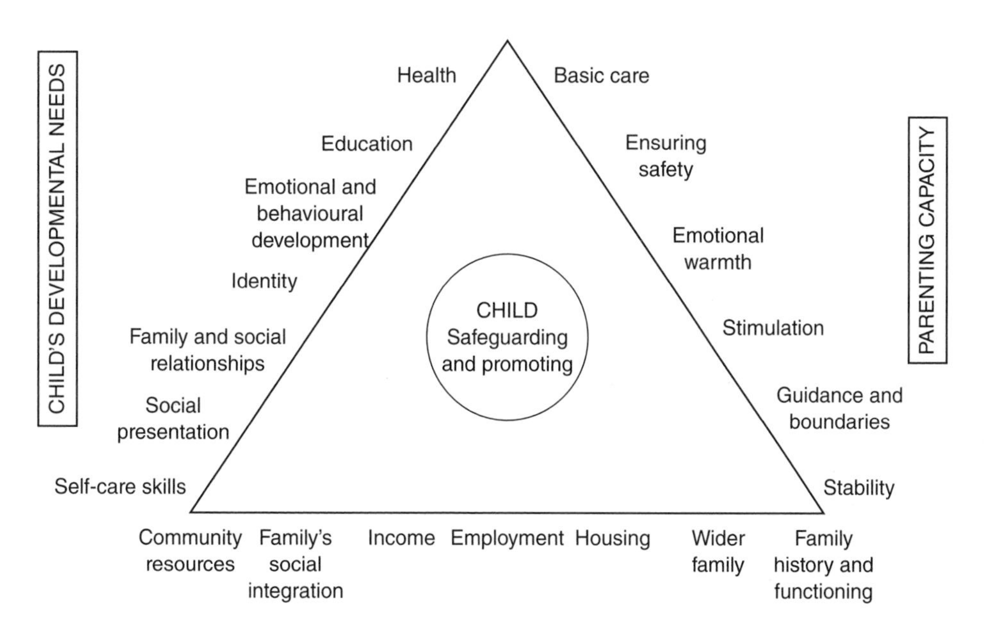

Figure 1.5 The assessment triangle (Department of Health, Department for Education and Employment, Home Office, 2000)

order to account for the complexity of the task, to gather and record information in a systematic and precise way, checking information with the child and parents. Where there are differences over information these should be recorded and strengths and difficulties should be acknowledged. The assessment should be child centred and therefore the impact of the situation on the child must be clearly identified (see Chapter 2).

The *Framework* follows a number of phases that each have clear timescales attached. The phases of the assessment concern clarifying the source of the referral and reason for it, gathering existing information, exploring facts and feelings, exploring differences between family, child and professional understandings and feelings, and drawing together an analysis of needs within the family and local community context. Timescales are tight and demand a high level of skill and good management of the process. A decision about the likely response should be made within one working day of receipt of a referral and an initial assessment should be completed within seven working days. If a core assessment is to be undertaken this should be completed within 35 working days of the referral being made. The core assessment is an important document for which the social worker has considerable responsibility. It may be used within family proceedings as evidence in support of threshold criteria or issues relating to the welfare checklist and as a rationale for the care plan for the child. This demands, therefore, that assessments should be planned, undertaken in partnership with children and families and recorded appropriately.

The *Framework* also acknowledges that assessment is a continuous process and that individual factors make assessments very diverse:

> *The Guidance has emphasised that assessment is not an end in itself but a process which will lead to an improvement in the wellbeing or outcomes for a child or young person. The conclusion of an assessment should result in:*
>
> - *an analysis of the needs of the child and the parenting capacity to respond appropriately to those needs within their family context;*
> - *identification of whether and, if so, where intervention will be required to secure the wellbeing of the child or young person;*
> - *a realistic plan of action (including services to be provided), detailing who has a responsibility for action, a timetable and a process for review.*
>
> (Department of Health, Department for Education and Employment, Home Office, 2000, 4.1, p53)

The *Every Child Matters* agenda seeks to improve opportunities, outcomes and services for children and young people in five key areas:

- being healthy;
- staying safe;
- enjoying and achieving;

- making a positive contribution;
- achieving economic well-being.

The thrust of this policy led to the development of a Common Assessment Framework (CAF) to aid the assessment of children's additional needs. It represents a standardised approach designed to promote inter-agency co-operation but is not an approach for use in the investigation of suspected harm or risk of harm, which would follow the agreed protocol of local safeguarding children boards. The CAF was introduced gradually until the end of 2008 within children's services (interdisciplinary children's teams brought about by the Children Act 2004 and *National Service Framework for Children, Young People and Maternity Services* [Department for Education and Skills/Department of Health, 2004]). It is likely that you will be able to note some of the common ground between the *Framework* and the CAF and the principles of assessment that underpin them both.

The CAF aims to be a comprehensive tool that, with training, will help practitioners identify children's additional or complex needs. It co-ordinates and complements rather than replaces specialist disciplinary assessments and is a voluntary approach that is careful to avoid stigmatising families requesting it (Department of Education, 2013a). The process is flexible but involves four clear steps:

1. an early identification of needs;
2. assessing the needs in a comprehensive way;
3. delivering services in an integrated way;
4. reviewing the progress.

It is the first and second of these that we are concerned with in this chapter. When identifying initial needs, maybe through the use of a checklist, which may, of course, prescribe or contain those needs, it is important that you, as a social worker, actively reflect on what this initial screening suggests to families you are working with and also for your own approach, thoughts and practice.

The documents and areas to be covered can be found at www.education.gov.uk/childrenandyoungpeople/strategy/integratedworking/caf/a0068957/the-caf-process. The CAF form covers the general details required in the assessment including the services already provided to the child and family before moving into three core areas:

1. child development;
2. parents and carers;
3. family and environmental factors.

The following case study introduces some of the issues that arise when using the assessment *Framework* or the CAF. This case study will develop throughout the book and it will be important to return to it at various stages in your reading to check how practice might develop with children and families.

CASE STUDY

Melissa is a single mother aged 16. She lives with her nine-month-old daughter, Rebecca, in a one-bedroomed flat owned by a local housing association. She has recently begun to spend an increasing amount of time with a young man, Ian, whom she met several weeks ago. Ian seems to be very attentive to both Melissa and Rebecca. Melissa's mother, Irene, herself in her early 30s, does not approve of Melissa seeing this man. She believes she should devote her time to Rebecca and mentions her own experiences as a young mother to back up this statement.

Melissa disagrees and she visits Ian and his father frequently for a number of weeks. It seems that Rebecca responds well to the introduction of another attentive person into her life. According to the health visitor, she is developing appropriately for her age and seems attentive and bright. However, she has been suffering from an increasing number of stomach bugs, and is not eating as well as she used to. In fact, Melissa has become a little concerned because Rebecca has lost weight consistently over the last two weeks. She has taken Rebecca to the doctor who suggested 'keeping an eye' on her.

A few days ago, Melissa's mother visited when Melissa and her young man were in bed smoking marijuana. Irene was horrified, it being two o'clock in the afternoon, and reported them to the police and social services. She insisted that her granddaughter was in 'moral danger and should be taken away and adopted'. Melissa said Rebecca was asleep and asked what harm there was in what they were doing.

The first action the duty social worker made was to explore with Irene, Melissa's mother, the substance of her concerns, to gather basic information and to ascertain whether Melissa was aware of the referral. The social worker, Mandy, then recorded this information on the childcare referral form used by her agency. A copy of this is shown opposite.

The information gathered from Irene was checked with her as the form was being completed. Mandy explained that she would need to speak to her team leader before deciding the next step. She also informed Irene of the department's policy of supporting children and families to stay together. Mandy then took the completed form to her team leader, Geoff, to consider how to proceed. Geoff and Mandy checked existing records to see if anything was known about Melissa, Rebecca and family but no information was found. Mandy and Geoff considered the information that had been given by Irene and, after beginning to complete a pre-assessment checklist (www.education.gov.uk/childrenandyoungpeople/strategy/integratedworking/caf/a0068957/the-caf-process) agreed, as Irene had indicated, that the referral did not constitute an urgent case. However, they also agreed that it was important to make further enquiries, to see Melissa and Rebecca and to check the concerns regarding stomach ailments. Since an allegation of potential harm was made and the referral had also been made to the police, Mandy's team leader spoke with the contact Inspector, Lynne Davies, to agree the proposed course of action. Inspector Davies informed Geoff that they were taking no further action in respect of substance use and had advised Irene to contact social services. It was agreed that there was no need for a joint investigation between social workers and police officers at this time. This decision was documented clearly and attached to the form.

CHILDCARE REFERRAL FORM 1 SOUTHSIDE SOCIAL SERVICES DEPARTMENT

New referral:	Existing referral:			Re-referral:			
Family Name:	Krajic			Given Name:	Rebecca		
Also known as (AKA):	N/A						
Date of birth/ Age:	9 months	Gender:	F	Ethnicity:	White British	Religion:	Not specified
Address:	Flat 10 Southfield South Street Southside			Recent address:	5 Northway Ave Southside		
Postcode:	ST1 1HS			Postcode:	ST3 2SW		
Tel. No.	N/A			Tel. No.	01111 234234		
GP/Health Visitor:	Dr Braye/ June Bridge			School:	N/A		

Members of Household

Family Name	Given Name	AKA	Gender	Ethnicity	Relationship	DOB	Parental responsibility
Krajic	Melissa	N/A	F	White Br	Mother	16 years	Y
Significant Others Krajic	Irene	N/A	F	White Br	Grandmother	34 years	N

Professionals involved

Name	Profession	Contact details
June Bridge	Health Visitor	Dr Braye's surgery 01111 321321

Source of referral: Grandmother

Reason for Referral

Grandmother believes her nine-month-old granddaughter is at risk of neglect from her mother, Melissa. She is concerned that Melissa's boyfriend has no experience with children and poses a threat to Rebecca. Grandmother thinks Rebecca should be adopted and has also passed on her concerns to the police who suggested contacting SSD.

The reasons for concern centre on Rebecca being left in her cot while Melissa and her boyfriend had sex in the adjoining room. She reports also an increase in the number of stomach complaints Rebecca seems to have.

Is client aware of referral?: Y

Receiving social worker: Mandy Jones

Date: 10.05.11

(Continued)

(Continued)

Childcare referral form

Melissa had no telephone and Mandy did not know whether she had any difficulties reading letters. However, she decided to send a letter stating a time and date for a visit as a matter of courtesy but was prepared to explain the reason for the visit when she arrived.

Geoff and Mandy set to planning an initial assessment of Rebecca's situation and needs. This would include the following:

- *a visit to Melissa and Rebecca;*
- *a discussion with Melissa and her boyfriend, and observation of their living situation focusing on the three aspects of the assessment triangle;*
- *seeking an agreement to contact the health visitor;*
- *contacting the health visitor and discussing Rebecca's development and the reported stomach problems;*
- *discussing and explaining the limits of confidentiality and the need to share information between health visitor and social services;*
- *sharing an initial assessment fully with Melissa;*
- *agreeing, where possible, any further action that might be necessary.*

Melissa appeared happy to see Mandy when she visited. She said she had not seen the letter but was aware that a social worker would be coming as her mother had told her of her concerns. Melissa stated that she wanted the opportunity to put her case forward, stating that Irene had continued to 'interfere' in her care of Rebecca since she was born and that Irene feels guilty in Melissa's view because 'she was so crap at looking after me'.

The initial assessment covered information taken from the three areas outlined in stage 7 of the CAF and in the assessment triangle – developmental issues, parenting capacity, and family and environmental factors. While these covered clear areas and the assessment could have been a simple 'question and answer' session, Mandy used her skills in forming relationships and communicating to develop her understanding of these areas. This was particularly important when discussing potentially sensitive areas such as parenting capacity and Melissa's own experiences of family life and functioning.

From the information that was discussed, Mandy began to form a picture of Melissa as a concerned young mother who was finding it difficult to care for Rebecca without some respite or support, especially when Rebecca was vomiting, ill or crying for long periods. The health visitor echoed this view and said she had tried to encourage Melissa to join a young mother's club that she ran but Melissa had said she did not see the point. The health visitor was, in general, fairly positive about Melissa's care of Rebecca but was concerned that she needed extra support, especially in keeping Rebecca's bottles clean. She thought it might be this that was leading to a number of stomach upsets. She was not unduly concerned, however.

Mandy agreed that it was sometimes difficult to look after Rebecca but said the best thing would be for her to have some rest by Rebecca being looked after two or three times a week.

It was agreed that Melissa harboured very negative views about her own upbringing, stating that her mother was never there for her and was too interested in her own life. She complained that Irene was now trying to meddle in her life and in her care of Rebecca.

At this point in the process, Mandy discussed with Melissa the possibility of some work with her and her mother, if Irene would agree, to re-establish the relationship and for Irene to take Rebecca twice a week to give her a break. At first Melissa was dubious, thinking that this might allow Irene to become more of an influence, but she agreed to consider this as a possibility.

Part of the plan for the initial assessment had been to speak with Melissa's boyfriend but he had not been present at any of the sessions. Mandy was concerned to get an all-round view and to ensure that Irene's concerns in respect of Rebecca were considered. When Mandy finally met him she found him to be a charming and personable young man. He told her that he had been 'in care' himself as a child and he gave her permission to consult with his previous social worker. Mandy did so and was assured that he presented no cause for concern.

The initial assessment recommended family work to re-establish the relationship between Melissa and Irene, for Irene to take Rebecca twice each week – either a morning, afternoon or evening – to give Melissa a break, and for Melissa to join the health visitor's group for young mothers to gain support and advice with childcare.

Community care assessment and the shift towards personalisation

We turn now to a second key area of practice, that of social work with older people, in order to help you broaden your understanding of the assessment process. We focus on older people since their perspective and needs form a large part of social care assessments, and these are drawn out and developed in an evolving case study in this and subsequent chapters. Readers who are interested in other adult service users such as people with mental health issues and those with learning difficulties should read other texts in the series, such as those by Golightley (2014) and Williams and Evans (2013) respectively.

Assessment within Adult Social Services (the statutory service for adults within local authority governance, set up following the structural changes resulting from the 2004 Children Act), known as ASS, has in fact been evolving over the past 20 years or so. It has developed from a system known as care management which was implemented in April 1993, following the NHS and Community Care Act 1990. Social workers carrying out assessments continue to be referred to as care managers, and this is the term we shall normally use, although other titles may apply. The principles and processes of care management that underpin current assessments include the referral of cases, case finding, assessment, care or support planning, monitoring and review. These processes are important to our understanding of assessments within adult services. Underlying principles and imperatives such as resource constraints and targeting services at those with greatest need help to explain why assessments have taken a particular form. Care managers will not necessarily be qualified social workers and this is increasingly the case, given the recent public expenditure cuts. These have fallen heavily on ASS and have resulted in the retrenchment of qualified posts in the sector (Lombard, 2011 in Lymbery, 2012). While it may not have been the government's intention (Department of Health, 2009 in Lymbery and Morley, 2012), qualified staff are now mainly used in complex assessments and when safeguarding is an issue. The shared vision for adult social care by the former Labour Government and more recently by the Coalition Government (Department of Health, 2010a) has been to focus on person-centred planning, on user self-assessment, on care facilitators, on maximising user choice and wherever possible devolving choice of services to users via direct payments (DP). This shift towards personalisation in terms of services for adults has been widely endorsed by local and national government (Lymbery and Postle, 2010). However, within a public sector culture of ever stricter debt reduction strategies, these more preventative initiatives create moral and practical conundrums, which we shall be drawing out as the complex case in adult care unfolds.

At this point we give you some background information on care management. We also put down markers which point to underlying tensions in social care for adults that are taken up in later chapters.

Historical background to care management and the single assessment process

Care management was introduced by the then Conservative Government following the NHS and Community Care Act 1990. The major initiative was in response to criticism of the way in which services, particularly for older people, were organised and to general concern that the cost of welfare provision was too high (Lewis and Glennerster, 1996). The Audit Commission (1986) held that it was cheaper to provide home-based care to enable vulnerable people to remain at home, where they preferred to be. However, the real price of care at home had not been fully costed, since account was not taken of the contribution made by informal carers (family and friends who provide the bulk of hands-on personal care on an informal basis). In spite of this anomaly, the message that services for adults needed to be changed within the context of a commitment to community care was well received. A key report was commissioned, known as the Griffiths Report (1988). It recommended that the government adopt a system of care management and that local authority Social Services Departments (SSDs – now ASS) should be given responsibility for implementing what was then a radical approach to delivering community care. Hence, on the back of little research, and following the 1990 Act, a system of care management was adopted throughout the UK.

The blueprint for care management (or case management as it was then known) was spelt out in the 1989 White Paper *Caring for People* (Department of Health, 1989). The main aims were to help people live as normal a life as possible; provide them with the right amount of care in order to promote independence; and give them a greater say in how services should be run (s.1.8). The principles which underpin these aims draw on theories of normalisation, targeting and efficiency measures, and user empowerment. They did not and do not always sit comfortably together and can lead to 'tensions and ambiguities' in practice (Postle, 2002). Nonetheless, the government was confident that skilled care managers who made *proper assessment of need the cornerstone of high quality care* (Department of Health, 1989, s.1.11.) would improve services for adults. This optimism was apparent when, in April 1993, the 1990 Act was implemented and predominantly qualified social workers were appointed as care managers, with many moving for the first time into local authority adult services (Bradley et al., 1996).

The process of care management for older people is linked with that of the single assessment process (SAP) (Department of Health, 2002b): a multidisciplinary approach to working that is designed to prevent unnecessary delays and duplication. A key aim of the SAP is to standardise the assessment processes for older people carried out by professionals working in health and social care. Principles that underpin care management are also common to the SAP, such as that of independence, and these are evident in policy documents such as the *National Service Framework for Older People* (Department of Health, 2001a). By introducing the SAP (see *The NHS Plan*, Department of Health, 2000a) the government was responding to many of the criticisms aimed at multidisciplinary working within the context of care management (Manthorpe et al., 1996; Quinney, 2006). The aim of the SAP is to *promote better care services and better outcomes for older people, and more effective use of professional resources*. Particularly, the SAP *should ensure that the scale and depth of assessment is kept in proportion to older people's needs, agencies do not duplicate each other's assessments, and professionals contribute to assessments in the most effective way* (Department of Health, 2002b, p1). When producing guidance on the SAP, the Department of Health was not envisaging radical change since many of the structures were already in place within care management.

The government appeared confident in the White Paper *Our health, our care our say* (Department of Health, 2006) that work on the SAP had been well developed and that initiatives were underway to build on this and develop a CAF to help root out duplication across different agencies and allow people to *self assess where possible* (p115). In practice there has been a level of drift in its implementation and the intention that the SAP initiative would be cost neutral has been met with a healthy scepticism (McNally et al., 2003). Progress has also been hampered by the fact that not all authorities have a shared data base and/or compatible electronic systems. On the other hand, local authority care managers can see the benefits of sharing assessments with allied professionals and these do take place within care planning. It could be argued that evidence that the joined up agenda requires more tinkering with may be found in the recent Health and Social Care Act 2012, since one of the key themes is to promote better integration of health and social care services (Department of Health, 2012). Perhaps a lasting legacy of the SAP has been its emphasis on a person-centred approach.

The personalisation agenda: history and critique

The personalisation agenda takes much of its philosophy from the Independent Living Movement that embraces principles of choice, control and actions of empowerment, active citizenship and advocacy for service users. You may ask why and how this philosophy has evolved. Why has it informed an agenda which is so important in the current welfare debate? We recommend you read Gardner (2011), particularly the first chapter that gives a résumé of the historical antecedents that informed this concept. Gardner puts forward a cogent argument from the Elizabethan Poor Law to the current day, that chronicles the shift from state welfare, based on concepts of deserving and undeserving poor, as demonstrated in the harsh interventions of the Poor Law and the workhouse, to one based on principles of choice, control and inclusion of service users in the welfare process. The critical antecedents are pulled together that help explain the journey of different adult service users in the twentieth century and beyond. So, for example, within the field of mental health, she cites the critique of the medical model, the campaigning that led to the closure of the psychiatric hospitals and the changes in the legislation that radically altered the perceptions of the needs of people with mental health problems. Deinstitutionalisation for those people with learning difficulties similarly informed the shift in welfare, and so too did the emerging concept of normalisation that reinforced the need for a normal life for such people in all its aspects. It was the disability rights movement that argued vociferously from the 1980s onwards that it was society that created the physical and social values barring people with a disability from being equal citizens. The movement strove to increase the number of organisations that could be controlled and run by people who are disabled. The Independent Living Movement spear-headed, in 1988, the introduction of the Independent Living Fund. The autonomy that this fund gave people with a disability to dictate how their support was managed presaged the introduction of DP in 1996 as a viable option which has become a *leitmotif* for personalisation.

In the recent past there have been key pieces of legislation and policy documents that underpin the concept of personalisation by the neo-liberal governments of the Left and of the Coalition Right, and Gardner (2011) also outlines these in the first chapter. Following the 1996 Community Care (Direct Payments) Act, two government White Papers in 1998 (Department of Health, 1998) and 2001 (Department of Health, 2001c) outlined the vision for user-centred services that promoted principles of independence, choice, rights and inclusion in the reworked landscape of welfare. Some six years later there was no doubt of the direction of travel of the former Labour Government when it published *Putting People First: A shared vision and commitment to the transformation of adult social care* (Department of Health, 2007). This agenda for social care was to be enabled through four key platforms: universal services; early intervention and prevention; self-directed support; and social capital. The latter is a way of enabling people to realise that their voice in their community can be heard and their input can make a difference to the type of social and cultural fabric around them. This transformative agenda that in its essence promotes the concept of personalisation and self-directed support in adult care has been taken up by the current Coalition Government. This is evidenced in the publication *A Vision for Adult Social Care: Capable Communities and Active Citizens* (Department of Health, 2010a), in its 'Big Society' slogans (more about these in Chapter 4) and also in the push to extend personal budgets (Gardner, 2011).

The shift in practice has been away from more prescriptive services often perpetuated due to bureaucratic expediency, to more personalised services that enable service users to find their own solutions. It was to mark a shift away from the more paternalistic and top heavy structures of care management, where decision-making ultimately rested with the professionals. The new emphasis is on self-assessment, person-centred planning, self-directed support and training for service users. Early intervention, prevention and keeping healthy are also important facets of this approach and, if services are required, they should be fitted around the individual (Department of Health, 2007). It could be argued that a person-centred approach that puts the individual at the centre of the assessment and helping process is at the heart of good care management and effective practice in social work generally. Indeed, the recent Munro Committee report into child protection (Munro, 2011) recognised and emphasised the importance of the quality of the relationship base to social work practice.

Nonetheless the personalisation agenda is not without its critics. Cunningham and Cunningham (2012) describe these concerns as both practical and ideological. From a practical perspective the debate is twofold. Firstly, the financial underpinning for these more preventative initiatives has never been clearly identified. This is particularly the case at the time of writing since stringent cuts to ASS often result in insufficient funds to meet even high levels of need (Dunning, 2011 in Cunningham and Cunningham, 2012). Secondly, they argue that some service users with needs that are complex are neither willing nor able to respond to the type of opportunities that personalisation may bring. For example, even with assistance some may view DP as too onerous to consider and for them the more traditional service is a preferred choice. However, if individual budgets become the norm, and if money follows user choice and the promotion of individual services, then more traditional services are likely to be run down in order to fund these developments, since the government has held for some time that implementation of the personalisation agenda should be cost neutral (Department of Health, 2005). This strategy is likely to lead to, for example, the closure of day centres and to increased social isolation for certain user groups who prefer and feel more comfortable with the known services. Schelly (2008) has long argued that it is the long-term interests of often the most needy service user groups that will not be best served by the removal of the more traditional supportive services and infrastructures. A linked practical point is that, from a social work perspective, it is known that there are fears within the profession that the practice of personalisation will erode their professional skills into a tick-box, functional activity (IBEN, 2008 in Cunningham and Cunningham, 2012). Further, Lymbery (2012) reflects that social workers in the UK, as a state mediated and controlled profession, will not be well served by the full implementation of personalisation, since their role in this process has never been made clear.

A critical ideological concern is that politicians have used the progressive language of social democratic principles of personalisation based on user empowerment and independent living to 'justify neo-liberal-inspired-strategies to reduce state welfare provision' (Cunningham and Cunningham, 2012, p151, drawing on ideas from Taylor-Gooby, 1994 and Ungerson 1997 and 2006). Not only is there no additional funding earmarked to promote the initiative, but it is also seen as a distraction from *costly and more fundamental reforms* that would place the economic and social well-being of adult service users on a sounder footing (p157). In essence, it is as if service users and social workers are colluding with the residualisation of welfare, as government deftly transfers responsibility for oversight and delivery of welfare from state and social worker to the individual. Scourfield's powerful argument is that we must not lose sight of the main reason why public sector welfare developed originally, that is to make certain those who are dependent and most needy are treated with dignity and respect, and that there is a *collectivised approach to risk* that ensures that *secure and reliable forms of support outside of the market or the family are available* (Scourfield, 2007, p112 in Cunningham and Cunningham, 2012, p157).

A further critique of the implementation of personalisation within adult services concerns its theoretical base, as outlined by Murphy et al. (2013). The authors hold that the theories that underpin the person-centred approach are taken from psychology, psychotherapy and counselling, theories moreover that are incompatible with current statutory social work practice. This is because the underlying ideology and ultimate goal of a person-centred approach, which draws on concepts of unconditional personal regard, respect and empathy, is self-actualisation through self-determination (Rogers, 1957 in Murphy et al., 2013, p708). They argue that statutory social workers cannot aspire to this goal; rather they use the tenets of a person-centred relationship in order to develop a rapport to gain the compliance of the service users. In other words, this approach has a utilitarian function that is dissonant with the conceptual framework on which the person-centred approach is based. They explain why at this juncture social work has needed to emphasise a person-centred approach, in part due to its poor public image and overly bureaucratic role. Nonetheless, it is the very nature of the statutory task of assessing, monitoring and auditing risks that is at the core of qualified social work with adults. In essence they hold:

> *... the term person-centred belies the function of modern social work in which the relationship is for utilitarian purposes of compliance and externally imposed direction on the service user.*
>
> (p717)

The concept of need

A key aspect of care management was that the process of assessment should be based on the expressed needs and preferences of the service user. It was clearly stated in 1989 (Department of Health, 1989) that services were to be *needs led* as opposed to being driven by services that were available to the local authority. Need, it was argued, should be separate from and should determine the level of care and service to be provided. In order to reinforce these demarcation lines between needs-led assessment and service provision, most local authorities with social services responsibility split their business. On the one hand, there was the assessment and purchase of service, on the other, the provision of service. These splits over time have become much less distinctive. Then as now, guidance and financial incentives encouraged local authorities to work closely with the private, voluntary and independent sectors in order to provide services within a mixed economy of care, and to move away from a market in which the former SSDs had monopolised provision. Assessment was to be based on principles of user empowerment and choice (Social Services Inspectorate and Department of Health, 1991a). But social care need was never clearly defined and it remains so in the revised policy direction (Department of Health, 2010b; Department of Health, 2010c; SCIE 2010).

Early guidance to managers (Social Services Inspectorate and Department of Health, 1991b) suggested that need would vary over time as a consequence of changes in local policy and national legislation, demand at local level and the resources available. In principle, therefore, councils with adult services responsibility can place limits on assessment by limiting the assessment of need. Indeed, when advising how practitioners should go about such work, under the revised fair access to care services (FACS) guidance we are informed that assessment and support planning are to focus on ways that achieve agreed outcomes rather than being driven by needs or impairments (SCIE, 2010).

Let us reflect on the concept of need. For a start, need is not a constant concept. It is dynamic and likely to change over time and its interpretation can be a very personal matter, dependent on personal and social expectations and influenced by current national and local culture. For example, in the 1930s most people did not have an indoor toilet. In some communities it was not seen as an essential need. Today attitudes have changed and the absence of an indoor loo would be viewed as an indicator of social deprivation and a public health hazard. The consensus would be that such a facility would be a need that should be met by our society. Other needs may be less obvious, more open to debate and personal interpretation. For example, some older people without personal means other than the state pension may argue that society should enable them to have a hot bath or shower every day and provide them with assistance to accomplish this activity, if this were required. They may feel and think that this is a personal need which would benefit their health and quality of life. Other older people, irrespective of their financial circumstances, may view this as a luxury not a necessity, or a need that should not be met by anyone other than the individual.

Do you view a daily bath or shower as a necessity or luxury?

If the former, who should pay and/or provide the service that may be required to assist this activity?

You will probably agree that perceptions of need can differ markedly between individuals.

Let us look at the case of Denise Lockwood and consider the extent to which you think (and feel) that her needs and preferences are reasonable and the extent to which she is approached and assessed in ways that are person centred.

CASE STUDY

Phase One: Denise Lockwood visits her general practitioner's surgery

Denise Lockwood (aged 65) retired a year ago from an administrative post in a large, local double glazing company. She had not planned to leave so quickly but the opportunity for voluntary severance arose and she put her name forward. For some time she had known she had not been performing well and was anxious about this. When she left work, she said she did not want a fuss, but was disappointed with the low key send off. It was not the way she wanted to end her working life. She had left the building with few contacts and little to show for nine

(Continued)

(Continued)

years with the company. As she returned to her small terraced house in a once gentrified but now run-down area of the city, she felt alone and dejected. Those feelings stayed with her in the months that followed. With time on her hands and few friends, she has become a loner. She got into the habit of watching late night movies, having long 'lie ins' and taking little exercise. Most of her time is spent trying to sort out personal and household paper work, but she never seems to get on top of it. She has always had difficulty throwing stuff away. But her main preoccupation is her health. She frequently has 'aches and pains' and thinks that her feeling of sadness and poor short-term memory are caused by depression. She talks to her general practitioner (GP), Dr Dyson, on a regular basis about how she feels. While he is sympathetic, he thinks that if she ate more healthily, got out more and took regular exercise her health would be much improved. He does not believe in prescribing drugs for mild depression, saying that it is a reaction to her life circumstances and that she can do something about it.

One Tuesday morning Denise visits the surgery feeling low after a poor night's sleep. She is quite forceful in her request for sleeping pills and to see a psychiatrist for her depression. She also says she is lonely and wants someone to visit her. Dr Dyson finally agrees to give her a prescription for some mild sleeping tablets, but does not think her symptoms are sufficiently severe to see a psychiatrist. He is feeling pressured that morning and does not have the time to discuss the merits of preventative health care. Hence he refers her to Amanda Thorpe, a care manager from ASS, who is attached to the surgery and is available to see her.

ACTIVITY **1.3**

1. *Do you think Denise's requests for help are reasonable?*
2. *Write down the reasons why you think Denise should be helped by the local ASS care manager.*
3. *Write down the reasons from a person-centred perspective why Denise should be helped.*
4. *Are there differences to answers 2 and 3, and if so what are they?*
5. *Are there reasons why you think this may* ***not*** *be the role for ASS involvement?*

CASE STUDY

Amanda's reflections and sequel

In the current climate of cuts in ASS an assessment interview with a qualified social worker may not always be an option, although qualified workers are still attached to health services and there is likely to be discretion at local level concerning how workers are employed. Amanda is a qualified social worker and a skilled interviewer. When talking with Denise she is person centred and focuses on her expressed wishes. She has also recently been on a person-centred training day and knows she should not filter out people too quickly who may have 'lower level presenting needs'. She knows that early intervention may prevent or delay a situation getting more severe. She may be able to 'signpost' Denise to other organisations to open up her opportunities and choices. Early on in the interview she asks if Denise would like to complete a self-assessment questionnaire and says she would help with this. Denise declines, saying that she just wants to talk. She appreciates being listened to and describes why she feels alone in the world and lonely, although her focus is on her early experiences, rather than the present. Nonetheless, she appears resolved to change her life that she feels is less than satisfactory. She thinks that she could best be helped by having a volunteer visit, but Amanda queries how this would help her wish to get out more and be active in her local community. In the event she gave her phone numbers for a local Pilates class and a choir and also details of a food bank in which Denise had expressed an interest (all good examples of 'signposting' she thinks). She took down details of her daughter who is next of kin and also made a brief note on the file. She wondered if she had been sufficiently 'outcomes based' in line with the revised thinking (SCIE, 2010). She shared her brief written record with Denise who signed and dated it. The note read:

> *Denise Lockwood lives alone in a small terraced house in Westfield. She has two grown-up children, Alice Richards and Sam Lockwood, whom she rarely sees following the break-up of her marriage 15 years ago. She regrets not waiting until they were older before she left. Nine years ago she changed jobs and moved to the area following the breakdown of a second significant relationship. She has lost contact with friends from that period and has not made new ones. This often makes her feel sad, particularly now she is retired. She plans to join some local activity groups. Details of local resources and activities have been passed on. A key outcome of this assessment has been to help Denise Lockwood strengthen her links with her community.*

ACTIVITY **1.4**

***The learning point** is that your personal and political values and preferences are likely to determine how you think and feel about Denise Lockwood's needs. Perhaps you could spend some time reflecting on the type of values which you drew on to form your opinion of her needs. Being clear about your own values, and recognising the extent to which personal values may affect professional judgement and practice, is an important part of developing your assessment skills (Banks, 2004).*

Care management and the process of assessment – the legal position

The Local Authority Adult Services, under section 47 of the NHS and Community Care Act 1990, have a legal duty to assess needs for community care services:

> *... where it appears to a local authority that any person for whom they may provide or arrange for the provision of community care services may be in need of any such services, the authority –*
>
> *a) shall carry out an assessment of his needs for those services; and*
>
> *b) having regard to the results of the assessment, shall decide whether his needs call for the provision by them of any such services.*

In terms of the community care legislation, the legal duty is primarily to assess where there is an appearance of need. This is not the same as assessment on request. Further, other requirements of the ASS are not laid down by legal statute, and are conveyed to local authorities through government guidance and circulars. As such, these documents are not as powerful and are more open to interpretation and local discretion. (Many of these discretionary powers are set to change with the new legislation following the Care Bill, 2013, which at the time of writing is making its way through the parliamentary process). Early guidance for practitioners (Social Services Inspectorate and Department of Health, 1991a, pp47–56) suggested that care managers should approach their work on assessment in a sequence similar to the following ten steps.

1. Negotiate the scope of the assessment.
2. Find the appropriate setting – ideally one which is most relaxing for the service user.
3. Clarify expectation.
4. Promote participation – users and carers to be encouraged to participate to the limit of their capacity.
5. Establish a relationship of trust – by drawing on helping skills.
6. Assess need – guided by the user's view of the problem and the clarification of the cause of the problem by the care manager.
7. Determine eligibility.
8. Set priorities.
9. Agree objectives – and how these can be achieved.
10. Record the assessment of need and share with the service user.

Supported self-directed assessment

At the heart of a person-centred approach is a belief that individuals are the experts on their circumstances and felt needs, that they know what is best for them and therefore should be responsible, with assistance if necessary, for driving the assessment process, as opposed to it being driven by a care manager. The shift in practice is away from seeing people as service users with needs towards viewing them more broadly as citizens within their local communities with rights and responsibilities. A fundamental premise of such an approach is conveyed in the self-assessment.

Ideally these are completed privately by the individual or with support from the care manager/advocate. The forms usually cover a range of domains such as those listed below. Normally the service user is asked to give a numerical score of importance, in terms of their need, against each domain and an overall score is reached. The domains listed by Gardner (2011, p41) are:

- personal care needs
- nutritional needs
- practical/daily living
- physical and mental well-being
- relationships and social inclusion
- choice and control
- risk
- family carer and social support.

The legal position of supported self-directed assessment

The term supported self-directed assessment is commonly used when a social worker/ care manager or advocate is involved in the process. After some deliberation the conclusion was reached by the Association of Directors of Adult Social Services (2009a) that self-assessment is not a lawful process if resources are required of the local authority, such as when applying for a personal budget in the form of DP through the local authority's resource funding known as the resource allocation system (RAS). This is a local centralised approach for allocating money for social care, either in the form of a direct payment or home care services. If this is the case, then it is the legal duty of the authority to require that officers (social workers/care managers), acting on their behalf, assess an individual under the current 1990 NHS and Community Care legislation. In light of this and the revision of FACS (see below), the government (Department of Health, 2010b) has sought to put into place a whole system approach to assessments that conflates both types of assessment and aims to make them outcomes based.

Eligibility criteria and fair access to care services

An important element of the assessment, and one which many would argue captured the spirit of the culture of care management, is that of targeting assessment and resources on those people with the greatest needs. In order to fulfil the targeting imperative, local authorities with responsibilities for adult services have been steered by government to implement assessment criteria, known as 'eligibility criteria'. These are scales in which levels of dependency are described in order of need and risk. The categories are then matched with a service user's profile of need as determined in the assessment.

The early recommendation was that the full eligibility scale should be used, but many authorities focused their attention on the higher risk banding, with stricter eligibility criteria for certain adult service users. The government was concerned about the inconsistency between authorities and thus a national system that was unfair (Department of Health, 2002c, p13). As a consequence it set a national eligibility framework based on risks that are linked with various forms of disability, impairment and difficulty. As part of the FACS (Department of Health, 2002b) local authorities were charged to review their eligibility criteria by April 2003. In implementing this guidance, local authorities were and are allowed to take into consideration their resources available for adult services. The government recognised that, as a consequence, services may differ between localities, but the aspiration is that *people with similar needs (are) to be assured of similar care outcomes* (p2). Resource issues within care management are a significant aspect (see section on financing care plans for adults in Chapter 3). The guidance on eligibility prioritises the risks faced by individuals into four bands: critical, substantial, moderate and low. These describe the seriousness of the risk which, if not addressed, will affect, for example, independence (Department of Health, 2003a).

In spite of the emphasis on fair access the continued drift, exacerbated by public sector spending cuts, was for local authorities to raise the eligibility thresholds and respond only to those people whose needs were in the higher categories. The Commission for Social Care Inspection (CSCI, 2008) wrote a critical review. It made the substantial point that by raising the thresholds without having preventative strategies in place would lead to higher and more expensive demand in the longer term. In 2010 the government redesigned fair access to care (Department of Health, 2010b), which was to be viewed within the context of public sector reforms. It urged local authorities to recognise and respond to the needs of the whole community as well as the individual when allocating resources. By responding to people in the lower bands of eligibility, it argued that universal and preventative services are promoted that should help sustain a more person-centred approach to adult care. The four eligibility bands remain the same as they were in 2003. They are:

Low

When:

- *there is, or will be, an inability to carry out one or two personal care or domestic routines; and/or*
- *involvement in one or two aspects of work, education or learning cannot or will not be sustained; and/or*
- *one or two social support systems and relationships cannot or will not be sustained; and/or*
- *one or two family and other social roles and responsibilities cannot or will not be undertaken.*

Moderate

When:

- *there is, or will be, an inability to carry out several personal care or domestic routines; and/or*

- *involvement in several aspects of work, education or learning cannot or will not be sustained; and/or*
- *several social support systems and relationships cannot or will not be sustained; and/or*
- *several family and other social roles and responsibilities cannot or will not be undertaken.*

Substantial

When:

- *there is, or will be, only partial choice and control over the immediate environment; and/or*
- *abuse or neglect has occurred or will occur; and/or*
- *there is, or will be, an inability to carry out the majority of personal care or domestic routines; and/or*
- *involvement in many aspects of work, education or learning cannot or will not be sustained; and/or*
- *the majority of social support systems and relationships cannot or will not be sustained; and/or*
- *the majority of family and other social roles and responsibilities cannot or will not be undertaken.*

Critical

When:

- *life is, or will be, threatened; and/or*
- *significant health problems have developed or will develop; and/or*
- *there is, or will be, little or no choice and control over vital aspects of the immediate environment; and/or*
- *serious abuse or neglect has occurred or will occur; and/or*
- *there is, or will be, an inability to carry out vital personal care or domestic routines; and/or*
- *vital involvement in work, education or learning cannot or will not be sustained; and/or*
- *vital social support systems and relationships cannot or will not be sustained; and/or*
- *vital family and other social roles and responsibilities cannot or will not be undertaken.*

(SCIE, 2010, p1–4)

SCIE (2010) reinforced the government's position by arguing that by responding to need across the spectrum, local communities would be strengthened (p3) and support planning, personalisation and preventative strategies would be promoted (p2). Commentators, however, have reflected (Lymbery, 2012) that there is a conundrum that pervades the eligibility criteria and FACS. At a time when ASS are pledged to embrace the tenets of personalisation in its widest sense, by promoting preventative initiatives that would fit well with moderate and low categories of eligibility, financial stringencies continue to erode public services, particularly in the adult sector, requiring an even greater tightening and raising of the eligibility criteria bar for service.

We return once more to the evolving case.

CASE STUDY

Phase Two: Denise Lockwood – an incident in the community

It was a year later, one evening in February, when Denise Lockwood surprised and disturbed her neighbours, Mr and Mrs Brown, when she banged loudly on their door. They had never seen her in such an anxious and dishevelled state. She said she had been shouted at and chased by a gang of youths when she was leaving the local supermarket. She did not want to call the police or make a fuss, but the Browns were concerned and invited her in for a cup of tea. After a while she seemed to calm down and then left abruptly. Mrs Brown called by the following day to see how she was. This was the first time she had been in the house, although they had been neighbours for many years. She was shocked by what she found. The house was in a chaotic state. There were piles of clothes and unwashed bed linen on the floor, dirty crockery was stacked high in the sink and all surfaces were covered with clutter. Denise appeared disorientated and subdued. She said she felt as if she was in a fog and had difficulty remembering things. She was reluctant but finally agreed that Mrs Brown could contact her GP on her behalf.

When the receptionist passed on the information to Dr Dyson, he said it seemed to be more a social problem, and passed the referral to Amanda Thorpe, since she already knew Denise. She arranged to visit her the following day.

The home visit

Denise did not recognise Amanda when she knocked on the door. At first she was apprehensive and withdrawn but her anxiety was allayed by Amanda's friendly manner. She had no recollection of their previous meeting, nor of their conversation. Amanda barely recognised Denise since her appearance was much changed: she looked unkempt; was several stones heavier; and seemed considerably older both in facial expression and gait. From the neighbour's description, Amanda was expecting to find the house in a mess, but she was still surprised by the scale of it. Her intention was to hear Denise's view of what was happening and to be steered by her. The local youths preoccupied her thoughts. She seemed to be in a state of crisis and was keen to talk.

The recent incident had upset her. While she knew the parents of the youths and where they lived, emotionally she felt threatened, intimidated and unable to deal with it. She said she also felt overwhelmed by her domestic chaos that was made worse by her not being able to concentrate, or remember things. She found the washing machine too complicated to use and could not find the instruction leaflet. The rings on the electric cooker were not working and she had not got around to having them fixed. Hence most days she phoned for a take-away. Of late she had forgotten the code to access her computer and practical things such as accessing her bank were not happening. She tended to pay for most items by credit card but admitted that some household bills were not getting paid. Some days she got up very late and never got around to opening the curtains. She had some local acquaintances but no close friends and felt she could not have anyone round, given the mess in the house. Recently her daughter Alice had moved into the area and seemed to want to be in contact. This has pleased her enormously, but she still feels guilty about how she left the family. When they had talked for a while and she had heard her story, Amanda asked Denise if she would like to complete a self-assessment form and said that she would help with this. She agreed. Most of the lengthy form is in a tick box format, broken down into sub-sections under headings such as those of the domains listed above, followed by an open-ended section for supporting information. In one of the latter she writes 'My main problem is that I can't remember things. I also can't stop thinking about the past and I think this is stopping me getting on with my life'. In another section she writes that one of the most difficult aspects of her life is sorting out ordinary tasks, such as laundry. There are gaps in the form and Amanda tells her not to worry since it is an ongoing process.

Amanda's reflections and decisions taken

While Denise is filling in the form (with some difficulty and much prompting) Amanda is thinking through how best to proceed. She knows from her recent training that self-assessment should come before formal assessment as a way of putting the person at the heart of the process, and that she should focus on strengths, assets and networks rather than on the deficits (SCIE, 2010). She is also aware of her legal duties to assess before she applies for resources through the RAS. Only when this process is completed will she need Denise to fill in a form about her personal finances.

Staying in the moment, Amanda and Denise work out an immediate plan based on what she has indicated on the form as most pressing. They attempt to word it in terms of outcomes. Denise wants help with managing her home and does not know if she can afford a cleaner. Amanda would like more knowledge of what she can do for herself. Hence she suggests that an OT attached to the surgery visits to help Denise work out what she can do for herself and where she really needs help. Denise likes the idea. She says that her daughter has already offered to 'declutter' the house, and now she is ready to agree to it. She also wants to know more about her memory problems and wonders if Amanda can have a word with her GP, since she feels he has not been responsive in the past. Amanda agrees. She wonders if Denise would like to talk in more detail about her current and past worries to a colleague, John Hughes, who could offer some counselling. Denise thinks it is

(Continued)

(Continued)

a good idea. Amanda leaves the house saying she will phone in a few days to see how she is getting on with the form.

Further reflections

As Amanda is walking away from the house she reflects that there are many uncertainties and things that just do not add up. Denise is an educated person who, in the recent past, has held down a responsible job. Now her capacity seems different and she has difficulty completing quite a basic form. She had expected her to be more depressed than she is. She seems to engage with people and yet actively seems to deprive herself of social activity. Why? The short-term memory loss seems significant and may explain the domestic disarray. Medical input and knowledge is necessary, but a full diagnosis may take some time, she muses. An OT assessment is going to be helpful to build up a fuller picture. She thinks she is in a state of crisis and may be receptive to change, which is why she suggested she see John Hughes. She knows he can offer some work on crisis counselling since she is his practice teacher and he is a competent student.

She wonders whether she steered the decision-making, rather than enabling Denise to maintain the control and direction. At the same time, she argues with herself, if Denise is becoming vulnerable in her community, then she has to balance potential risks with her personal choices. She thinks Denise's needs, in FACS terms, are on a continuum somewhere between moderate and substantial, but she will know better as the assessment unfolds. She remains uneasy and thinks a tipping point may be reached quite quickly that would move her into a higher category.

ACTIVITY 1.5

In light of Denise's expressed wishes and circumstances as described in the home visit, complete a self-assessment form in the eight domains listed above and grade or mark each category in the way you think reflects Denise's felt needs.

What are the strengths in this case as you see it?

What type of universal services and/or preventative intervention would benefit Denise at this point?

If you had to identify self-directed support for Denise, what would it look like?

To what extent do you think and feel Amanda is running with the person-centred agenda? List your reasoning.

From the information disclosed so far, give your reasons why you think Amanda is thinking of banding Denise as indicated (see details above of the four bands)?

Conversely, if you disagree with Amanda's evolving assessment, explain your reasoning.

If you are able to share this activity with a colleague it will help you to identify some of the complex issues involved in determining eligibility and a person's needs. Undertaking this activity will also help you to recognise the centrality of values and ethics for good social work practice.

ACTIVITY **1.6**

How GPs and care managers co-ordinate their work is often a consequence of local arrangements. In this activity in the first chapter, we ask you to find out how similar care managers in your own locality cover health-related work. We also ask you to reflect on whether you think the reasons they give for co-ordinating/transferring work in a particular way is in the best interests of the service user.

ACTIVITY **1.7**

Reflective journal

We have spent some time writing about the reflections of Amanda Thorpe on her work. Developing skills of reflection, as mentioned in the introduction to this textbook, is essential to a critical and planned approach to your work and to your continuing professional development. In order to heighten your skills we strongly recommend that you begin a reflective journal that chronicles your thoughts, perceptions, doubts and queries as you progress through the chapters. We also would like you to complete the activities set in a section of the journal in such a way that you can return to them to edit, amend and critique as you progress through the book.

CHAPTER SUMMARY

In this chapter, you have been introduced to some of the complexities and uncertainties involved in social work assessments. Different understandings and approaches have been introduced and the importance of working together with service users and carers has been promoted. Assessment in social work is both an art and a science, demanding skills and knowledge and requiring a sound value base from which to act. It was stressed that good assessment is the cornerstone of further successful social work. It is important to note that when assessment is separated from the overall social work process, and becomes an end in itself, it creates unnecessary dilemmas that have the potential to harm rather than help (Parker and Doel, 2013). By way of helping you to determine how this knowledge is relevant to the PCF and SoPS, case studies have been developed. You have been able to consider how to assess needs and options and recommend a course of action, and the importance of written

(Continued)

(Continued)

assessments, assessing risk and using your knowledge to assess as part of a wider social work process that involves planning, intervention and review. In the next chapter we will explore a range of helpful techniques to assist you in developing the skills to make effective assessment. Whenever you are involved in assessment work, ask yourself the following questions:

- *What information do you think you need?*
- *Why do you think this is important?*
- *How will you collect it?*
- *How will you make sure that service users are involved at all stages?*
- *How will you construct an assessment report from this information?*
- *What skills are involved in undertaking an assessment?*
- *Write a plan describing what you intend to do on an assessment visit.*
- *What ethical considerations do you need to take into account when conducting a social work assessment?*

It is also important to bear in mind the following:

- *know why you are making an assessment;*
- *know the reasons why your agency makes assessments and to what purpose an assessment will or might be put;*
- *plan carefully for all assessments;*
- *be aware of the power you have as a social worker;*
- *check your assessments carefully with service users and others contributing to the process;*
- *treat the information gained with care and sensitivity – know the bounds and limits of confidentiality.*

Department of Health, Department for Education and Employment, Home Office (2000) *Framework for the assessment of children in need and their families.* London: The Stationery Office.

The Framework provides a comprehensive introduction to assessment in childcare social work, paying attention to theory, practice and the inter-professional context in which social workers practise.

Department of Health (2010) *Prioritising need in the context of putting people first: A whole system approach to eligibility for social care – guidance on eligibility criteria for adult social care.* London: Department of Health.

This is an updated and broader view on how FACS should be implemented within the revised vision of social care for adults.

Gardner, A (2011) *Personalisation in social work.* London: Sage/Learning Matters.

We recommend you read Chapter 1, which provides an informed and succinct explanation of how and why the concept of personalisation has evolved and taken on such importance within the current culture of welfare.

Lymbery, M (2012) Social work and personalisation: Fracturing the bureau-professional compact? *British Journal of Social Work,* 42(4) 783–792.

This is a critical article that puts forward a thought-provoking argument to the effect that social work in the UK will not be best served by the implementation of the personalisation agenda that is set, within a public sector climate of austerity measures, to transform social care.

Milner, J and O'Byrne, P (2009) *Assessment in social work.* 3rd edition. Basingstoke: Palgrave.

This book provides an in-depth and critical treatment of assessment, highlighting the central importance of anti-discriminatory practice and values for social workers undertaking assessment.

Chapter 2

Tools and diagrammatic aids to assessment

ACHIEVING A SOCIAL WORK DEGREE

This chapter will help you to develop the following capabilities, to the appropriate level, from the PCF.

- **Professionalism**
  Representing and being accountable to the profession.
- **Values and ethics**
  Apply social work ethical principles and values to guide professional practice.
- **Diversity**
  Recognise diversity and apply anti-discriminatory and anti-oppressive principles in practice.
- **Knowledge**
  Apply knowledge of social sciences, law and social work practice theory.
- **Critical reflection and analysis**
  Apply critical reflection and analysis to inform and provide a rationale for professional decision-making.
- **Intervention and skills**
  Use judgement and authority to intervene with individuals, families and communities to promote independence, provide support and prevent harm, neglect and abuse.
- **Professional leadership**
  Take responsibility for the professional learning and development of others through supervision, mentoring, assessing, research, teaching, leadership and management.

It will also introduce you to the following academic standards as set out in the social work subject benchmark statement.

5.1.4 **Social work theory.**
5.1.5 **The nature of social work practice.**
5.5 **Problem-solving skills.**
5.5.2 **Gathering information.**
5.5.3 **Analysis and synthesis.**

Introduction

There are a number of aids, activities and tools that can be employed to gather and represent the data social workers may collect in order to complete initial and ongoing assessments. In this chapter, we shall consider five particular tools that can help in making assessments and beginning to analyse information collected from service users and carers. These are:

- genograms;
- ecomaps;
- culturagrams;
- flow charts;
- life road maps (the latter two will be considered together).

Making an assessment is not a value-neutral activity and your prior experiences, thoughts and beliefs will influence the process and your understanding of the information gathered. The fundamental importance of a critically reflective approach is central to social work, partly because it is a human-to-human interactive and relational activity (Ruch, 2013). Therefore, when undertaking an assessment, it is helpful to ask yourself the following questions throughout this chapter:

- Why am I collecting this information?
- What right have I to collect this information? Is it by legal mandate or by request (see Marsh, 2008)?
- To what purposes will this information be put?
- How would I react if asked to undertake these activities?
- How might I react if someone was collecting this information about me or members of my family (especially those who may be vulnerable in some way)?

It is also important to keep the person using social work services at the heart of the assessment as we have seen in Chapter 1, something reiterated by Eileen Munro in her report on child and family social work (Munro, 2011). It will help, therefore, to ask yourself, 'How can I best include the person requesting or receiving a service?' At times throughout the section you will be asked to complete activities about your own family, lifestyle and networks. Undertaking this work may raise issues that you have not thought about before or trigger quite deep-seated feelings. Be prepared for this and, if you are affected, seek some support from colleagues, friends or other trusted people. Remember, assessment is not an emotionally neutral area; professionals are also human beings and looking after yourself is important too (Howe, 2013; Thompson, 2013). If you are challenged in some ways by information about your family and life, consider how much greater these feelings might be for someone who is volunteering this information in a social work relationship. In this chapter we are deliberately using a different case study to the ones used throughout the rest of the book. This will help to demonstrate the versatility of the tools, and hopefully allow you to envisage how they may be applied in your practice. At the end of this chapter you will be asked to review what you have learned by applying your knowledge to what you know about one of the other developing case studies employed in the book.

Genograms

The uses of genograms

A genogram is a type of family tree, something that many of us are familiar with from such websites as Genes Reunited® (www.genesreunited.co.uk) or ancestory.co.uk (www.ancestry.co.uk). The genogram provides a technical application of these popular tools, and offers an immediate visual representation of the individual or family being assessed. It is a 'snapshot' of how that person or family is structured and viewed at a particular point in time. As such, it can be useful in highlighting to social workers those areas that may cause concern and information that is lacking and needs to be sought. It may also identify areas or themes for further exploration with the service user. Furthermore, as it is a family tree, it presents a historical picture or document from which the social worker can gain insight into a variety of patterns regularly occurring within that family unit and that may still influence the way in which that family operates. Thus, as Hartman (1995) states in her classic paper, the genogram can be useful in portraying the family unit across time.

Genograms are not undertaken solely for the benefit of social workers, however. Using genograms is a participative activity that can help you to form a working relationship with service users. This is, of course, beneficial in forming constructive working alliances, and encouraging the development of service users' motivations to work with you. Involvement in an interactive and practical activity, which compiling a genogram can be, may help to reduce nervousness and anxiety by placing something between the service user and yourself as a social work practitioner. This can act as a focus of attention rather than the people compiling the genogram. Being actively involved in the genogram's construction may enable service users to feel better as a result of 'doing something'. This active approach can help to restore confidence in the service user's ability to take a degree of control in their life. It has the additional benefit of helping the service user to recognise patterns, to face difficult areas and to consider their family history as a process in which they are intimately involved. Hodge (2005) adds an important perspective to the use of genograms, and other tools, to assess spiritual needs. Unfortunately, his paper does associate spirituality rather too easily with religious belief but genograms can be used to identify these belief systems and patterns important to those families and individuals completing them.

The construction of a genogram on paper is a fairly simple task. However, it can be a very powerful process and may raise a number of varying emotions within those completing the task. Social workers need to be mindful of this and to be sensitive to the emotions of the subject. This, of course, can add to the assessment process. An additional benefit of the genogram can be its capacity to engender discussion and to raise important issues that social workers need to deal with and which may not have been recognised, or the opportunity to explore would not have arisen if the activity had not been undertaken. However, this cannot be done at the expense of the service user's level of comfort with the process. The pace of the work must take its lead from the service user and, especially in the case of children and young people, it must take into account the age and development of the service user. People will need time to assimilate information about themselves, their lives and their families. The social worker who allows this time is likely to be appreciated by service users for respecting their feelings and situations. This can add to the development of a positive working relationship.

Symbols used in developing genograms

There are a number of almost universally accepted symbols used in the compilation of genograms. These can be found in most books concerning systemic family therapy, but an especially good point of reference is McGoldrick, Gerson and Petry (2008), which details the many different symbols and indicators to be used. The most common symbols are shown in Figure 2.1.

The relationship between generations is shown by lines connecting parents to children. This is shown in Figure 2.2 that includes further common symbols used in genograms.

When collecting the information and compiling the genogram with the service user, it is important that you collect full names, dates of birth, and the exact dates of significant events within the family life history. Asking service users for the dates when their parents married, divorced, or when grandparents died, the dates of separations and divorces, dates of marriages, or having children helps to map out significant historical events and contextualises them. This is important for the social worker and equally important for the subjects of the genogram. However, it is not always easy to ask questions about the intimate details of a person's life or family. Sometimes using a genogram can help the social worker overcome these difficulties and ensure that a comprehensive assessment has been undertaken.

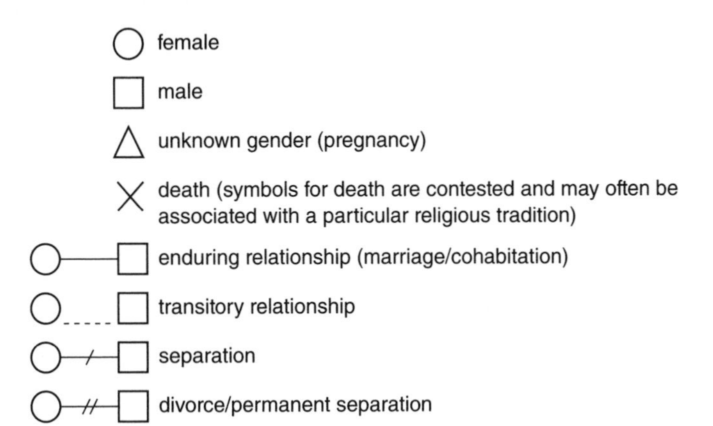

Figure 2.1 Genogram symbols

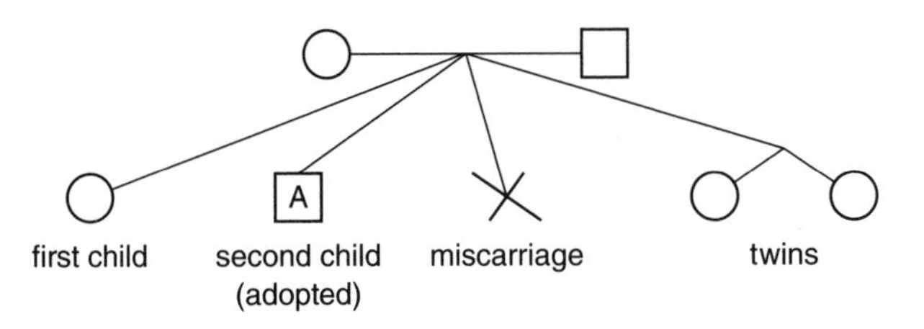

Figure 2.2 Developing connections and relationships using genograms

Assume, for instance, that you are working with the Pritchard family and their concerns about Tom, their second child, who is adopted. Eleanor and James Pritchard are worried that Tom is not settling in with the family. You have been asked to make an assessment of their current situation and have begun to compile a genogram. You have explained to the family that in order to help with their situation in the best possible way you will need to look widely at the family, its history, composition and present situation. Eleanor and James agree, being aware of assessments from their adoption of Tom. Constructing a genogram can be an interactive activity that helps families and social workers engage with one another. Therefore, you might ask James and Eleanor to draw their family situation. Let us consider that the following information is provided (see Figure 2.3).

You note that the date of Tom's adoption is not mentioned nor is the date of the miscarriage. Also, there is no information about James' or Eleanor's parents or siblings or, indeed, dates of birth. In identifying this missing information you are formulating possible further questions to ask or avenues to explore. In this case it would be helpful to point to some of the missing information. Perhaps you might say 'I see you have put down Tom's year of birth, and it is the same as Alicia's. However, I wonder if you could tell me when he was adopted?' You may also wish to ask directly if James and Eleanor have any brothers or sisters, and about their parents. In asking for this factual information you will then be in a position to search more deeply and to look at the involvement of grandparents, uncles and aunts in the life of the family. This depends on the information being gathered and, as a social worker, you need to develop the skills to determine where, when and how questions should be asked. As a start, the genogram allows you to identify gaps in information and to clarify your understanding.

It can be hard to ask difficult and personal questions but harder still to answer them. Remembering this when making an assessment will help. It is useful to acknowledge how difficult it might be to answer a question when asking it. If, for instance, you

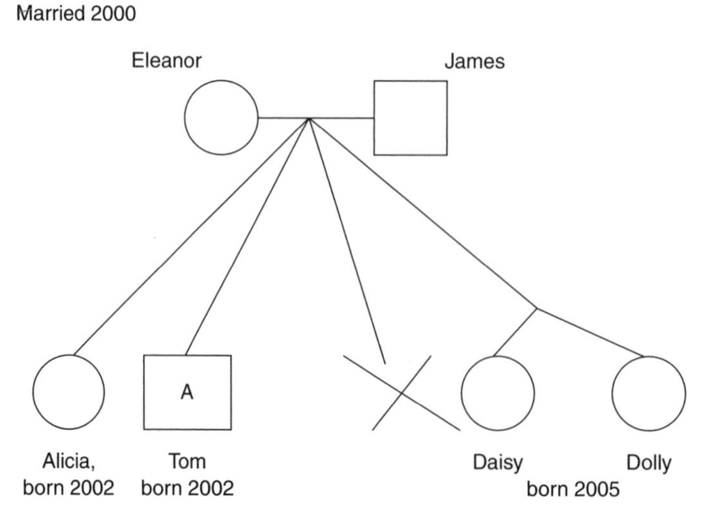

Figure 2.3 James and Eleanor

wanted to know a little more about Eleanor's miscarriage and how it might have impacted on the family, you might ask 'I recognise that this might be a difficult thing to talk about, but you have included having a miscarriage in your genogram. Could you tell me when that happened?' Depending on the answer, and how it was conveyed, you may wish to explore matters further.

Imagine that your questions provided the following information: Eleanor had a miscarriage in 2003; Eleanor's parents both died in a car crash in 1990 when she was 13. This was six years before she and James met in 1996 when she was 19 and he was 20 years old. Eleanor is an only child. James' parents are still alive and are involved in the family. However, since Tom's adoption in 2009 they have tended to argue more with James and Eleanor and are convinced that they are 'storing up trouble' by adopting Tom. His difficulties settling down at home and reports of unacceptable behaviour at school confirm their view to James' parents. James' brother and partner are described as very supportive. The genogram has brought more information to light that could be used to help Tom settle into the family. The genogram itself now looks like Figure 2.4.

Genograms in family therapy

The work of Burnham (1986) and Hartman (1995), working from a systemic perspective in family therapy and social work respectively, is extremely relevant to our discussion. The use of the genogram began to be debated in these texts. Barker (1986) places genograms in the context of assessment prior to intervening with whole families in a therapeutic context. He places the genogram in the wider perspective of family assessment.

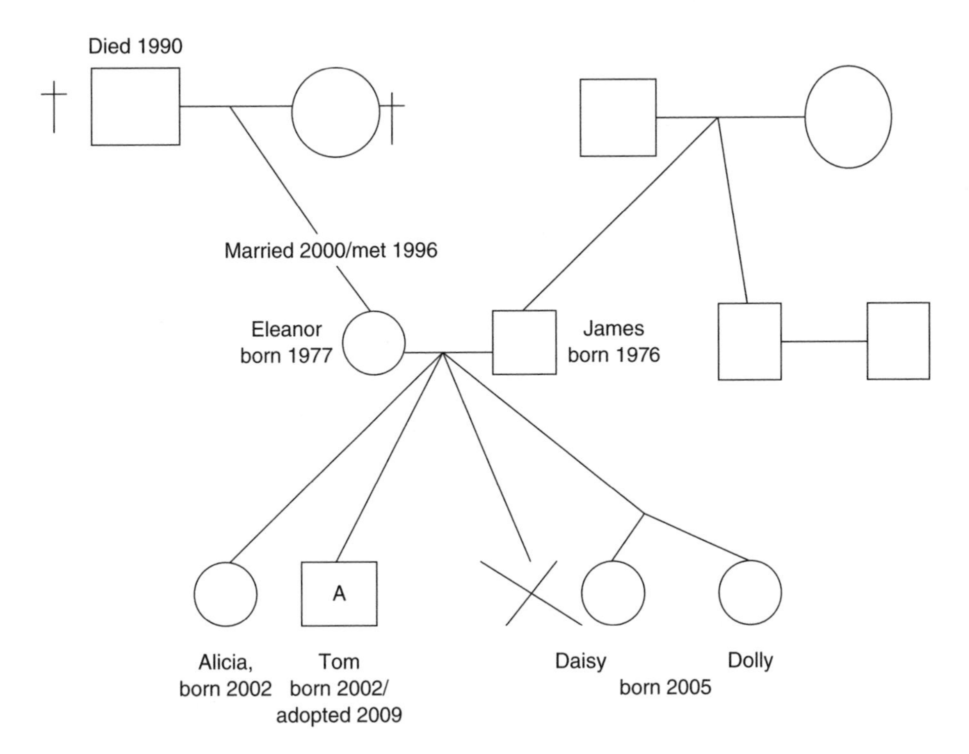

Figure 2.4 James and Eleanor across three generations

In his work, he reviews one of the key models family workers have employed in assessing the functioning of families – the circumplex model – which examines how cohesive or adaptable family members are. Barker also considers a range of different assessment models. The genogram contributes to whichever model of assessment is employed. It is now considered central to working in child and family social work, when undertaking comprehensive assessments and in direct work with children and young people.

Given the range of emotions that may surface and the potential for uncovering previously unconsidered patterns in a service user's family history, it is important for the social worker to have some idea of how this may feel for service users. By completing the following activity, you will have a chance to explore some of these emotions.

ACTIVITY 2.1

Using the symbols outlined above, construct your own genogram. Do this for at least three generations in your family. You can place yourself at any generational level depending upon your circumstances. For instance, if you are the child in your genogram, you will need to include grandparents and parents. If you are a parent you might be 'sandwiched' between your parents and your children. However, if you place yourself at the grandparent level please include a fourth level to indicate your parents. This will give a sense of change over history.

When you have completed your genogram, examine it closely for patterns or norms of behaviour or event. Some examples may help here:

- *If there are no separations or divorces in your family history, does this suggest an unspoken rule about commitment to relationships?*
- *If daughters tend not to marry/cohabit until late, does this explain the hostility to your sister leaving home to live with a partner at the age of 18?*
- *Might the family approach to death and bereavement be influenced by the fact that males have tended to die in their early 60s, while females have lived until their late 80s?*

Think about how the process of constructing the genogram made you feel. Was it sometimes an emotional and painful experience? In what ways was this painful, exciting or simply informative and interesting? Can you think of some ways in which some of the strong emotions that may be raised when constructing a genogram can be ameliorated? Did you discover things about your family and your own attitudes and values that now seem more understandable? How does this make you feel?

COMMENT

Common reactions and thoughts often reflect a mix of sadness, when thinking of relatives who may have died or relationships that have ended, and enjoyment and fascination, when learning things about one's own family. Perhaps some of the ways in which painful memories can be ameliorated include having another person with you to share feelings with, by writing down thoughts about losses, by slowing the pace or by leaving aside aspects of one's family history until feeling more comfortable. Olsen, Dudley-Brown and McMullen (2004) extend the use of genograms into areas of health which may be of increasing importance when undertaking multidisciplinary assessments which feature highly in contemporary practice.

By attempting this activity you may learn ways of using genograms in sensitive and empowering ways with service users, as well as for the professional purpose of collecting and analysing information. You may wish to write down your answers and add to them as you complete this chapter.

The following case study demonstrates some of the uses of a genogram in both collecting information and beginning to establish an understanding of situations in which people find themselves. This is something that needs to happen before being able to plan and intervene to bring about change.

CASE STUDY

Damien Jones was referred by his mother who was concerned that he seemed to spend long periods on his own and was not developing in the same way as her other two children. Given this scant information it was necessary to make arrangements to conduct a comprehensive assessment of the situation. At the first interview a social and personal history was taken. Part of this process was achieved by the compilation of a genogram. In the first instance this was done to help elucidate the composition of the family. It was explained to Mrs Jones that it was important to see the family as a whole and to consider how Damien fitted in.

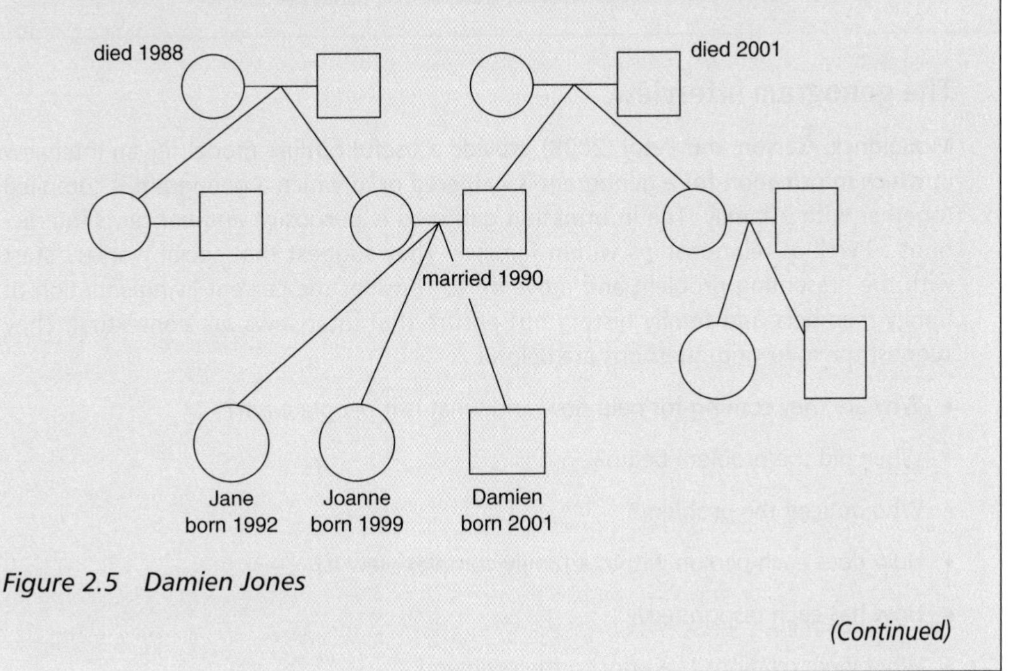

Figure 2.5 Damien Jones

(Continued)

(Continued)

During the course of the interview it transpired that Mrs Jones was, in fact, concerned that her mother-in-law appeared to favour the other two children and to ignore Damien. The genogram helped the social worker to question in a focused manner and to make a hypothesis relating to the death of Damien's grandfather in 2001 and Damien's birth. It is not always the case that such hypotheses work. However, in this particular case it was found that Damien was born only one week after the death of his grandfather. This had led to several ramifications in an otherwise fairly well functioning family. Mrs Jones had enjoyed a good relationship with her mother-in-law who had helped with the care of Jane and Joanne over a number of years, especially during the pregnancy with Damien. During this pregnancy Mrs Jones had been quite ill and at times was incapacitated. Mr Jones' mother helped out when it was not possible for him to take time off from work. Unfortunately, Mr Jones' father became ill and, after only a short illness, died. Mrs Jones' mother-in-law now blamed her for being ill when her husband was ill, and Damien served as a constant reminder of her bereavement. As a result, Mrs Jones no longer received help from her mother-in-law, and when she did visit, she ignored Damien while lavishing attention on Jane and Joanne. The increased demands on her time meant that Mrs Jones herself could not spend as much time with Damien as she had with her other two children and, upon further exploration, she felt guilty about this.

The genogram taken in this case study provided useful visual information, an opportunity to form a working hypothesis, and it created an atmosphere conducive to frank and open discussion. It did not say anything directly about the networks of support available and utilised by the family, however. This information had to be sought, initially, from careful questioning. A way of gathering such information in a visual way is contained in the eco-map. It is to this particular assessment tool that we will turn next.

The genogram interview

McGoldrick, Gerson and Petry (2008) provide a useful outline model for an interview in which information for a genogram is gathered or in which a genogram is compiled together with a family. The information gathered is purposive and concerns interactions as well as relationships within families. They suggest that social workers start with the presenting problem and move on to consider the current living situation of family members and family history but ensure that interviews are contextual. They suggest the following questions are helpful.

- Why are they coming for help now and what is it people want?
- When did the problem begin?
- Who noticed the problem?
- How does each person within a family complex view it?
- How has each responded?
- What were relations like prior to the problem?

- Has the problem had an impact on relationships? If so, in what ways?
- What will happen if it continues?

During the interview social workers will explore deeply the living context and the rituals, beliefs and expectations within those families with whom they are working. McGoldrick, Gerson and Petry (2008) see the genogram as part of the process of working towards change and include service user strengths to enable an analysis of the information and potential for change. Other suggested questions include the following.

- Who lives in the household (names, ages, gender)?
- How is each related?
- Where do other family members live?
- Were there any similar problems in the family before?
- What solutions were tried in the past (therapy, treatment, hospitalisation, etc.)?
- What has been happening recently in the family?
- Have there been any recent changes or stressors?

The depth and purposes to which the genogram interview and its development can be put are manifold. This can include:

- tracking individuals' lives over time, and examining patterns, commonalities and differences;
- identifying location, space and movement such as where people have lived, how often they have moved and so forth;
- illuminating family functioning and highlighting areas for further exploration;
- encouraging exploration and feelings therapeutically;
- family research.

Ecomaps

The genogram placed the family in a temporal context demonstrating its links with history and connections across and between generations. The ecomap is another visual representation useful in assessment and analysis but locates the family and/or individual members within it in a spatial context; it looks at the networks available in the environment in which the person using social work services lives. These networks may represent individuals or organisations and agencies with whom service users interact. Ecomap templates can be downloaded from the internet, but sometimes it is better to develop your own tools, as long as you are keeping to some basic format that will be more widely understandable. This is because it will afford you a greater degree of flexibility in developing the ecomap and using it for assessment, planning and charting change. However, the use of computerised approaches is growing and can be helpful (Gustavsson and MacEachron, 2013). To reflect the focus on social networks, Coulshed and Orme (2006) refer to them explicitly as 'network maps', and others as 'network diagrams'.

Based as it is upon systems thinking, the ecomap seeks to show the various connections and interrelations between a range of systems and sub-systems involved with the family and/or individual members. This means that an ecomap seeks to show how family members act on and react to each other and how the family as a whole relates to other families, groups and organisations in society. It can also be used to demonstrate interrelations between various levels within environmental living systems. A visual representation of the way systems and sub-systems interact may be helpful here.

Figure 2.6 may look, at first glance, very complex. However, it shows the different levels at which individuals and families interact on an everyday basis, considering the influences that come from individuals and families and in return have an impact upon them. For instance, individual family members have a mutual or reciprocal influence on one another, but in turn each family member is influenced by and has an influence on other individuals, families and organisations with whom they have contact. They are also influenced by wider society, portrayals of issues in the media and social policy issues of the day. Part of this wider social view itself stems from the collective influence that individuals have on each other and on the development of wider 'common-sense' or shared understandings.

In the same way that genograms can help the process of engagement with families, so too can the use of ecomaps. Ecomaps provide an 'at-a-glance' perspective, showing who is involved with whom and in what ways. They are participative and can

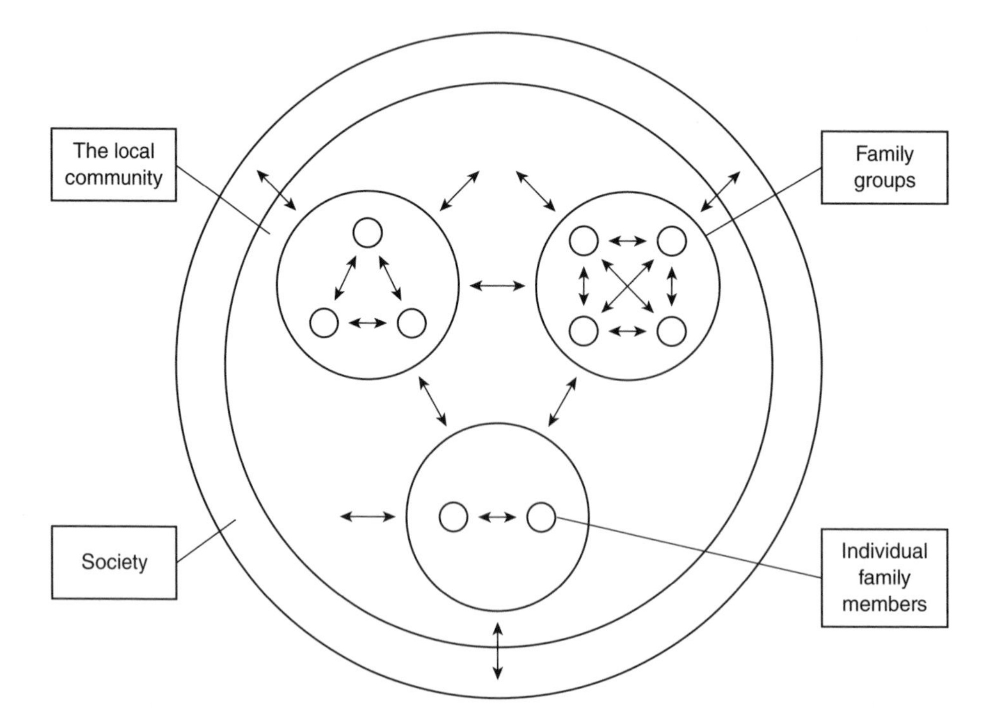

Figure 2.6 Systems and the ways they might relate

foster constructive discussion during their compilation if undertaken together. For instance, the following question may result from using ecomaps with families: Why is it that one member of the family feels that the next-door neighbour represents their strongest support while other members of the family believe her support comes with a high degree of stress? Compiling ecomaps as a family unit can also encourage debate and discussion concerning beliefs and disagreements between members that can be used to deal with issues arising. Just as genograms can show the assets and spiritual interactions across generations, Hodge (2005) also demonstrates how an ecomap can demonstrate spiritual support and connections between people. It must be remembered, however, that just as constructing an ecomap can foster positive debate and discussion, it may give rise to matters that evoke strong feeling and conflict between family members. You need to be aware of this when working with families in this way and to consider ways in which you may lessen tension arising from disagreements, while acknowledging the value of each person's contribution and understanding. Setting some ground rules first may help. Acknowledge that there may be disagreements and state that this is healthy and should be allowed. By making people aware of possible differences and encouraging participants to discuss them you may find a greater willingness to explore issues in more depth.

How to construct an ecomap

Ecomaps or network diagrams are fairly easy to construct. On a large sheet of paper draw a circle in the middle and place the family or individual member's name within it. Following this, a series of smaller circles can be placed around this circle. In each of these place the name of the organisation, institution, social group, family or individual with which the family has connections. The nature of the relationship between the individual and 'circle' can be made clear by the line linking the two. Thick lines indicate strong connections, broken lines indicate weak connections and wavy or crossed lines indicate stress associated with the connection. The following ecomap (Figure 2.7) concerning Mark provides an example.

The ecomap is valuable because of its direct and immediate visual impact. A wealth of information is presented concerning relationships and important individual perceptions

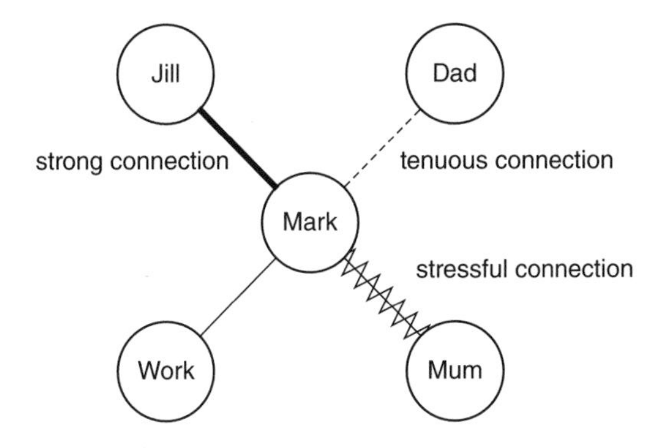

Figure 2.7 Mark's relationships

of these. While it was originally developed as a tool to aid social workers' and family therapists' assessments of family situations, it has, as noted above, value in creating a working partnership in which the service user takes an active role in the assessment. The result of this has been that shared insight has aided planning and subsequent interventions are located firmly within the living space of the service user. The first composition may help the initial assessment but, as we know, human life is never static and changes occur continually. Therefore, constructing further ecomaps at various points throughout the interventive phase can help social workers and service users to evaluate outcomes together. It can also identify possible sources of support to assist the family or individual in working towards change. It is important to note, however, that an ecomap leaves out certain information. For instance, in the above, we are not told Mark's age, where he lives or anything about his family history or life experience. These are questions that can be asked during the construction of the ecomap. However, by combining the ecomap with the genogram we begin to get a more rounded picture of an individual's or family's life and relationships. Hartman (1995), again in her seminal paper, describes the development, construction and uses of ecomaps in social work settings.

It is important to gain an understanding of some of the possible implications and impacts of the models and tools used to make an assessment. This helps us to tailor the tools to particular circumstances and to ensure that issues arising from the process are effectively dealt with. The following activity gives you an opportunity to compile your own ecomap.

ACTIVITY 2.2

Take a piece of flip chart paper and place your name in a circle at the centre of it. Draw circles around the outside of your circle and place the names of family, friends, acquaintances and clubs or organisations with whom you are involved. In this way you will begin to construct your own map. Consider carefully the relationships and connections you have with the various organisations, agencies, groups, families and individuals that you have placed in the outer circles. By using a combination of different lines, thicknesses and comments, show the strength of these relationships and your feelings towards them. You may be able to compile a retrospective ecomap that may help, in some way, to demonstrate changes that have occurred throughout your life. Of course, when drawing such ecomaps retrospectively you are open to interpreting the past in the light of the present. However, for experiential purposes it forms a useful exercise. Keep your ecomap for later consultation and adaptation if you wish. It may be useful to compare the ecomap with your genogram to see how they fit together, what different information each map includes and what each says about you. Ask yourself how these tools might add to an effective assessment when working as a social worker.

The genogram was extremely useful in the case study of Mrs Jones and her concerns with regard to Damien. The case study continues below to demonstrate what additional information could be gained from an ecomap.

CASE STUDY

At a later assessment session it was agreed to construct an ecomap (see Figure 2.8). The intention was to find out exactly what levels of support Mrs Jones now had, how she felt about the support and how this compared with the support she had enjoyed previously. It was also thought likely that in the compilation of the ecomap it may be that further sources of support would be discussed, identified and an interventive strategy determined.

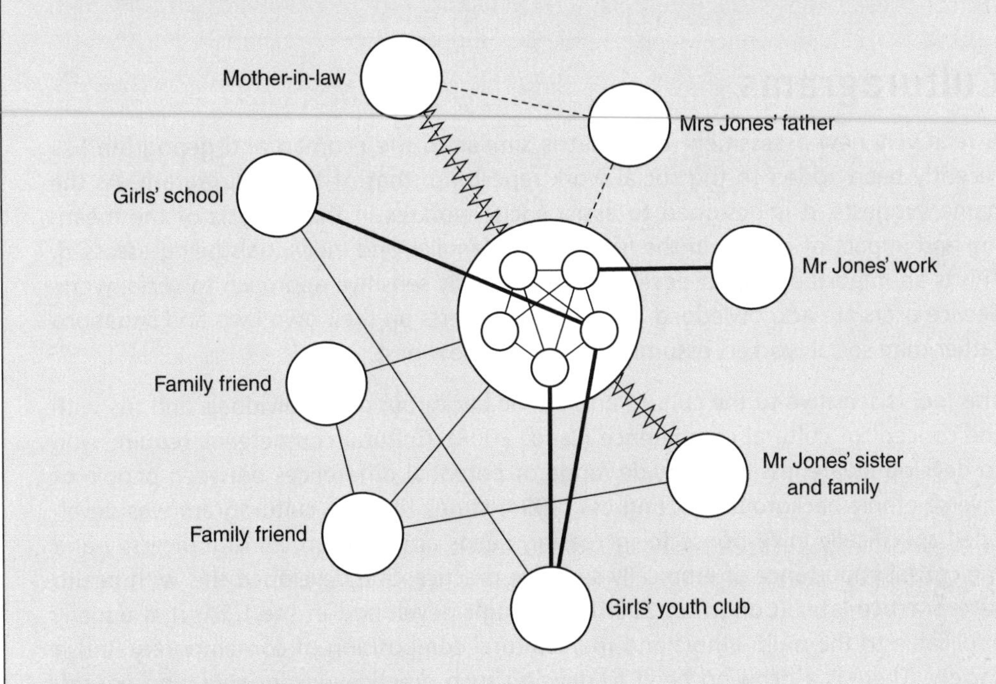

Figure 2.8 Mrs Jones' ecomap

It quickly became apparent that Mr and Mrs Jones had mutual friends, Mr Jones worked and enjoyed this, and the girls enjoyed good relations with their school and youth club. Mrs Jones, however, had little if anything to occupy herself outside of the family unit. In fact, since the deterioration in her relationship with her mother-in-law she had little support within the family. Her father had not seen her for some years. She described her relationship with him as stormy in the past. On further exploration it seemed that they disagreed on most things since the death of her mother. This culminated in her marriage two years after to Mr Jones. They had been seeing one another for some time but Mrs Jones' father had never approved of the relationship. When she married Mr Jones her father visited only rarely until he ceased visiting completely some years ago. A source of support and friendship in Mr Jones' sister had been lost after an argument following the death of Mr Jones' father.

The ecomap proved extremely useful in presenting a visual and pictorial display of relationships and isolation. It gave rise, also, to the beginning formulation of an interventive strategy aimed at securing positive and supportive connections for Mrs Jones outside of the family environment and within her control.

An interesting variant of the ecomap or network diagram is that of the Outcomes Star™. This represents a system of measuring the various social and professional supports available to people in a range of situations they may be experiencing as problematic such as substance use, homelessness or mental health issues (www.outcomesstar.org.uk/about-the-outcomes-star/). What the various Outcomes Star™ approaches tell us is that these visual aids to assessment are flexible and it is possible for you to adapt them to the particular social work situations in which you find yourself.

Culturagrams

A relatively new assessment tool that is similar to the ecomap and genogram has recently been added to the social work repertoire: that of the culturagram. As the name suggests, it is designed to assist social workers in the analysis of the meaning and impact of culture in the life of those families and individuals being assessed. This is an important tool in developing a culturally sensitive approach to social work. Service users are acknowledged as being the experts on their own lives and situations rather than social workers assuming that they know best.

The tool is sensitive to the culture and ethnic background of individuals and fits with the concept of cultural competence (Laird, 2008). Cultural competence requires you to develop awareness of the wide range of potential differences between people of diverse ethnic backgrounds. Congress (1994) states that the culturagram was developed specifically in response to increasing needs arising from cultural diversity and the crucial importance of ethnically sensitive practice. She developed this with health care practice later (Congress, 2004). Although developed in the USA, it is equally applicable to the multi-ethnic and multicultural composition of contemporary British society. There is a growing need to develop such practice with people who are refugees or asylum seekers and this assessment tool allows a social worker to gather information on the impact of the move for individuals involved and to gain the story of people at first hand (Parker, 2000). A culturagram can allow practitioners to ask questions and can allow others to be the experts on their own lives, assisting the development of cultural competence (Laird, 2008).

RESEARCH SUMMARY

Yu and Tran (2011) state that the culturagram represents an important tool when working using a diversity-based approach that recognises the fluidity of difference within cultures as well as across them. They acknowledge in their conceptual paper that a culturagram as an assessment tool highlights that different members of the same ethnic minority group may attach significance in different ways and to different aspects in respect of their cultural heritage. Given that such differences may be affected by length of time in the new or host community and whether or not people have been able to obtain legal status within that country, a culturagram can illuminate a family's or individual's situation.

They stress also that culturagrams support the concept of fluidity of culture, recognising that culture can be created and re-created in different aspects of life and during different times. A third important point that Yu and Tran raise is the capacity for culturagrams to identify structural issues that affect people's quality of life as members of an ethnic minority group.

There are ten important factors about which information is gathered in the culturagram. These are:

- the reasons for immigration;
- length of time in the community;
- legal or undocumented status;
- age at time of immigration;
- language spoken at home and in the community;
- contact with cultural institutions;
- health beliefs;
- holidays and special events;
- the impact of crisis and significant events;
- values held about family, education and work.

Constructing a culturagram involves using excellent communication skills. Asking sensitive questions is not easy in any situation. Where people may be suspicious of authority figures asking questions, sometimes because of particularly traumatic past experiences, great sensitivity is necessary. Social workers must explain very clearly why such information is needed, what it will be used for and who will have access to it. This may slow the process of assessment but it is important if the information is going to be used in the most effective ways. Rushing or pushing too hard may result in spurious information being given or may indeed impede the development of constructive working relationships. Sometimes working at the pace of service users will involve you developing and using skills of assertion within social work teams, especially when you are being pressed to achieve objectives and targets within specified timeframes.

It is also important to be mindful of language and communication issues, especially where English is a second language. Social workers will need to ask careful, concrete questions and be prepared to repeat or put certain questions to one side. Summaries of discussion, paraphrasing and sharing written copies of the information can help in developing good practice. The information gathered in response to the ten areas highlighted above is drawn together to form a culturagram in a diagram similar to the ecomap (see Figure 2.9).

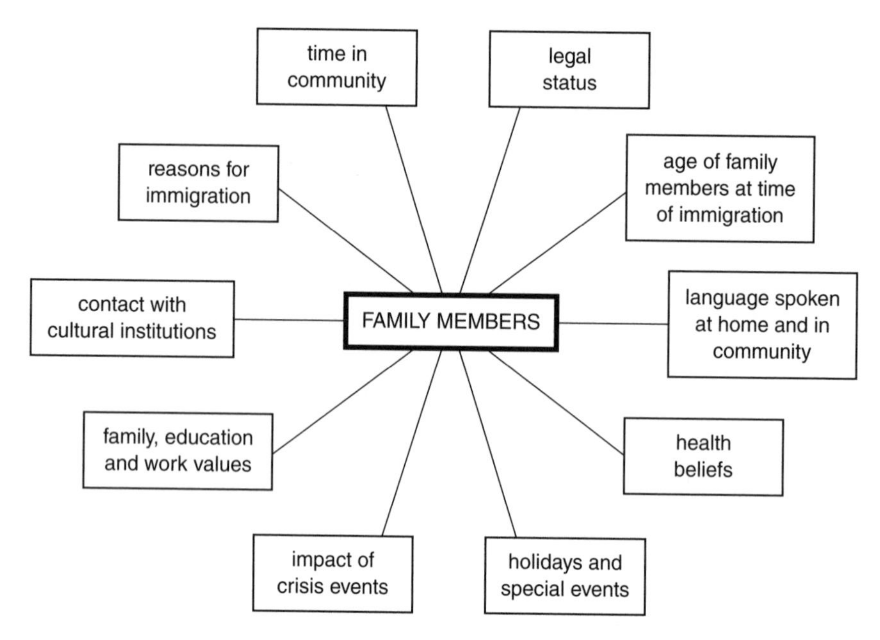

Figure 2.9 Culturagram

The use of the culturagram is important to the social worker in demonstrating the significant differences between family members that may have an impact on acculturation – how individuals begin to fit in to a new culture – and family functioning. The diversity of beliefs among family members may become very clear. This knowledge can be used to understand and reconcile differences between family members.

Congress (1994) believes that the use of the culturagram may empower family members by helping them to see their cultural background as important and may point to areas within the family and to external social institutions that need social work involvement and support. The following case study exemplifies some of the uses such an assessment may have.

CASE STUDY

Baljinder was 18 years old and was hoping to study law at university in the coming year. She had been asked by her mother to visit her uncle and brothers in a small village in Bangladesh in the summer before going to university. Baljinder was nervous about this request and although her mother had promised her that it was just a visit, she did not wish to go. This nervousness stemmed from the experience a friend of hers had had the previous summer. Baljinder's friend had been forced into marriage, but had escaped later in the year and had returned to England. She now had few friends within her family or community. Baljinder's mother promised her that during her visit she would not ask her to marry against her will. A social worker from the local area working specifically with the Bangladeshi community assisted Baljinder and her mother to work through these anxieties. By compiling a culturagram, Baljinder was able to see the process of her family moving to

England, the importance of consultation within her family and the strong Islamic faith that guided family decisions. As a result of this, Baljinder was convinced that her mother was indeed proposing a family trip and was able to go and enjoy this summer prior to going to university.

As Congress (1994) states:

> *The culturagram is a powerful tool for helping social workers assess and intervene appropriately with culturally diverse families. It is rooted in a model of cultural pluralism which stresses the intrinsic value of culturally diverse families pursuing their own styles, customs, values and language while recognising that different degrees of acculturation do occur ...*
>
> (p538)

This case study demonstrates how culturagrams can identify changing attitudes and influences of culture between generations.

Baljinder's mother was pleased that her daughter could see that she would not be forced into marriage. The move to England in the 1970s to gain work and support her husband's mother and father back in Bangladesh was significant to her. Completing the culturagram allowed her to see the changes in attitudes between her and her daughter's generation. The expectation that she would move and that her husband would support his parents was never questioned at the time. While she would not have changed her move to England or the reasons for it, she was convinced that her desire to support her daughter in what she wanted came in part from her own experiences. It was the completion of the culturagram that helped her to understand this.

COMMENT

It must be remembered that events do not always work out so well. Compiling a culturagram can give rise to conflicts and tensions within families. It is important that social workers do not fall into the trap of working through conflicts in a way that reflects their own cultural values and position but to work at the pace of service users and show respect for their value systems.

Culturagrams in working with abuse

Culturagrams have been employed in the sensitive area of elder abuse and domestic violence (Brownell, 1997). It is possible to use a culturagram as a screening instrument to assess and detect abuse and to promote culturally sensitive practice. Brownell suggests that it is an adjunct to professional assessment that allows the social worker to gain a clearer understanding of cultural values, belief systems and experiences and so to intervene more effectively in a person-centred way rather than one based on an appreciation of one's own values. She reports on a number of case examples including the Chinese–American community, the Polish community, Latin American and Indian/South Asian communities. The culturagram helped to identify particular aspects of culture and values that were important in planning further work and developing culturally sensitive approaches to practice. What must be remembered, of course, is that this tool was developed in the US context and may need some adaptation for use in the UK.

ACTIVITY 2.3

Often, our own culture is taken for granted because we live within it and reproduce it from day to day. In this activity you are asked to compile your own culturagram and to examine how this tool can bring to the fore aspects of your life and culture that were perhaps buried beneath the surface or taken for granted.

Using the areas identified in Figure 2.9, construct a culturagram for your family. Pick out key points and issues. It may be that you have not moved country but perhaps moved town or county. This too can demonstrate cultural issues that are important to the way you see the world and respond to it. For instance, the terms we use for the meals we eat differ across different parts of the UK. Other aspects of language may be specific to a region. These all help to identify us and can lead to assumptions being made about who we are. By identifying our own cultural values we can begin to recognise the importance of everyday rituals in others.

There has been very little further research into the use of culturagrams, and many of the cultural nuances of families can be picked up by the use of genograms (McGoldrick, Gerson and Petry, 2008). However, it is a tool that has untapped potential when used with sensitivity, and one that can show respect for diversity (Yu and Tran, 2011).

Flow diagrams and life road maps

The previous assessment tools can provide a wealth of information concerning the ecological location of the individual and family, family histories, patterns and norms. The flow diagram and the life road map stand at a mid-point between the person's living system and the patterns and norms that develop within families. They can be used to provide a chronological history of significant events and moves in the family's and/or individuals' lives. These tools also serve to locate the person in space and time in the present, giving a snapshot look at how the individual came to be where they are and what experiences have had an impact in making them so. Like the genogram, flow diagrams and life road maps can demonstrate the various routes a person has taken to where they are today, and like the ecomap, they firmly locate the person or family unit in a specific context in place and history. Their use demonstrates matters of importance to individual service users.

The number of movements that a family or individual has made in a given space of time may be of great significance to understanding the particular situation for which they are now seeking help from a social worker. This information may also identify patterns and events that were not consciously considered by service users. One interactive way of charting movements that can be employed with adults and equally so with children is the construction of a flow diagram. Starting from birth or, indeed, some other specified and agreed point, the individual or family is asked to complete a box for every place where they have lived. It is important to include dates, as the length of time spent in places can be of the utmost significance. If possible, it is useful to provide information of the family composition at these various stages to consider the various expected and unexpected transitions that the family may have undergone. In this way, the compilation of a flow diagram can be undertaken alongside the construction of a genogram. The boxes of the flow diagram are connected to one another until the present in terms of time and location is reached (see flow diagram, Figure 2.10).

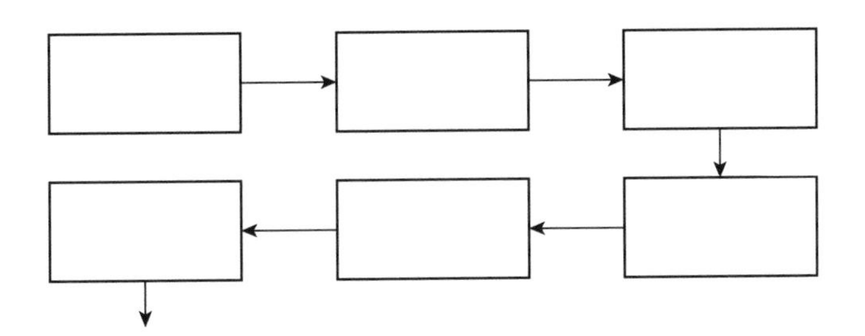

Figure 2.10 Flow diagram

Again, like genograms, ecomaps and culturagrams, the flow diagram has great potential for making a visual impact. It can locate times of turbulence and upset, times of change, and consistencies and inconsistencies in a family's pattern of life. This can have an immediate impact on service users when completing the flow diagram. They may be encouraged, by seeing the results of their diagram, to express a range of issues and concerns connected with these moves and their own histories. The patterns that emerge can help explain how and why the person is located where they are today. At the very least, the flow diagram allows for the formation and further exploration of hypotheses. As such it is a valuable assessment tool in the social worker's repertoire.

ACTIVITY 2.4

Take a large piece of paper and draw as many boxes as you think you might need to detail your moves. Complete a flow diagram representing all the house moves you have experienced by filling in the date and place of move in each of the boxes. Wherever possible, add information that you remember from the move. For instance, who was with you when you moved and did anyone stay behind? You might have moved because of your parents' jobs, or perhaps moved into a place of your own for the first time. What roles did

(Continued)

(Continued)

each person involved in the move have? This could relate to the role of a parent, a partner or a child among others.

Try to think about the experiences associated with these moves and the people who were involved, what changes there have been in your family or living group composition and your associated feelings. Again, this activity can evoke strong feelings and reactions. These may appear when using such techniques with service users, and being aware of this yourself is good preparation for an understanding and sensitive response.

Repeat this activity for someone you have worked with or someone you know well from your past. (Remember to ensure the anonymity of the person.) Does the diagram assist in your understanding of their present situation? It may bring to light points for further exploration. For instance, a reasonable hypothesis to make about a homesick person who has experienced very few moves during their life but has just begun a university course away from home may be that the homesickness is connected. Of course, this need not necessarily be the case and you would need to ask further questions to check this idea, but seeing the pattern can help you forge these questions.

What information did completion of this activity provide you with that you were not aware of beforehand? You may have found out something about your own life and moves or those of the other person you have considered. Think about the possible ways in which the completion of a flow diagram may help you in formulating questions to extend the depth of an assessment.

We can see how the use of a flow diagram assisted in the continuing assessment of the Jones family case study.

CASE STUDY

A flow diagram (see Figure 2.11) was completed with Mrs Jones and her present family. This indicated that in the two years prior to the death of her mother she had moved frequently, living in a variety of locations in the country. It was at this time that she met her present husband and began to lose more contact with her father. She expressed a belief that her father blamed her for not being with her mother during her last two years of life. This seemed to have some substance but more importantly it brought up an issue warranting further exploration.

There was a further period of frequent moves that seemed to the social worker to have significance. In the year immediately after the death of Mr Jones' father and the birth of Damien, the family moved three times because of Mr Jones' job. Since that time, however, they have settled in one place.

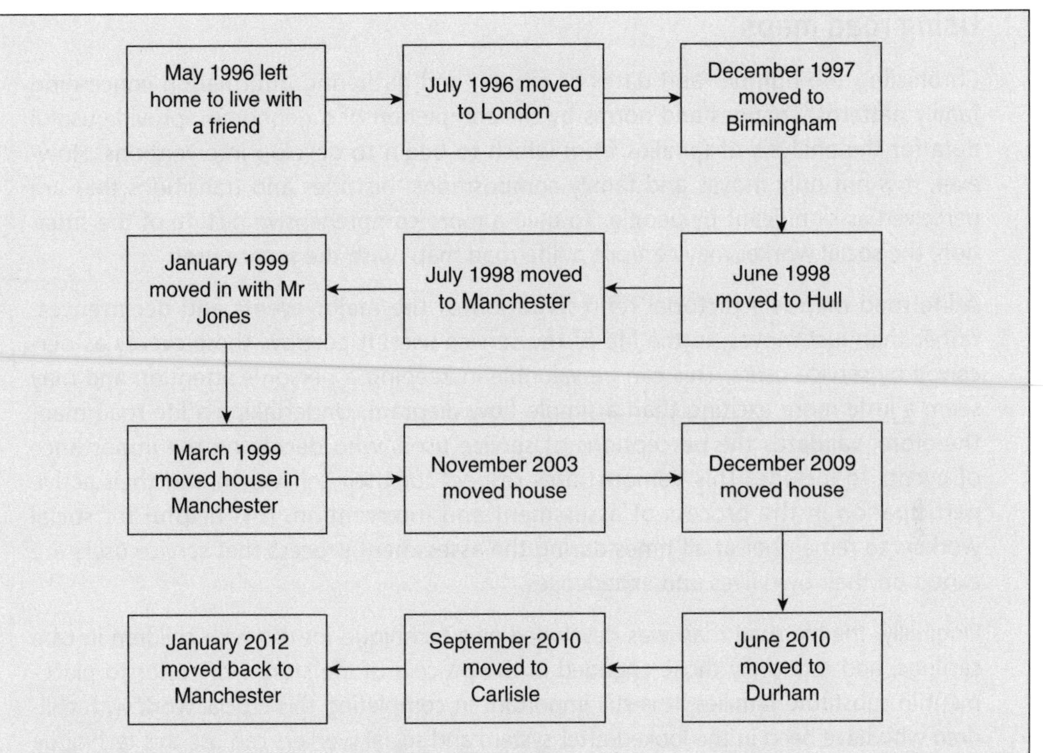

Figure 2.11 Mrs Jones' flow diagram of moves

The information collected provided the social worker with areas to explore further. It gave Mrs Jones a level of insight and understanding into her life that she had not had before and the process helped establish a working relationship between her and the social worker.

Two significant points were raised by this exercise. First, it was apparent that Mrs Jones' stormy relationship with her father and disagreements with him were long lived, and, in fact, began some time before the death of her mother and before she met and began living with Mr Jones. Also, it seemed potentially significant that there were so many moves in the year following Mr Jones' father's death. This provided opportunities for further discussion and exploration. Prior to such a focused consideration of her life's events and chronology, Mrs Jones did not realise the potential significance of these. She said she was so wrapped up in the events themselves that she paid little attention to the details.

COMMENT

The above case study exemplifies not only that such tools can aid the collection of useful information as part of an assessment but also that they can act as an aid to deeper exploration and analysis. They can also, at times, engender self-knowledge that can also be useful in developing a positive working relationship between social workers and people who use their services.

Using road maps

Chronicling the number and dates of moves, and gathering information concerning family patterns, changes and norms by the completion of a genogram, provide useful data for the analysis of families from which to begin to develop interventions. However, it is not only moves and family compositions, histories and transitions that are perceived as significant by people. To gain a more comprehensive picture of the situation, the social worker may compile a 'life road map' with the service user.

A life road map is a pictorial representation of the major events and occurrences, rather than just moves, in the life of the service user. It portrays these events as perceived by service users. This can be valuable in keeping a person's attention and may seem a little more exciting than a simple flow diagram. Undertaking a life road map, therefore, validates the perceptions of service users who decide on the importance of events to include. This demonstrates respect for their self-worth and their active participation in the process of assessment and intervention. It is helpful for social workers to remember at all times during the assessment process that service users are expert on their own lives and experiences.

Originally, the life road map was developed as a technique for use with children in care settings, and especially those engaged in the process of life story work prior to placement in substitute families. It is still important in completing this crucial work with children who have been in the looked-after system and social workers can use this technique effectively, as with other tools, to establish positive working relationships. However, the use of life road maps can be much wider. It has been used successfully with a range of service users: adults and older people as well as young people and children.

It is useful to take a little time to consider some of the ways the use of life road maps can contribute to the compilation of a life story book. For instance, can you think of possible dangers and limitations in using this technique? Are there likely to be differences between completing a life road map as an adolescent and as an older adult other than the length of time that can be covered?

It is clear that focusing on major events in a person's life will provide rich material that forms the backcloth against which that individual may view their life. It can form an immediate visual display that can itself be included in the life story book and can identify events to be explored in more depth. It may be, however, that the activity raises very painful memories and social workers must be aware of the need for sensitivity and be able to work with distress. It may also be the case that some aspects of a person's life have been forgotten or mistaken and it is again important that people feel comfortable enough to leave out areas of their lives. This may present some differences depending on the age and developmental stage of the individual completing the life road map.

Limb et al. (2013) have developed a particular use of the spiritual life map assessment tool to engage with people from the Mormon Church in the USA developing Limb and Hodge's (2007) work with Native Americans. They state that this tool allows social workers to develop their cultural competence with diverse populations and with a particular facet that can often be ignored or misunderstood.

A life road map is fairly simple to construct (see Figure 2.12). The social worker asks the service user to draw a 'road' on a large piece of paper. The road will have a number of bends and turns in it. The social worker then asks the service user to write a brief comment about an event in their life that they themselves perceive as significant at each turn and twist in the road. As events are being written onto the road, the social worker and service user may talk about them and weigh up together the significance of each. This will help to identify further areas for exploration and clarify other points.

It is not strictly necessary for events to be written in chronological order but the idea of a road may lend itself to this. When seen as part of a larger assessment, it may be more useful to link data from each session and activity. If this were to be the case, then a chronological account would be preferable. However, it is, in the end, the information gathered for the assessment that is of paramount importance whatever service user group you are working with, or whatever the purpose of your assessment. In this instance the information relates to the perceptions of the service user and tells you something about their construction of the world, how they perceive it working and how they themselves interact with it. This material can be used, again, to stimulate conversation and analysis of issues, to gain insight for the service user and to prepare the ground for intervention. Bear in mind the following questions when completing a life road map with service users.

- What is it that service users want to change?
- What is of concern to social welfare institutions?
- Is there anything within the assessment we can use as a basis for, or to measure, change?

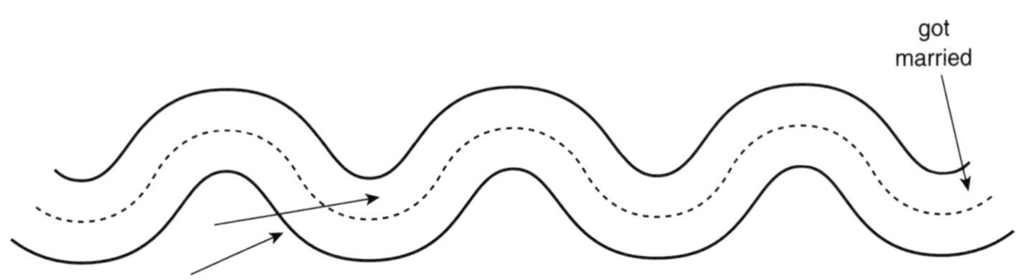

Figure 2.12 A life road map

ACTIVITY 2.5

Again, it will be useful to your development and for your understanding of the process of undertaking an assessment using these techniques for you to compile a life road map representing some of the significant events that you have experienced. Remember the 'significance' is based upon your perception of events and not what you think might be

(Continued)

(Continued)

considered significant by others. Try to think about the experiences associated with these events and the people, times and settings involved. If you need to use more than one piece of paper to complete your map, this is all right. It can provide a useful learning experience for applying the technique later with service users.

How might you employ this technique in a practice situation?

You would need to be prepared with paper, pens and perhaps some ideas for starting the map. Depending on the age and understanding of the person involved, you could use the time drawing the 'road' to build a relationship and to put the individual at ease. With an older person the process could take a more matter-of-fact approach. As with all techniques, a clear explanation of the task and its purpose is essential.

List some of the ways a life road map may help in identifying areas to work upon following the assessment.

You might include the identification of strengths, individuals important to the person completing the map or specific events that have occurred in the life of that individual in your list.

In our continuing case study we see how Mrs Jones used the life road map to explore events and issues in her life.

CASE STUDY

In order to complement and add to the data collected from Mrs Jones and her family she completed a life road map with the social worker (see Figure 2.13). This brought to the fore a number of issues not previously mentioned. The genogram presented her family history as reasonably stable. However, when completing the life road map, it was clear that a significant event for Mrs Jones was that her father left her mother for a period of a year when she was 11. Not surprisingly, her illness during the pregnancy with Damien figured highly in her perceptions of significant events. Apart from this, little other data emerged. However, even the incidental material has value; it demonstrates that the feelings

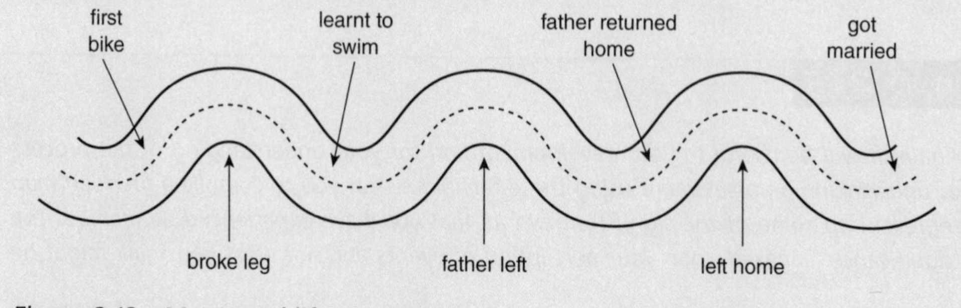

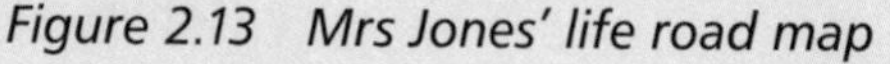
Figure 2.13 Mrs Jones' life road map

invested in certain things and events add to the overall picture of the subject of the assessment.

This conflated view of part of the life road map drawn by Mrs Jones demonstrates some of the important events that help the social worker make sense of who she is and what is important to her. The map is interesting. Mrs Jones included the positively perceived aspects of her life towards the top of the map and the negative ones towards the bottom. While too much significance can be read into this, life road maps can be used in ways to discuss the significance of events and the value attached to them.

CHAPTER SUMMARY

Assessment is a skilled professional process. The collection of information is integral to the completion of an effective assessment. The manner of the assessment and the methods employed to gather information, to synthesise it and to begin to form hypotheses for further exploration are all important factors to take into account. This is recognised in the educational requirements for social work. Models and tools must be chosen with sensitivity and with a clear purpose in mind. It is useful to bear in mind the following questions:

- *Why am I collecting this information?*
- *What right have I to collect this information? Is it by legal mandate or by request (see Marsh, 2008)?*
- *To what purposes will this information be put?*
- *How would I react if asked to undertake these activities?*
- *How might I react if someone was collecting this information about me?*

You may also wish to add:

- *Who will see the information?*
- *How can I involve those people who are the focus of the assessment?*

The five tools we have discussed in this chapter help to structure the process of assessment. Not only do they provide an interactive and participative way of collecting information, they also elicit important topics to explore further and to determine the focus of future assessment. Using these tools can also provide key insights for service users completing them. Although insight into one's situation is unlikely to promote change in itself, it can encourage motivation to work towards change and by doing so assist in planning and implementing effective intervention strategies.

These tools and techniques form a useful adjunct to the use of interpersonal or communication skills, such as exploration, questioning and probing. It must be remembered that they form part of an overall and comprehensive approach to assessment that will also take

(Continued)

(Continued)

into account case files, reports, third party statements, verbal and written communications from others involved, and full and candid discussion with the subjects of the assessment.

It is imperative that social work is seen to be a discipline that is effective. It should do what it claims to be able to do (while allowing for human changeability). Essential to this is promoting a model of practice that is research-minded and that evaluates the effects of its interventions. The use of these techniques to collect data at a cross-section in the life of the family or a family member enables the social worker and the subject to monitor change in some small way. This is integral to the development of good social work practice but further research into the efficacy of these models is also needed.

Assessment is and should be purposeful, as we saw in Chapter 1. It is undertaken in order to determine targets and goals for change to improve the quality of life of those involved. The tools introduced here are important in providing data to enable the planning and implementation of social work interventions designed to achieve desired and agreed change. We saw the tools being used with Mrs Jones and her family. A genogram assisted in beginning to compile information about the family's history and highlighted other information that may have been important, especially Mrs Jones' relationship with her mother-in-law. In later sessions an ecomap was used to look at support and other family relationships, and the completion of a flow diagram and life road map highlighted other significant aspects of her life. All the activities undertaken helped the worker to engage with Mrs Jones and her family, to encourage participation in the assessment and to begin to focus on areas of concern and issues that could become targets and goals for intervention. They provided also a baseline from which change could be measured. This could not be done in a rigorous scientific and quantitative way. However, qualitative change could be measured and alterations to her and her family's life space, patterns and development could be explored, discussed and promoted.

Before we turn in the next chapter to a discussion of how we use our assessments to plan for effective practice with service users and carers, consider the following activity.

ACTIVITY 2.6

Read through the case study material that you were introduced to in Chapter 1. Using your knowledge of the tools for assessment discussed in this chapter, compile a genogram, ecomap, culturagram, flow diagram or life road map for these service users as far as you are able.

This activity will help to consolidate this knowledge. We have not provided examples of the information you may have found to complete this activity as this gives you an opportunity to check through your understanding of this chapter and the models employed. You do need, however, to bear in mind the following questions:

- *What further information do you think you might need or wish to explore?*
- *How might you get this information?*
- *How would you seek to involve the service users as fully as possible in collecting this information?*

Barker, P (1986) *Basic family therapy.* Oxford: Blackwell.

While this text discusses the principles of family therapy and is quite old, it remains useful for social workers because of its treatment of diagrammatic tools for assessment.

McGoldrick, M, Gerson, R and Petry, S (2008) *Genograms: Assessment and intervention.* 3rd edition. New York: Norton.

This updated book represents an essential text for those social workers and students who want to expand their knowledge of and improve their practice in the use of genograms for assessment.

The Social Work Toolkit (2012) Palgrave Macmillan, online resource. Available at: www.socialworktoolkit.com/assessment_and_intervention (accessed 13.1.14).

The toolkit offers a wide range of excellent resources for use in social work. It is provided on a subscriber basis and many universities have elected to purchase it for students. The use of diagrammatic assessment tools is helpful.

Chapter 3

Developing, making and writing plans for effective social work

ACHIEVING A SOCIAL WORK DEGREE

This chapter will help you to develop the following capabilities, to the appropriate level, from the PCF.

- **Critical reflection and analysis**
  Apply critical reflection and analysis to inform and provide a rationale for professional decision-making.
- **Intervention and skills**
  Use judgement and authority to intervene with individuals, families and communities to promote independence, provide support and prevent harm, neglect and abuse.
- **Professional leadership**
  Take responsibility for the professional learning and development of others through supervision, mentoring, assessing, research, teaching, leadership and management.

It will also introduce you to the following academic standards as set out in the social work subject benchmark statement.

5.1.5 The nature of social work practice.
5.5 Problem-solving skills.

Introduction

Assessment, as we noted in the previous two chapters, is the keystone holding together effective social work practice (McDonald, 2006; Parker, 2013). However, it is not in itself a professional social work method, rather it is part of a non-linear process which necessarily involves planning and development for future work (Parker and Doel, 2013). While the recommendations of the inquiry into the death of Victoria Climbié emphasised the importance of assessment, they also highlighted the importance of subsequent planning and the need to include and consult with the child and carers when developing action plans (recommendation 25).

Once information is gathered and an ongoing engagement with service users established, it is important to make plans to determine what can be done, how it can be done and who will do what and in what ways. In this chapter you will be introduced to the development of plans in social work based on assessments, which may be specific and time limited or may involve continued work. You will explore key issues arising in respect of ethics, power, professionalism in social work and anti-oppressive practice. In making plans, you will be asked to consider the effects of working with other professions and with informal carers and service users as well as recognising some of the ways in which you might 'measure' or qualitatively evaluate change, which will be dealt with more fully in Chapter 5.

Students will be invited to consider how a plan is made in child and family work and work with adults. Contemporary guidance and advice on care planning will be provided and activities will help students to make links between knowledge and practice throughout this chapter. A critique of the language of 'care plans' and the importance for students of being aware of the centrality of service user involvement will permeate the discussion. A particular focus will concern the writing of care or service delivery plans, and the importance of accessibility and involvement to make plans effective will be emphasised through student-centred activities. Students will question the purpose and use of plans, and how they can be person focused and proactive in achieving agreed aims and in charting a course for intervention.

What is a plan?

Perhaps the immediate thing that comes to mind when thinking about plans is the scale drawing made when building a house or extension. These plans provide details of what would have to take place to reach the desired outcome – building the house or extension. They provide a visual map of the elements making up the plan and a view of what that outcome would look like. They also include an element of risk analysis in that plans must take account of standards and expectations and mitigate possible risks or dangers. This is a useful analogy for considering social work plans. They are also 'maps' based on prior and ongoing negotiations with those involved. A social work plan, however, is wider still. It presents a detailed picture of a situation, those involved and what action might be taken, and by whom these actions might be taken in order to meet assessed or identified needs.

One useful element that can be taken from plans for a building is the notion of 'planning permission'. The negotiation of a plan with those who would be involved from a professional angle is clear. If services and agencies cannot contribute in the ways you have identified, the plan is unlikely to be effective. Also, if the service user is not involved in the negotiation and agreement of the plan then plans may either ignore and contravene the rights of the service user or be doomed to failure. So plans, like assessment, must be built on a developing relationship between you as a social worker, the other agencies and professionals who might be contributing to the plan and service users. It is important that an ethical approach be taken from the outset.

To help you think about the process of planning and to consider what negotiations, agreements and actions might be involved try the following activity.

ACTIVITY **3.1**

Think back to the time you decided to study to become a social worker. Write down how you came to that decision. Who did you talk to when making your decision? What plans did you have to make? For instance: Did you have to plan moving house or area? Did you have to examine how you might manage financially? Were there any family or relationship considerations that needed to be taken into account before deciding where you might apply, what type of programme you would study and who would be central in helping you achieve your goals?

You may have written how the first rush of enthusiasm to study was tempered by the practical and emotional considerations that arose when planning how to achieve your aims. You may have needed to speak with parents, partners or children and to come to some understanding with people close to you. You may have had to consider the financial implications of studying. Would the bursary be enough to help you study? Are there other financial commitments that need to be dealt with? You may also have had to plan with others to take on roles and responsibilities that you have assumed but would not be able to continue to do while studying. The range of matters to think about mirror many of those that occur when negotiating social work plans with service users and with other professionals. It is important, therefore, that you understand some of the complex issues raised when making plans.

SMART planning

A useful way of remembering the core elements involved in planning can be found in the mnemonic SMART which relates to the following:

> **S**pecific in respect of aims and objectives of the plan and the roles or tasks undertaken by those involved.
>
> **M**easurable in terms of the outcomes and goals that are agreed upon.
>
> **A**chievable goals and outcomes so that those involved are likely to succeed and enhance their motivation for change.
>
> **R**ealistic and **r**elevant outcomes that maintain a focus on the core issues identified by those involved.
>
> **T**imely and **t**ime limited in addressing current issues and setting in train a plan that has a review point not too distant in the future.

This mnemonic allows you to transfer planning skills into any setting in which you may be working. It is important to remember that, while our two following examples relate to children and families, and adult social work mainly within statutory local authority services, much social work is undertaken outside in the third sector. Whatever your setting, good planning is important in helping you to detail, explain and check what it is that you have agreed to do with those people with whom you are working.

Plans for children in need

The *Every Child Matters* agenda and the Children Act 2004 section 10 led to a joint planning and commissioning framework for Children's Trusts that considers the planning and provision of children's services as a whole in a local area. This approach has been continued by the Coalition Government, but the ways in which it is implemented have been made more flexible and adaptable to local contexts. The mandate for the development of a Children and Young Person's Plan has been revoked. However, the emphasis on planning services remains and it is now up to each area to agree how this should be done. It is focused on and attempts to involve those using services, based on local needs assessment and agreed by a range of stakeholders integral to the process. Planning at this level aims to be preventive and the granting of greater flexibility amplifies the need to plan effectively for children and young people. The original Children and Young Person's plans were strictly monitored, in the belief that plans for working with children in need are central to measuring the success of any subsequent work that is undertaken. Where they were used as a measure, they needed to be both clear and feasible. It could be argued that the current prevailing austerity measures make the need for planning for children and young people more acute.

However, there are a range of plans in childcare social work that need to be taken into account. We must also remember that it is the assessment and analysis undertaken with children, young people and families that forms the basis of the plan which will be attuned to meeting the specific needs and circumstances of those in question. The plan will also differ according to the reasons for undertaking an assessment, and, as we saw in Chapter 1, will be driven by particular purposes of which you, as a social worker, need to be aware. The Box 3.1 shows some of the different plans identified by the Department of Health, all of which have accompanying guidance linked to them.

Box 3.1: Types of social work plans for children in need, following Department of Health, Department for Education and Employment, Home Office (2000)

Children in Need Plan *Negotiated with child, family and contributing agencies (see Department of Health and Cleaver, 2000).*

Child Protection Plan *After a child protection case conference and assessment under s.47 of the Children Act.*

Care Plan for Looked-After Children

Care Plans *For a child who is the subject of a supervision or care order or for whom adoption is planned.*

Pathway Plan *For a young person in care or leaving care.*

Of course, as we noted above, not all children and families social workers practise in local authority social work teams, and it is important to rehearse good practice in negotiating and developing plans in non-local authority agencies as well. The general principles outlined for making plans with children and families include the importance of negotiations and agreement, where possible, with the child or young person and key family members. Also, the objectives agreed should be reasonable and achievable, and sufficient time should be allowed to achieve these outcomes as suggested by SMART planning. The question of resources and appropriate services is important. A plan will be unlikely to succeed if it needs particular resources that are in short supply or difficult to obtain. A further central concern is that, while it is important to take into account everyone's views, the child or young person must be the focus of the plan. Practice guidance from the Department of Health and Social Services Inspectorate (1995) and repeated in the *Framework for the assessment of children in need and their families* (Department of Health, Department for Education and Employment, Home Office, 2000) outlines the following elements to be included in plans:

- the objectives of the plan;
- what services will be provided and by whom;
- the timing and nature of contact between professionals and families;
- the purpose of services and contact;
- the commitments to be met by the family;
- the commitments to be met by professionals, including attending to matters of diversity and equal opportunities;
- specification of those parts of the plan which can be renegotiated and those which cannot;
- what needs to change and what goals need to be achieved;
- what is unacceptable care;
- what sanctions will be used if the child is placed in danger;
- what preparation and support children and adults will receive if they appear in court as a witness in criminal proceedings.

Plans are part of the overall social work process as noted earlier and as stated in the following quotation:

> *It is essential that the plan is constructed on the basis of the findings from the assessment and that this plan is reviewed and refined over time to ensure the agreed case objectives are achieved. Specific outcomes for the child, expressed in terms of their health and development can be measured. These provide objective evidence against which to evaluate whether the child and family have been provided with appropriate services and ultimately whether the child's wellbeing is optimal.*
>
> (Department of Health, Department for Education and Employment, Home Office, 2000, 4.37)

Part of the purpose of assessment is to create a baseline of information and knowledge from which social workers can plan with children and families. Indeed, as part of the current Care Planning, Placement and Case Review (England) Regulations 2010 it forms an integral continuing process. The importance of good planning has been re-emphasised in a consultation on the regulations started in June 2013, designed to ensure that children and young people are adequately supported in placements and post-placement (Department for Education, 2013b).

When working with looked-after children under the 2010 regulations, the care plan must consider the suitability and geography of the placement, the child or young person's health, education, ethnicity, religion and culture and the importance and/or risks of maintaining contact with family and friends. Care planning in this context is a collaborative venture involving the person at the centre of the plan (the child or young person), the parents or carers and the child's social worker. Issues of power abound in the planning process, and it is important to reflect on how the collaboration can be made as genuine as possible while acknowledging the imbalance in the weight of participants' power.

ACTIVITY

Reflection point

Put yourself in the position of a child or young person and write down three or four concerns you might have in expressing your views and making plans for yourself. Repeat the exercise by putting yourself in the position of parent or carer. Consider what you might do as a social worker to limit negative consequences of this power imbalance.

COMMENT

You may have suggested that you would be at a loss when identifying plans and goals to achieve, or that you did not trust others with greater power to listen or treat your views seriously. Continued reflection and asking yourself questions relating to the process and how others may be experiencing it are important, as is being honest about your authority as a social worker. While this will not create equal power relations in the process it may assist in building trust and that, in itself, is a step in the right direction.

In respect of child protection plans, the purpose of a child protection plan as outlined by HM Government (2013a) is to:

- *ensure the child is safe from harm and prevent him or her from suffering further harm;*
- *promote the child's health and development; and*
- *support the family and wider family members to safeguard and promote the welfare of their child, provided it is in the best interests of the child.*

(p42)

The role of the social worker is to lead this process of planning and to outline the inter-agency plan. There is also recognition, however, that the plan should lead to further intervention and work with the child or young person and family, that it should develop a communicative relationship, and review and re-assess needs. The guidance promotes a more integrated approach to the social work process.

RESEARCH SUMMARY

Whyte and Campbell (2008) examine the importance of assessing and planning to meet the mental health needs of looked-after children. They describe a research study using a screening instrument, the Strengths and Needs Questionnaire, with 37 male and 39 female children aged 3 to 17 years who were living with relatives or foster carers, mainly as a result of neglect. The questionnaire was used with a further 76 carers, 64 teachers and 32 children aged 11 and over.

The usefulness of screening for the care planning process was illuminated by conducting pre-test and post-test audits on the plans. Following this, three focus groups were held with social workers and managers who recognised the usefulness of the questionnaire and recommended its use routinely in the care planning process with looked-after children.

A plan made to assist a child in need should have a statement recording the timing for its review and how this will take place. Regular review is counted as good practice. The processes of review will be considered in Chapter 5. Before we return to the case of Rebecca and Melissa, it might be helpful to consider the following plan in respect of another service user, Peter.

CASE STUDY

Peter was ten years old. He had recently been diagnosed as having attention deficit hyperactivity disorder (ADHD), a condition that meant he had considerable difficulty staying focused and a tendency to become very angry about seemingly minor things in a short space of time. He was not able to control his anger and was often physically violent to his mother and broke his toys, glasses and pots in the house. He had recently been excluded from school for hitting a teacher in one of his outbursts.

With the agreement of his mother, the school had contacted the local social work team. A case discussion including Peter himself, his teachers, an educational psychologist, general practitioner, his mother and a social worker had been called following an initial assessment of his situation. A plan to return and support him at school was developed. The plan was written and recorded as a form of agreement. This plan, which was made accessible to Peter as the focus of the work, follows.

Care plan for Peter

Aims and objectives

The aim of this plan is to set out the ways in which Peter can return to school and learn to control his behaviour.

By each person agreeing to the actions set out in the plan, Peter will be able to return to school and be supported in controlling his behaviour.

Who will do what

After this meeting Peter will attend an appointment with Dr R (GP), who will discuss possible medicine with Peter and his mother.

Peter's mother and Mrs B (teacher) will meet with Dr G, educational psychologist, who will discuss ways of managing his behaviour in the classroom, and consider any special needs and requirements to maintain him at school.

Peter will attend meetings as arranged and will work with everyone trying to help him control his temper.

Susan F (social worker) will discuss with Peter and his mother ways of managing his behaviour at home, reducing the number of times Peter gets angry and hits out.

When we will meet

Susan will visit Peter and his mother at home after school on Thursday evenings. Susan will visit weekly for the first four weeks of this agreement and a fortnight after this before the first review.

What are we meeting to do?

When we meet we will discuss how things have changed, what we want to achieve and look at ways in which Peter can recognise when he is about to become cross, what happens inside when he gets cross and what he might do instead of hitting out or breaking things.

Susan, Mrs B, Peter and his mother will work out a plan to reintroduce Peter into school over a period of four weeks. Mrs B will be informed about the ways Peter might control his temper and will make this possible within school.

What we expect

Everyone involved in this plan can expect to be listened to and taken seriously. We will all attend arranged meetings promptly and if, for any reason, someone cannot attend an arranged meeting, this should be discussed with all involved as soon as possible.

Review and renegotiation

This agreement will be reviewed by a meeting of all people involved in six weeks' time.

If there is a need to get together prior to this, a review can be requested by any person involved in this agreement by asking the social worker.

ACTIVITY 3.2

In Chapter 1 you were introduced to Rebecca, her mother, Melissa, and grandmother, Irene. An initial assessment, using the CAF and the assessment triangle from the Framework, was carried out and recommendations were agreed:

- *to undertake family work with Melissa and Irene;*
- *for Irene to take Rebecca twice each week and offer Melissa a break;*
- *for Melissa to attend a young mothers' group to gain support and advice.*

This initial assessment saw the first stages of planning. Indeed, without prior planning the assessment would have been unfocused and unlikely to be effective in considering Rebecca's needs. However, the development of plans for social work intervention takes place in earnest following the completion of an initial assessment. Your task as a social worker now concerns the discussion and negotiations necessary, assuming you have the agreement of your team leader, service users and carers, with the services who will carry out this work. In this particular case, you may look at a 'continuing care' or 'family support' team within the local authority or in a voluntary agency with which the authority has a service agreement. Such teams have different names, and indeed, different functions in different areas. Considering the above recommendations, begin to draw together a plan for Rebecca using the elements outlined above.

You may have produced something akin to the following plan. However, note where there are similarities and where there are differences between your plan and the one outlined, and consider why these might have occurred and what they might mean for the people involved.

CASE STUDY

Care plan for Rebecca Krajic

Aims and objectives

This care plan aims to:

- *provide Melissa with a break from caring for Rebecca;*
- *provide Melissa with an opportunity to gain support and advice from other young mothers;*
- *work towards improving the relationship between Melissa and Irene.*

The objective of the plan is to offer the best possible start in life for Rebecca.

Services

A member of Southside Family Support Team will work with Irene and Melissa to identify causes of friction and to find ways in which they can reduce tension and support each other in caring for Rebecca.

June Bridge, health visitor, will secure a place and introduce Melissa into the young mums' support group.

What will happen

The social worker will meet with Irene and Melissa at the family support team office for one hour for the next four weeks. Childcare support will be arranged for Rebecca within the team for the duration of these sessions.

These meetings will be used:

- *to explore the family history and relationship between Irene and Melissa;*
- *to identify tensions and strengths in their relationship;*
- *to seek alternative ways of negotiating and behaving towards each other;*
- *to develop an agreement to work together for Rebecca;*
- *to negotiate the best times to create a regular slot for Irene to look after Rebecca.*

What we all expect

It is expected that Melissa and Irene will attend each session promptly, informing the social worker as soon as possible if it is not possible to attend.

The social worker will attend each session promptly and will inform both Melissa and Irene if it is not possible to attend.

If any session is missed, this will be rearranged as soon as possible.

The social worker will ensure that childcare is provided for Rebecca during these sessions. Melissa will attend the young mums' support group regularly.

Melissa will ensure that Rebecca has clean nappies, clothing and a bottle when she attends the family support sessions and the support group.

The social worker will help Irene and Melissa agree the best times for Irene to look after Rebecca.

Renegotiation and review

This plan will be reviewed by everyone involved after the four sessions have taken place at the family support team office.

If anything happens that may affect this plan, this can be discussed at the following session or, if necessary, by contacting the social worker, Melissa or Irene between sessions.

Any changes or amendments to the plan should be agreed by all involved if at all possible.

Outcomes

At the end of the four sessions we will review how Melissa and Irene feel about their relationship and where to proceed from here. We will discuss whether arrangements for providing Melissa a break from Rebecca are working. We will review Melissa's attendance at the young mums' support group.

Care plans are central to building on assessments and producing an effective map for the intervention to proceed. Care plans are not, however, the property and preserve of the social worker and, to work best on behalf of your service users, they must be negotiated and jointly agreed. Of course, as we have seen, plans will need to include some aspects of social work that are not open for negotiation. These need to be clearly explained. Indeed, when social workers are honest and open about sensitive, difficult and non-negotiable areas of practice, service users are able to appreciate this. What is not acceptable is keeping hidden any sanction or aspect of the plan that might have to be used under certain circumstances. For instance, it is important to qualify issues of confidentiality. A service user might want to be assured that whatever they say will be treated as confidential to the session. This is not always possible. A service user who talks about their own experiences of child abuse when the abuser still has contact with and access to other children will not be able to have that information kept confidential. This kind of situation can be spelt out clearly in agreed plans. SMART planning can assist in dealing with some of these issues, such as keeping a focus on relevant issues that can be achieved ethically, legally and practically in the timescales allowed. Using such a mnemonic as a set of guiding principles with people using services can assist and enhance their involvement.

An effective plan is a blueprint for action that looks two ways. It is retrospective looking towards the assessment, while recognising that an assessment should also be an ongoing process, and it is prospective in looking forward to working with service users to effect change (see Figure 3.1).

We will now explore the use and development of care plans in care management practice with adult service users.

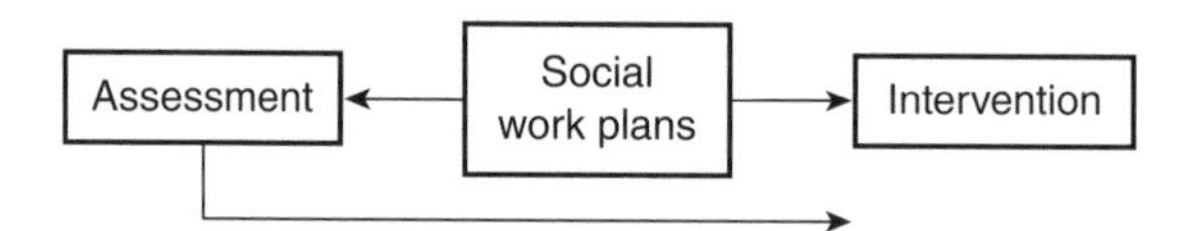

Figure 3.1 Plans as retrospective and prospective

Care planning in adult services – historical context

Making and writing plans for adult service users has been known for some time as care planning. Within the context of care management, it was the dynamic process that followed assessment of need and the vehicle for achieving the agreed outcomes. Early guidance (Social Services Inspectorate and Department of Health, 1991a) drew on theories of user empowerment. The service user and carer were at the heart of the process and their preferences and choice were to steer how the package took shape. The first three action points on the checklist for practitioners reflect these precepts.

1. Has the user been involved to the limit of their capacity in the implementation process?
2. Have the inputs of users and carers been maximised and have formal service inputs been geared to their support?
3. Has the pace of implementation been agreed with the user?

(Social Services Inspectorate and Department of Health, 1991a, p76)

Good practice required the development and implementation of codes of practice and procedures that helped identify ways in which minority or disadvantaged groups were not directly or indirectly discriminated against (Orme, 2000). The emphasis was to build on the strengths and abilities of individuals and the part they would play in the execution of the plan. Service requirements were to reflect the level of risk assessed and agreed between all parties. Objectives were to be clearly spelt out together with the criteria for measuring a positive outcome. Payne (1995) described the need to have a *sense of strategy* in order to understand *where the care plan is coming from and its future overall direction* (p112). Differences between the user, carer, practitioner or other agency were to be recorded; details of the named person responsible for implementing, monitoring and reviewing the care plan were to be provided; factors which may trigger an early review were to be known; and the user was to have a copy of the document (Social Services Inspectorate and Department of Health, 1991a, p67). Further, the cost of the care plan was to be fully recorded, reflecting costs to user and agencies. The process was intended to be systematic and transparent.

As with the assessment process, care planning was viewed as an art as well as a science. Care managers were to use their judgement, practice skills and experience to decide how the process should be completed. It was not and is not always a straightforward procedure. Then, as now, much depends on the quality of the relationship between the key workers and the service users. Care managers need to develop a trusting and sincere relationship with the service user, drawing on skills referred to as 'helping skills' (Egan, 2001; Bradley, 2007). These skills are based on values such as trust, compassion, empathy and openness that have long been at the heart of social work practice (Payne, 2005), particularly practice that is anti-oppressive and person centred.

Underpinning concepts that inform the care plan and self-directed support

When putting together care plans and when discussing self-directed support, the practitioner needs to be aware of underpinning concepts that inform good practice. For example, the concept of normalisation, which we referred to in Chapter 1, aims to enable people to live a life with similar day-to-day rhythms to others in their community. This approach was developed with the needs of people with learning difficulties in mind (Wolfensberger, 1972). It is equally valid when considering care plans for older people who may not wish, for example, to rise or go to bed purely at the convenience of the service providers. Being required to go to bed early and not being able to do ordinary things in habitual ways, such as watching a favourite late night TV programme from the comfort of a particular chair in a known room, may be a high price to pay and may send the signal that life is no longer 'normal'. Similarly, when drawing up a care plan for a person with severe disabilities, care managers should be aware of the models of disability which inform our perceptions. The challenge is not to fall into 'disablist perceptions' by accepting the medical model of disability which focuses on physical deficits and on individual health needs. Oliver (1996) encourages us to look more objectively at the extent to which our society has helped to compound disability through insensitive and inaccessible infrastructures, such as public transport systems, for example buses that are not constructed to be used by people in wheelchairs. Drawing on ideas from the social model of disability may help practitioners challenge why, for example, particular forms of public transport are inaccessible for service users. As care managers employed by a local authority, practitioners are in a strong position to raise concerns through their line managers that may be taken up at director level between appropriate agencies.

A critique of the practice of care planning

There are challenges in putting good practice precepts and the interests of the service user uppermost into care planning practice. User empowerment implies power sharing and self-management by users and involves a philosophy which spurns unnecessary bureaucracy (Adams, 2003). Care planning within a system of care management operates within a 'top down' system of local authority power and control in which, according to Lymbery (1998), *the professional components of care management are clearly subordinate to the administrative and managerial requirements* (p873). In other words, the role of the care manager has become rule bound and bureaucratic. Research (Postle, 2001; Bradley, 2005) points to care managers becoming overwhelmed by bureaucracy and paperwork with a decreasing amount of face-to-face time spent with service users and less opportunity to use their interpersonal skills.

Care support planning, self-directed support and personal budgets

There are links between care planning, as it was formerly known, and care support planning. Both are expected to be systematic and transparent. The new emphasis is on specifying the practical results of the process still known as the outcomes, and the care manager needs to be clear about the criteria for measuring them.

Both promote and foster independence and run with the expressed wishes and needs of the individual and these inform the plan and the services to be tailored to need. The important shift, however, in person-centred care and support planning, according to Morris 1993 (in Gardner, 2011, p40), is to look again at the concept of independence and not link it to intellectual or physical capacity to care for oneself without assistance, *but it is about having control over that support and when and how that assistance is provided*. This, it is argued, is the very nature of self-directed support. In other words, we have to move away from delivering services that normally focus on a person's physical deficits, from viewing people as having things done to or for them, and from a professional worker taking the final decisions about the care plan. We need to think beyond adult social care services and consider options such as smart technology and equipment, suitably adapted housing, improved health care, robust benefits take-up and community support when co-producing flexible, personalised solutions. The shift that is needed on the part of the professional is to see people first and foremost as citizens with rights (Gardner, 2011, p20) and not as users of services within a top-down professional bureaucracy.

As mentioned in Chapter 1, once a person has assessed their needs by completing a personal assessment form, a social worker will still have to complete a formal assessment of need under the NHS and Community Care Act 1990. Not to do so would be an abdication of the legal responsibilities of the local authority (Leece and Leece 2011). Drawing on these two assessments (some authorities now conflate them into one), a person with or without help from family members and/or a professional can then put together a plan of support. Once this plan has been agreed, the eligibility assessment needs to be completed. Eligibility assessment *precedes* financial assessment since an individual's financial situation must not pre-empt or influence the assessment of the cost of their social care needs (SCIE, 2010).

Once this is in place an application is normally made to the RAS, which is fast becoming the standard way for allocating finances locally in adult social care. Gardner (2011) describes it as *simply a framework to understand and describe needs and provide a methodology for the conversion of needs to money* (p45). Points taken from the self-assessment questionnaire are converted into money known as the 'indicative allocation'. Once the allocation has been decided then the person's personal finances can be assessed in accordance with recent guidance (Department of Health, 2010c).

The person will then be informed of the amount of money available to help meet the costs, either in the form of a personal budget or more standard services, to fund their care and support needs. The care manager will need: to explain to the person concerned and perhaps their family the different ways in which a personal budget may be held; agree the preferred way; establish the support they may need to set it up; and also manage it securely and in ways that fit the local authority's financial systems. Arrangements for monitoring the use of the budget need to be established and also information provided concerning what action individuals and carers can take if they have difficulties managing the personal budget, and what options the authority may consider as a consequence (SCIE, 2010).

This is a significant shift in practice since such resources were less transparent within the care management system of service delivery, although increasingly in local authorities both systems of funding social care are through the RAS as mentioned. The Association of Directors of Adult Social Services (2009b) in conjunction with In Control (set up in 2003 to promote self-directed support and to find ways of organising this type of social care) produced a framework to help local authorities deal with the legal, financial, administrative and policy implications when operating the RAS.

The new Care Bill (2013) refers to the processes described in this section as *care and support planning* (p22). The intention is to put in law for the first time the process of such planning that will include entitlements to personal budgets and to ongoing reviews.

Direct payments

The personal budget described above is normally received as a DP. The legislation for DP is embodied in the Community Care (Direct Payments) Act 1996. The Act gave local authorities the power (not as strong as a duty and therefore less enforceable) to implement DP. It was not until 2000 that the service was extended, through Statutory Instrument 2000/11, to people over 65. Policy and practice guidance that actively encouraged take-up was introduced. There has been no let-up on the part of government to run with this initiative for older people. It is viewed as a way of enabling them to manage their own care and to some extent their health conditions, and as a right not a privilege; it is also seen as a service that is provided not only on the basis of need and disadvantage but also on the grounds of rights, duties and participatory citizenship. The strategy for developing DP for adults was emphasised in the Green Paper *Independence, well-being and choice* (Department of Health, 2005) and in the subsequent White Paper *Our health, our care, our say* (Department of Health, 2006). DP is described in the latter as the *payments given to individuals so that they can organise and pay for the social care services they need, rather than using the services offered by their local authority'* (p210). More information and easy-to-read leaflets on DP, such as the Care Services Improvement Partnership (CSIP) Direct Payments Uptake Project can be found on the following website:

http://webarchive.nationalarchives.gov.uk/20120503022308/http://www.dh.gov.uk/prod_consum_dh/groups/dh_digitalassets/@dh/@en/documents/digitalasset/dh_073355.pdf

By promoting concepts of recovery and inclusion DP may be seen to support the social model of disability. Nonetheless initial take-up was not robust, due in part to the lack of active promotion of the scheme by social workers and their apparent lack of knowledge about it (Glasby and Littlechild, 2002a; 2002b). Early research indicated that practitioners viewed DP as: too bureaucratic (Leece and Leece, 2006); not relevant to core business; consuming of staff time; and threatening to job prospects (Spandler and Vicker, 2005). Some commentators are of the view that DP has the power to dismantle ASS (Mandelstam, 2007), since professional roles and known bureaucratic infrastructures may become redundant. Others take a more balanced view and see it as a component of the care system and not an alternative to it (Lyons, 2005).

A more recent study (Leece, 2010) considers and compares the experiences of DP relationships with those of traditional service delivery homecare relationships. A key recommendation highlights the need for a funding increase in the DP rates to enable better pay and terms of service for the personal assistant (PA), in order to make both parties less vulnerable in the relationship and to address the power imbalance which she argues is in favour of the service user (see Research Summary in Chapter 5). Whatever the concerns, criticisms and opportunities of DP, what is clear is that it has long been held by the government as the norm rather than the exception (Carmichael and Brown, 2002) and remains the direction of travel in current policy documents.

Individual budgets

Piloted in 2005–2007 (Glendinning et al., 2008), individual budgets (IB) are more flexible and seen as more imaginative than DP for funding a wide range of personal and social care for disabled and vulnerable adults' domestic, social, leisure and educational activities. Bureaucracy is viewed as less intensive, for example receipts are not required for individual expenditure. Funding streams differ from those of DP. The latter, as discussed, are keyed into levels of statutory care provision. In contrast, IB has been set up to make use of a resource allocation system that draws on a wider range of funding, for example the Independent Living Fund (ILF), Supporting People and Access to Work, although (as with DP) no extra funding has been allocated by government to the project. Glendinning et al.'s (2008) evaluation is that users of IB are more likely to feel in control of their daily lives compared with conventional services and that there is little difference between IB costs and standard social care costs. Nonetheless, the study illustrates that the lowest level of satisfaction with IB was among older people for whom the process of planning and managing their own support appeared more burdensome (Manthorpe et al. 2009a). The real implications of IB on social work and care management practice continue to be under scrutiny.

Charging for services: resource constraints then and now

Care management has always been viewed as the vehicle for targeting services within a framework of welfare which is driven by resource constraints and accountability (Hughes, 1995; McDonald, 2006). Commentators such as Waterson (1999) reflected that community care assessments focused on risk management and limiting services to those cases that carry a high risk, and that this approach of *containing risks becomes a means of rationing scarce resources* (p276). Indeed, when setting the eligibility criteria the local authority was able to put constraints on need by taking into account what can be afforded before a need is assessed. Similar discretion would appear to continue with the latest update on FACS. SCIE (2010) informs us that the national eligibility banding and criteria are for councils with adult social services responsibilities (CASSRs) to interpret according to the needs of the local community and local budget considerations.

If a service user thought they needed and would be better off in a desirable (more expensive) residential home for adults with a sea view, their ASS may define their needs in the light of local resource constraints, and decide that a different (less expensive) home is appropriate and write the care plan accordingly. The service user would, of course, be able to live in the home of their choice, provided they could pay the difference between the two fees.

Under FACS (Department of Health, 2002c), the government increased ASS spending power in real terms by six per cent per annum to enable more people in genuine need to receive support. However, the public sector spending cuts of the former Labour

Government that have been doubled by the current Coalition Government (Lymbery 2012) will likely negate this gain.

Financial assessment of a service user's means is an integral part of support planning, as it was of the care plan. Some practitioners view charging for care services as difficult since it does not rest well with some social work principles. Trained to help service users to maximise their income through, for example, the take-up of benefits, they find themselves, often uncomfortably so, in the role of gatekeepers to scarce resources (Bradley and Manthorpe, 1997). Research indicated (Bradley, 2003) that practitioners sometimes experience dilemmas and conflicts of interest between older people, their relatives and the local authority when undertaking financial assessments for long-term care. Variations in charging for care were identified in two official reports: the Royal Commission on Long Term Care's *With respect to old age* (1999) and the Audit Commission's *Charging with care* (2000). Reports such as these have prompted the government to act to make the system fairer (Department of Health, 2001b), no more so than in the revision of fair access to care (Department of Health, 2010b) and the 2013 Care Bill (see below) that is currently going through parliament.

Charging service users for services within the care support plan

Once the care support plan, the level of service and the RAS have been agreed, the care manager will consider whether a financial assessment of the service user is required. Charging for services continues to be the subject of much debate. At the time of writing, NHS services remain free of charge at the point of entry and ASS normally operate a means-tested charging policy for home-based care, whether it be for DP or standard services. Charges for the non-nursing component (that is personal care and residency costs) of care in long stay homes in England and Wales are levied on a means-tested basis using nationally agreed thresholds. There are two areas where ASS are not allowed to charge and these concern the assessment of need and general advice on community care, (under s.47 and s.46 respectively of the NHS and Community Care Act 1990) and also after care services of mental health patients under the Mental Health Act 1983 s.117. Further, people who are terminally ill with a prognosis of less than six weeks to live normally receive a free service and those eligible for intermediate care (a service that provides for intensive support and rehabilitation following hospital discharge) normally receive a free service for the first six weeks.

Under the guidelines (Department of Health, 2002c; Department of Health, 2002d; Department of Health, 2010b), which promote fairer charging policies for home care, charges levied by local councils must be reasonable, consistent with good practice in social care and must not result in the service user being worse off financially than they were before the changes. As mentioned earlier, the aim of FACS (Department of Health, 2002c) is to create a more consistent and equitable approach to implementing eligibility criteria by introducing a national framework within which local authorities should establish local eligibility criteria. Thus it stopped short of establishing national criteria on eligibility, which is seen as a limitation (Lymbery, 2005). Nonetheless, significant progress was made. Firstly, local authorities were required to act by October 2002, and remove charges from service users in receipt of a range of income- and disability-linked benefits. As part of the financial assessment of income, service users with a significant disability receive *an individual assessment of their disability-related expenditure* (Department of Health, 2001b, s.2.3) since it is assumed that having a disability is likely to give rise to more expensive living costs, such as heating charges. Secondly, more sensitive approaches to charging for home care were implemented by April 2003. Good practice dictates that following the decisions reached concerning the care plan, service users will be assessed on their ability to pay and given information on the charges before the service is provided. Details of the charging policy should be published and made available to the public (Department of Health, 2002c). In spite of the considerable developments in fairer charging, this area of work can be challenging for practitioners. Adults in England who currently have savings over £23,250 in 2013/14 (Age UK 2013) are viewed as 'self funders' and while they may opt to purchase services privately, without a formal assessment, care plan or system of monitoring services, they may be vulnerable. On the other hand, they are likely to have more choice than people on a low income. The latter can be at the mercy of some local authority policies that, for example, may only deliver frozen meals, never provide a cleaning service, and only offer assisted baths on a limited basis. Recently ASS have found that a fairer system generally can operate if all cases are taken through the RAS. Whether this will continue is uncertain, since how care and support is funded is set to change in light of the reforms that are likely to be introduced when the Care Bill 2013 is implemented (see below).

The funding of social care and the Care Bill 2013

How social care should be reformed and funded in the longer term, given the predicted increase in the number of older people in the population, has been a matter of concern and some urgency to the Coalition Government (Humphries, 2013). Shortly after taking up office in May 2010, the government set up an independent commission with the brief to make recommendations concerning how to achieve affordable and sustainable systems for funding care and support. The Dilnot Report, as it has become known (Commission on Funding of Care and Support, 2011) put forward ambitious ideas for funding social care and made many recommendations. We draw your attention to two substantial ones. Firstly, there should be a cap on the lifetime contribution to the cost of adult social care in order to protect people from extreme care costs. Where an individual's costs exceed the cap then they would be eligible for full support from the state. Secondly, it was recommended that protection be extended to people falling just outside of the means test for charging for residential care, by lowering the asset threshold. The government have acted on these recommendations. In February 2013 it accepted that social care costs to the individual should be capped at £75,000 (this excludes the charge for personal care within residential care) and that this should be operational from 2017. It was also accepted that the upper capital threshold for means-tested support will rise, as from the financial year 2016/17, to £118,000 and the lower threshold be lowered to £17,000 (Humphries, 2013). These ambitious central proposals of the Dilnot Report that underpin social care reform are to be found in the White Paper *Caring for our Future* (HM Government, 2012a), the *Draft Care and Support Bill* (HM Government, 2012b) and, more recently, as the Care Bill 2013 (HM Government, 2013b). Humphries describes aspects of these initiatives as enlightened, in that they seek: to promote well-being and strengthening of capacity at individual through to community level; to offer choice and control through personalised approaches and access to personal budgets; and to provide advice, information and assessment to all irrespective of financial means.

The Care Bill 2013 has incorporated the responses to the consultation on the Draft Care and Support Bill. It was included in the Queen's Speech (May 2013) and at the time of writing is currently going through parliamentary stages with a likely implementation date of April 2015. It is viewed as the largest reform of social care in the past 60 years. The Bill places new duties on local authorities and also simplifies and modernises aspects of the existing adult social care law into a single statute. The Bill seeks to:

- clarify entitlements to care and support;
- provide for the development of national eligibility criteria;
- treat carers as equal to the person they care for, by putting them on the same legal footing;
- reform how care and support is funded, to create a cap on care costs which people will pay;
- rebalance the focus of care and support by promoting well-being and preventing or delaying needs, in order to reduce dependency;
- provide new guarantees and reassurance to people needing care, such as supporting them to move between areas;
- simplify the care and support system to provide flexibility needed by local authorities and care professionals to integrate with other local services (see HM Government 2013b, section 20, pp10–12).

Government money to finance the new reforms includes £1bn a year to establish the cap on care costs and an extension of means-tested support to people in residential care, and £175m a year to support carers. The costings point to a national minimum threshold of eligibility that will be set at the equivalent of 'substantial'. Groups such as the Care and Support Alliance, that represents key charities for older people, carers and disabled adults and care provider associations, have stated that the threshold is too high and should be set at the level of 'moderate' (Community Care, 2013).

Humphries is of the view that there is likely to be trouble ahead, since it is unlikely that these ambitious plans could ever be funded. Due to current spending cuts the actual financing of adult social care is falling, although the need for such care is growing. In real terms, citing statistics from the Association of Directors of Adult Social Services (2012, in Humphries, 2013), he demonstrates that in these stricken times, 87 per cent of councils are only responding to substantial or critical needs. Thus he argues that the main challenge for many within the reformed social care culture is the exclusion from eligibility for help, since the bar is likely to be set too high, and not the protection from care costs.

These concerns were further elaborated in the ADASS's survey to April 2013 (ADASS, 2013). The views of 145 out of a possible 152 'top tier' social services authorities were logged. It was confirmed that, despite resources being transferred from NHS to local authority funded social care, in the three years since the current austerity measures they have had to impose saving cuts of 20 per cent of net spending. Looking ahead to the next two years, 50 per cent of those surveyed were of the view that fewer adults would be able to access services and the same percentage feared that personal budgets would get smaller.

The more enlightened reforms, that aim to bring on broader, universal, preventative services, may have to be funded, Humphries argues, by looking creatively at the relatively high levels of property wealth among some older people and redirecting existing expenditure on current universal benefits such as bus passes and winter fuel allowances for the better off pensioners (p20).

The point of view of the carer

When the success of the care package relies on the goodwill and input of an informal carer, talking to them about their wishes and preferences and undertaking a separate assessment of their needs under the 1995 Carers (Recognition and Services) Act (CRSA) is likely to be of vital importance. Under the provision of the Carers and Disabled Children Act (2000) (CDCA), local authorities can take preventative and supportive action to help carers by, for example, making payments to them directly for their services, and stepping in to allow them to take a break. The right of carers to have their own independent life fully recognised has become a statutory requirement in the Carers (Equal Opportunities) Act 2004 and accessing services that enable them to have a more balanced life needs to be an integral part of assessment and care planning. Further good practice guidance that emphasises the full involvement of the carer alongside that of the service user in assessment and care planning has been placed within a legal framework following a local authority circular (see Department of Health, 2004). Although this guidance has now been around for some while, the research by Glendinning et al. (2008) found that carers of people accessing IB were more likely to have been engaged in the process of support planning, compared with carers involved with the more traditional form of service delivery. In the original evaluation of the IB pilot programme the focus was on the individual in receipt of personal budgets, and the following year Glendinning et al. (2009) paid particular attention to its impact on and the likely output for carers. They reported both positive and negative findings. On the one hand, carers of service users were more engaged in the support planning and their needs were listened to, particularly those caring for older people. This resulted in their being given opportunities to take up other activities that would enhance their lives, while others were paid to do their tasks from the IB fund. The downside was that the payment to carers from the service user's IB was either minimal and/or they were not paid for the full amount of time worked.

Good practice views from SCIE (2010) are that practitioners need to view carers alongside personal and community networks as partners in care within the personalisation vision, and as such they need to be valued and supported. Guidance by NICE (NICE–SCIE, 2007 in Moore and Jones, 2012, p36) draws attention to the need to take account of the psychosocial impact on the carer and their psychological distress in the carer's assessment. This can particularly be the case when caring for a person with dementia. The new Care Bill 2013 reinforces the status and recognises the importance of carers by placing them at the centre of the law and on the same legal footing as the person for whom they are caring. Section 53 (p17) refers to *a single right to an assessment for adults and one for carers, based on having an appearance of need for care and support*.

With the perspective of the carer in mind, we include below a research summary concerning an aspect of caring that does not always have a high profile, that of lesbian carers of parents with dementia.

RESEARCH SUMMARY

Price (2011) reports on the experiences of eight lesbian women who are caring or have cared for a parent who has dementia. It forms part of a qualitative study that considers the care-giving experiences of 10 gay men and 11 lesbian women. A snowballing technique was used to gather the sample, which took four years to establish, from what is described as a 'hard to reach' population. Participants signed a consent form and the study was set up in accordance with ethical guidelines as published by the British Sociological Association. Semi-structured interviews were held in a 'guided conversation' format (Kvale, 1996 in Price, 2011). Interviews were recorded and transcribed and respondents were allowed to vet them. A constant thematic comparative method (Glaser and Strauss, 1967 in Price, 2011) was used in the data analysis. Themes that emerged concerned the different ways in which respondents had become carers; the quality of the relationship they had with the person cared for; and the extent to which the cared for person and the wider family were supportive of the sexuality and lifestyle choices of the respondents (p1293).

The focus of the article is on the findings and linked discussion relating to the sub-group of eight lesbian women who were caring for (or had cared for) a biological parent with dementia. All were educated, white, British women between the ages of 23 and 62 and three were in long-term partnerships.

All eight had made decisions to accommodate their caring role and this had been life changing. Some had been pressured by family members to take on what appeared to be gendered caring roles and some were made to feel that their needs were of less importance compared with heterosexual married siblings. Gendered expectations were felt by the lesbians without children, particularly from older family members and neighbours in the locality of the cared for parent. There was also evidence of lesbians becoming carers because they wanted to, or because there was an element of reciprocity and expectation. As one carer said, 'I needed mum to be happy and so I needed that to happen and I knew I could make that happen' (p1294). On occasions the act of caring and working alongside other siblings had improved relationships, where in the past it had been strained due to the sexuality of the carer. Similarly, there was evidence of change, when a former difficult relationship between the carer and the parent became 'a catalyst for renegotiation', (p1295). This may have occurred due to the changed personality of the parent with dementia or from the parent forgetting that there were unresolved issues with the offspring in the first place.

Price comments that support for the lesbian carers was likely to be from friends, who may also be ex-lovers, and that such people were more likely to be their 'family of choice', rather than their biological family (Weston, 1991, Weeks et al., 2001 in Price 2011). This led to a discussion on 'the lesbian experience' (p1298) and ways in which it affects family relationships and friendship networks. As one respondent commented 'your friends become maybe more central to you than straight people's friends do' (p1298). Such friendship networks were also seen as more helpful to carers than support received from the statutory and voluntary sectors.

Price comments that while we cannot generalise from such a small sample, the findings convey important messages from lesbian carers attempting to cope with people with dementia. She does not presume that most social workers work within a 'hetero-normative framework or are exclusively heterosexual' (p1301). Nonetheless, she reflects that practitioners working with lesbian carers need to understand the variety and complexity of family dynamics and the type of expectations placed on them. She is also of the view that the notion of family needs to be conceptualised in its broadest forms.

CASE STUDY SEQUEL

Denise Lockwood: Support planning meeting to set up self-directed support?

Several weeks have passed and Care Manager Amanda Thorpe has been gathering additional information as follow.

1. *GP Dr Dyson has seen Denise a couple of times in the surgery and she has been to see, accompanied by daughter Alice Richards, a psychiatrist and a consultant neurologist at the local hospital. He has given Denise the feedback and she has agreed that his short report may be shared at the planning meeting. The report confirms that she is not depressed but that her language is less fluent and her physical reactions and gait have changed. Results from a standard memory test are that her short-term memory is in the lower band; for example, she is not able to recall the date or the name of the current or previous prime minister. No abnormalities have been found following a brain scan and some blood tests. The GP pointed out that while this may seem to be good news it still does not explain her symptoms and she may have a degenerative condition.*
2. *In a confidential aside to Amanda, Dr Dyson has said that conditions such as dementia rarely show up on such tests and that a diagnosis is often reached when other medical*

(Continued)

(Continued)

conditions are ruled out. He is not yet at the point of making a statement that Denise has dementia type symptoms, but he thinks it is likely. If such a diagnosis begins to shape, then he would consider prescribing a recent drug for early onset dementia. His counsel is not to tell Denise what he thinks, in case he is wrong and Denise takes a turn for the worse on the basis of misinformation. Amanda can accept his logic but she is perturbed by what she has heard.

3. *Amanda has spoken to Denise's daughter. She has been upset by the change in her mother following the long gap when they did not see each other. She has recently had two children and has realised that she would like her mother, and their grandmother, in her life once more. She now lives five miles away, wishes to be helpful, and is a busy mum who works full time for a building society. She definitely wants to attend the meeting. She is aware of 'Lasting Power of Attorney' and the capacity requirements to register this. Amanda is relieved that Alice is thinking ahead and hopes that, given her work experience, she may be willing to help her mother sort out her affairs.*

4. *Denise's neighbour, Susan Brown, has gone out of her way to contact Amanda. She has been a volunteer for Age UK for 18 months and feels that she too would like to be helpful. She has taken a course in advocacy and is familiar with self-directed support. She knows of volunteers who may be interested in some paid work were Denise to be given a personal budget.*

5. *The OT David Hobson works closely with Amanda in the surgery and is familiar with the person-centred approach. The two colleagues view their brief as complementary and overlapping. David sent Amanda the following report for the planning meeting. He has highlighted points to be raised, since he is not able to attend in person.*

Report on home visit to Denise Lockwood on 22 February 2013

David Hobson Occupational Therapist

I spent three hours in the home of Denise Lockwood on 22/2/13. She was welcoming and amenable to answering questions about her normal personal and domestic routines.

Personal care needs

Denise says she is confident using the shower and there is evidence that it is in use. She has not been to the hairdresser for some time, since the shop is two bus rides away and she has recently become uncertain of the route. She has also lost/mislaid her bus pass and gave this as an additional reason. ***Denise would benefit from finding a mobile hairdresser to visit her at home.***

Nutritional needs

The amount of food in the house was sparse and some of the perishable items in the fridge were well past the sell-by date. At lunchtime Denise started to make sardines on toast but did not remember to switch on the toaster. There was mould on the half-used tin of fish that she was intending to eat. The rings on the electric cooker are not working but she has a microwave oven and is content with this, since she mainly heats up 'ready meals' or has take-away food. ***It would be helpful if Denise could get to a local supermarket on a regular basis to stock up with more nutritious and cheaper food. Without transport she would need help with this.***

Practical/daily living skills

There is a lack of order in the house and few places where personal possessions can be stored. Denise responded well to suggestions to buy transparent plastic boxes that could be labelled clearly. She admitted the clutter was getting her down. She has mislaid the instruction leaflet for the washing machine and does not feel able to sort out and organise her laundry. It is likely that official letters that require attention are being overlooked along with the piles of junk mail. ***Denise recognises that she is probably avoiding dealing with her affairs and recognises that she needs assistance with this and managing her finances.***

Physical and mental well-being

Denise is mobile and has no apparent physical difficulties. She takes little physical exercise other than walking to the local shops. She appears forgetful and her short-term memory is poor. Her mental stimulation is mainly from watching television. ***She said she knows she should get out more and is interested in joining a local choir.***

Family carer and social support

Denise's neighbour, Mrs Susan Brown, has started to call by from time to time and sometimes bakes her a cake. Since her daughter has re-established contact she normally phones on a Sunday morning and has visited once in the past month. Denise very much appreciates these developments.

Risk assessment

Denise appears responsive to receiving assistance to help sort out her life. The risks are potentially considerable and will increase if some form of intervention is not provided soon. ***Assistive technology may be helpful to prompt her with security matters and storing and accessing important items for daily living.***

Pre-meeting reflections

Amanda is about to arrange a support planning meeting at Denise's house. She is not yet certain where it will lead and whom she should invite. Should it be a meeting that helps to set up more traditional services or one that is orientated towards self-directed support and DP? She knows she wants this to be Denise's decision and needs to be clear in her own mind how the two possible meetings would shape up and what the outcomes would look like.

ACTIVITY 3.3

What is your view?

List the reasons for and against either type of meeting.

CASE STUDY

A hypothetical planning meeting linked to standard home care services

As part of Amanda's deductive reasoning she considers how a traditional care planning meeting, leading to homecare services, would look like and whether it would be helpful to Denise. As a care manager she is familiar with the following questions and procedures.

Common questions posed:

- *What is the level and frequency of the help required?*
- *Which agency would be responsible for what service and why?*

In order to think through this task Amanda considers the ways in which Denise wishes to live her life as indicated in the self-assessment form she completed earlier. She goes over her strengths, weaknesses and level of motivation, and her personal and physical needs. She thinks of things that could go wrong and contingencies she could draw on to build in more support. She drafts a day-to-day plan of agency/worker involvement that may be acceptable to Denise, one that takes into account her health needs and is realistic in terms of managing risk without stifling her independence. Is security of the house an issue and if so how would professionals access her home? Will a care plan enable Denise to be safe, comfortable and as independent as possible at home or would such a plan stifle her independence?

Likely key objectives for a standard service plan:

- *To help Denise set up systems for managing her day-to-day life given her short-term memory lapses – an immediate short-term goal would be to help her manage her finances and bills and 'declutter' her home.*
- *To actively seek to help Denise change her diet and take more exercise.*
- *To encourage Denise to lead a more creative and positive life in her community.*
- *To review the care plan in six weeks or sooner if the arrangements change/break down for any reason.*

ACTIVITY 3.4

- *If you were helping Amanda to draft a daily/weekly chart that demonstrates a support plan linked to a standard service for Denise, what would it look like?*
- *On the basis of knowledge to date on Denise's needs, what type of professional and informal help would you envisage? What would be the level and frequency of help?*

Is the daily plan sufficiently structured? Is it professionally dominated? Would it stifle Denise or enhance the quality of her life?

- *Would Denise actively want the plan and sign a written agreement for it?*
- *Have a go at completing the chart below.*

Draft plan for home-based services: schedule of daily and weekly tasks

Date compiled:			**Service user:**		**Overall level of need:**		
	Monday	**Tuesday**	**Wednesday**	**Thursday**	**Friday**	**Saturday**	**Sunday**
Early morning							
Mid-morning							
Lunch							
Mid-afternoon							
Late afternoon							
Evening							
Bedtime							
Night							

CASE STUDY

Amanda's thoughts on facilitating self-directed support and support planning

Setting up self-directed support is relatively new territory for Amanda, particularly for people, such as Denise, who have memory difficulties. She has read about some of the difficulties in Moore and Jones (2012), particularly the section on 'Obstacles to using self-directed support for people with dementia' (pp72–76). They refer to work by Kinnaird (2010) and Lightfoot (2010) that reinforces the point that assumptions are made by practitioners that people with dementia are not capable of managing a personal budget through a DP, nor have they the interest in such support and therefore it is not promoted by the profession. Nonetheless, at an ideological and practice level, Amanda believes in self-directed support and thinks that at this stage in Denise's life it may free her up to have more control over her life and gain pride in so doing. She has known for some time that all adult service users are eligible to receive DP providing they are willing and able with assistance to cope, and that this should be taken into account when making an assessment. She has also recently been on a course linking DP with adult protection issues and knows about some of the potential pitfalls. Hence, if Denise selects this route, Amanda wants her to be selective in her choice of PA. She has also been made more

(Continued)

(Continued)

aware of the need for financial safeguards and has been encouraged to become more knowledgeable about and engaged with 'sorting out' personal finances for people who are known to be vulnerable adults, since this is an area that can be open to abuse (Manthorpe et al., 2009b). Recently her line manager has become keen that she should raise the profile of DP in her work since its take-up is linked to external performance indicators. Amanda normally ignores this type of comment as too 'managerialist' but she likes the sound of DP. She has read some leaflets in the office that are written from a user perspective that describe its pros and cons and refers to a local support service that would help people like Denise to manage the paperwork and the responsibilities of being an employer. She can also see the relationship with the neighbour, Susan Brown, working well, particularly given her progressive work with Age UK and her links with trained volunteers locally who are CRB checked and who may make good PAs. She knows that the process can be slow going through the RAS and she fears Denise's circumstances may change significantly in the meantime. There is also a matter of whether she will meet the eligibility criteria since it may be difficult to place her in a high category of need. However, she tells herself that the earliest possible intervention is required since Dr Dyson would not have shared such a confidence with her lightly. If it is a diagnosis of dementia then the best and most humane course is to help Denise while she has capacity to put structures in place that are the least restrictive and most helpful to her. She thinks she can argue the case with her line manager for this type of preventative work. The report from the OT, that catalogues mainly deficits and difficulties in Denise's life, disappointed her since it felt like 'old speak', but nonetheless it has spurred her on to help set up systems that will serve Denise's best interests.

On the basis of these thoughts and reasoning Amanda is reluctant to go down the planning route to access standard services, since she thinks that this is more likely to 'box in' Denise. In reality, there may also be less money to draw down, given the more expensive on-costs of a more conventional service-led care package. She argues to herself that Denise is still a 'young old' who needs to be in charge of her life as much as she possibly can, and that self-directed support, with the right level of funding, could work if this is what she wants.

She shares these thoughts with Denise in preparation for the meeting (leaving out the confidential conversation with Dr Dyson) and asks her to think through the pros and cons of both types of support plan and how each could work for her. Denise decides on self-directed support. She reads the report from the OT and agrees that the content of it may be shared. She likes Amanda's suggestion that the support meeting be in her house and that numbers be kept low. They agree on four.

ACTIVITY 3.5

Think about and make a list of the pros and cons of Denise being in receipt of DP. Pay particular attention to Denise's strengths.

CASE STUDY

Self-directed support planning meeting in Denise Lockwood's home

***Present**: Denise Lockwood; Amanda Thorpe, social worker; Alice Richards, daughter; Susan Brown, neighbour*

Amanda opens the meeting saying that it has been set up to help Denise decide on the type of help and support that is best for her. Amanda uses her social work skills to encourage Denise to do the talking and go over the points she raised in her self-assessment form. She also agrees to take brief notes on decisions made.

Denise's view is that she wants help to sort out her life and regain some control over it. She feels she should get out more and meet people. However, she knows she has short-term memory lapses, difficulty remembering numbers and that often she feels muddled and unable to think clearly. She reflects that she thinks she may have dementia, having listened to a recent radio programme on the subject. This is a powerful moment in the meeting. Amanda feels a sense of relief for this being voiced – it feels very real. After a pause she says softly, 'Maybe, but I don't think anything is certain – you need to keep talking to Dr Dyson'.

Denise confirms she likes the idea of DP as described to her. She has tried to read the leaflets but has not remembered much, and says she will need a lot of help completing the forms. Susan is confident that Rachel Armitage, who volunteers with her at Age UK, would be willing to help and may be interested in the PA work. It is agreed that she will introduce her to Denise in the coming week. Amanda reminds everyone that accessing DP can be slow; that there is uncertainty about the amount of funding Denise is likely to receive and hence the number of hours of a PA's time that can be funded. She does not want to lose Denise's enthusiasm and suggests they make positive plans now in the anticipation of getting DP, think about how a PA's time could be used and also consider the support that needs to be in place now.

With Denise's permission Amanda gives a brief outline of the OT report and asks Denise where she feels she needs most support. Denise says her main frustration is the mess in the house. This prompts Alice to confirm that she will help with the 'decluttering' and she commits to the following two Saturdays. Amanda suggests they contact the OT regarding his offer to help. Denise likes his suggestions regarding transparent systems and daily prompts, but is less keen about assistive technology and feels it is not necessary. Alice also says she will help her mother sort out and manage her finances since she knows this needs attention. Denise's face lights up at the thought of spending more time with her daughter. Amanda asks some thoughtful questions about how Denise's finances will be sorted. She thinks Alice is trustworthy but she also wants her to know that she is alert and is likely to continue to ask pertinent questions. Alice does not appear phased by this and Amanda takes this as a good sign. Alice comments that she may need additional legal powers to enable her to manage her mother's finances if her memory does not improve. This is not spelt out; it may be too much for Denise to cope with in this more public

(Continued)

(Continued)

arena, but Amanda knows that action may be required soon while Denise still has capacity to comprehend the process. Finally, Alice suggests that once the house is more sorted, her mother may have enough money to pay for a private cleaner and her mother thinks it a good idea.

Amanda steers the meeting back to Denise's immediate support needs. Denise says that following some helpful crisis counselling sessions (see Chapter 4) she is determined to be more positive and have a healthier lifestyle. She tells the meeting she is planning to go with Susan to an informal choir each Wednesday afternoon that is in walking distance, and that she is also going to help her run a local food bank each Friday between 10am and 1pm. But she still feels that there are many days when she sees no one. Susan says she is happy to call by for a chat and to check she is okay on the days when nothing is planned. Denise seems relieved about this and spontaneously asks if there is something she can do for Susan, such as take Lucy, her dog, for a walk. She knows it would help Susan and would help her fitness regime. One outstanding matter concerns buying healthy food that is easy for Denise to prepare, and Susan offers to take her once a week on a Thursday when she does her own supermarket run.

Towards the end of the meeting Amanda returns to the type of support required using DP funding. She suggests it may be better to have two PAs to help cover holidays and sickness. She senses that Susan may be interested in a time-limited PA role and she confirms this. Amanda talks positively about taking up PA's references and having CRB checks and why this is important when working with adults who may be vulnerable.

It is confirmed there will be a review in eight weeks' time to report on progress.

Amanda's reflections on self-directed support following the meeting

Amanda is pleased with the outcome of the meeting while wondering if it has been in sufficient depth. She knows that self-directed support should be closely linked with the self-assessment of the service user at the heart of the process (Social Work Task Force, 2009 in Lymbery and Postle, 2010). But then she wonders if the mainly tick box form is too simplistic. She argues to herself that Denise is the expert on her own needs, but wonders whether she has sufficient insight into her current state, her wishes and her preferences, given her cognitive difficulties. Did the meeting address the real issues? Were there potential conflicts of interest between parties, perhaps between mother and daughter, which were not aired? Was there too much reliance on the goodwill of her neighbour? Her counter-argument is that she knows she has helped Denise understand the complex world of care for adults and enabled her to complete a self-assessment. She has enabled her to think more broadly about her personal capacity and what she can, with help, achieve each day to enhance her life. She has also encouraged her to build links and capacity within her community, by gently promoting and reinforcing positive activities and relationships within her network. Additionally, she is a skilled assessor, and throughout the process and the recent meeting she has been mentally filling in the community care assessment form that she will need to complete in order to make representation to the RAS and make sure that it is pitched at the right level to meet the eligibility criteria – then hopefully the finances can be agreed. It also has to be written in such a way that Denise can agree to it.

But what exactly is her role now and subsequently? Is a professionally trained social worker needed? Her line manager may well argue that since there is no clear diagnosis for Denise, no clear safeguarding remit, then there is not a need for a professional worker. So why not close the case given the resource constraints? Amanda's professional 'nous' tells her otherwise. She predicts that the nature of Denise's health condition is likely to change in the not too distant future. She thinks her role as link worker with the surgery and her close working relationship with Dr Dyson will enable her to keep the case open. Her knowledge of dementia and possible links with safeguarding issues should be sufficient to make a persuasive case with her line manager to keep the case open. At this point she thinks that there is sufficient support for Denise. She trusts her neighbour and although she has never met Rachel Armitage, she assumes she has been 'vetted' by Age UK when working for them as a volunteer and advocate. Her challenge, as she sees it, is to enable Denise to have as much autonomy as she can manage and cope with, while having the right amount of protection and support should her health take a downward turn.

Some of the practice dilemmas highlighted in the case to date are addressed more fully by Lymbery and Postle (2010) and are raised by Manthorpe et al. (2009b).

ACTIVITY 3.6

In light of the planning meeting we would like you to write the notes from the meeting concerning decisions taken. Try to be succinct, while being clear about everyone's roles that are linked to the decisions and include timescales if appropriate.

Finally, map out the support plan that includes all the weekly events mentioned. You could use a template similar to the draft schedule plan for a more standard service that you worked on above.

Does the support plan look robust enough for Denise's needs?

Give your reasons for and against.

ACTIVITY 3.7

Reflective journal

There have been many activities in this chapter linked to planning and the new vision for delivering social care through self-directed support. We hope that the work you complete for the set activities is also written up and reflected upon in your journal.

CHAPTER SUMMARY

In this chapter we have considered how information gained and negotiated during an assessment contributes to the development of a plan to meet needs. Again, it is important that social workers practise in ways that include service users at the centre of the work. Plans in respect of child and family social work and work with adults have been introduced and illustrated by reference to case study material. These are set within their changing contexts, many of which you will be working within. Following the development of a plan, social workers and service users work towards its implementation. In the next chapter we will consider some of the ways in which plans can be operationalised through intervention.

It may help, in any plan that you are involved in constructing, to remember the acronym HOSEC:

- *be **h**onest about the reasons for the plan;*
- *be **o**pen about who does what and what 'comebacks' there might be;*
- *be **s**imple in your use of language;*
- *be **e**xplicit about what it is that you are communicating;*
- *be **c**lear in your written expression.*

FURTHER READING

Department of Health, Department for Education and Employment, Home Office (2000) *Framework for the assessment of children in need and their families.* London: The Stationery Office.

Laming, H (2003) *The Victoria Climbié inquiry report.* Cm 5730. London: The Stationery Office.

The report into the tragic death of Victoria Climbié is essential reading for all social work students and qualified practitioners regardless of area of practice. The lessons learned for assessment, planning and communicating must be learned and applied.

Lymbery, M and Postle, K (2010) Social work in the context of adult social care in England and the resultant implications for social work education. *British Journal of Social Work,* 40: 2502–22.

Within the changed and changing policy landscape of social care for adults, Lymbery and Postle highlight a range of practice dilemmas and incompatibilities such as between preventative work and restricted budgets, and between autonomy and protection.

Moore, D and Jones, K (2012) *Social Work and Dementia.* London: Sage/Learning Matters.

This text provides an excellent overview of working with people with dementia. It addresses the transformative agenda of self-directed support, while not holding back on the obstacles to using such support for people with dementia.

Holloway, M (2009) Planning, in Adams, R, Dominelli, L and Payne, M (eds) *Social work themes, issues and critical debates.* 3rd edition. Basingstoke: Palgrave, pp229–43.

Holloway's chapter provides an extremely useful and accessible introduction to planning in social work and social care, and while generic in scope, demonstrates the benefits of planning across disciplines and agencies (for service users with a range of needs).

Chapter 4

Intervening to make a difference

ACHIEVING A SOCIAL WORK DEGREE

This chapter will help you to develop the following capabilities, to the appropriate level, from the PCF.

- **Values and ethics**
  Apply social work ethical principles and values to guide professional practice.
- **Diversity**
  Recognise diversity and apply anti-discriminatory and anti-oppressive principles in practice.
- **Rights, justice and economic well-being**
  Advance human rights and promote social justice and economic well-being.
- **Knowledge**
  Apply knowledge of social sciences, law and social work practice theory.
- **Intervention and skills**
  Use judgement and authority to intervene with individuals, families and communities to promote independence, provide support and prevent harm, neglect and abuse.

It will also introduce you to the following academic standards as set out in the social work subject benchmark statement.

5.1.4 Social work theory.
5.1.5 The nature of social work practice.

Introduction

In this chapter you will explore some ways in which social workers put in place plans made with service users to achieve agreed goals. The chapter will introduce you to a range of interventions including task-centred practice, cognitive-behavioural approaches, crisis intervention, networking and advocacy. You will be asked to consider and reflect on these interventions. It is important to remember that interventions are simply tools for a particular purpose and that the intervention, model or approach should not lead, but that the service user's needs remain paramount. There is some debate about the power implications of using the term 'intervention', that may convey the work of experts on the non-adept or a degree of professional knowledge that sets apart social workers from service users (Parker and Doel, 2013). However, we should not be afraid of acknowledging social workers' expertise or, indeed, their authority, as long as this is tempered by a commitment to those people with whom social workers practise, using their knowledge as well as relationship skills.

You will be invited to consider how to construct and implement an intervention plan in child and family work and work with adults. Issues arising from 'voluntary' and 'involuntary' use of services will be explored. Guidance, research and advice on intervening effectively will be provided and activities will help you to make links between knowledge and practice throughout this chapter. A particular focus will concern the recording of interventions and associated processes. The importance of simple recording schedules and making your written recording style easy to read will be considered. Service user involvement in the intervention process will be emphasised through student-centred activities.

Theory, methods and models: contested debates

Debates about theory, models and methods in social work practice are complex and contested. It can be a difficult and taxing area for students to make sense of. It has, unfortunately, led to many students abandoning an explicit use of models and methods in practice and a false and unhelpful divide being created between theories, models, methods and practice. Some of the initial comments made by the former Minister for Health, Jacqui Smith, when the social work degree was introduced, appeared to echo an anti-theoretical approach. However, in the foreword to the Department of Health (2002a) *Requirements for social work training*, the emphasis is on competence in practice which necessarily employs knowledge, theories and methods.

> *The new award will require social workers to demonstrate their practical application of skills and knowledge and their ability to deliver a service that creates opportunities for service users. It will require all social workers to demonstrate their knowledge of human growth and development, particularly development of children and other vulnerable groups, their communication skills and their ability to work confidently and effectively with other professionals. The emphasis must be on practice and the practical relevance of theory.*
>
> (Department of Health, 2002a, pi)

With the rise in 'fast-track' programmes in social work education in England, it appears even more important that robust theoretical approaches are championed. The importance of this cannot be underestimated in respect of providing the best possible services, based on evidence (however that contentious word is interpreted), for the people who use social work services.

Trevithick (2005) considers three interconnected domains of knowledge that are important in social work practice:

- theoretical knowledge;
- factual knowledge;
- practice knowledge.

It will be useful briefly to explore each of these in turn (see Box 4.1).

Box 4.1: Types of knowledge in social work

Theoretical knowledge

In social work the theoretical base is predominated by knowledge borrowed from other disciplines. It has been suggested that this might make the interpretation and use of such knowledge difficult because it is taken out of context. It may also be the case that the knowledge is limited as it generally developed within Western frameworks and assumptions and may not apply to diverse cultures and societies. The core elements of borrowed knowledge come from psychology, sociology, law, philosophy, medicine, and political and economic science.

Theoretical knowledge may also refer to theories that analyse the tasks and purposes of social work, or to approaches to practice, sometimes called practice theories or models. Theoretical knowledge relies on theory. Theories themselves remain hypothetical rather than absolute, attempting to explain, predict and illuminate from a range of perspectives.

Factual knowledge

Factual knowledge refers to data, statistics, figures, records and research findings. It is important not to be immediately accepting of the veracity of these 'facts' or the implications that might seem to arise from them. Trevithick (2005) points to the important rule of 'falsification' attributed to Karl Popper. Data must be able to be scrutinised, checked and be open to falsification if it is to be accepted as scientific. There are elements of factual knowledge that, for social workers, are crucial. One might immediately think of knowledge of legislation relating to your particular field of practice, knowledge of resources available in your area, knowledge of the procedures of the agency that guide practice.

Practice knowledge

Finally, practice knowledge relates to the use of self and the importance of a critical perspective in your use of knowledge, skills of reasoning and practice. Pawson et al. (2003) recognised that practitioner knowledge is usually passed on in a tacit way and acquired through practice and sharing collective wisdom, through training and formal and informal consultation rather than being judged against any specific standards. Practice wisdom and working intuitively lie at the heart of reflective practice, which underpins much of what social workers do and how their practice develops. However, it does not make explicit why social workers do what they do and what works in practice.

It is important that we add another form of knowledge to this tripartite model, that of *experiential knowledge*. This form of knowledge comes from people's experience of life and its events that leads them into contact with social workers and other helping professions. The integration of service users and carers in the social work learning process, at all levels of study, is established (see Webber and Robinson, 2012). It is now important to acknowledge that the knowledge service users and carers bring is the flip side of the coin of social work practice wisdom and must be taken into account when planning to deliver services or interventions.

One of the difficulties when considering social work methods is highlighted by Marsh and Triseliotis (1996) who found that students and practitioners could identify many different models and methods for social work practice, but there was no agreement on which should be used in which circumstances. The 'art' and 'science' debate that we referred to in Chapter 1 permeates the argument about and use of theories and methods. Arguments have become polarised to some extent between those who point out that social work is an ever-changing profession and those who have adopted an evidence-based approach to practice. The former group would suggest that, because social work responds to uncertainties, complexities and contradictions in human life, it cannot be bound to a particular model for practice. The latter group might, on the other hand, suggest the only models for practice are those which can be shown to do what they say they will do.

RESEARCH SUMMARY

Trotter's empirical model of social work practice

Trotter (2004) proposes a model that is based on empirical evidence of success. It involves practitioners carrying out their own single-case experiments on their casework.

He argues that critics of empirical practice:

- *state that it is reductionist – it breaks human life into small chunks without seeing the wider perspective;*
- *state that it is value-based and individual objectives might be ignored because they are not open to the measurement demanded by evidence-based practice;*
- *provide one best answer, and therefore downplay diversity.*

Social work, however, is a complex activity and often workers and service users have multiple objectives to pursue. Empirical models of practice, in fact, rest on the values of starting where the service user is at, of acknowledging the importance of presenting problems, and working together openly and honestly to find solutions.

Approaches that work are characterised by clear, honest and frequent discussions about the role of the worker and the client. There is an important focus on modelling and encouraging the expression of pro-social behaviours and actions by the client. The use of a collaborative problem-solving approach that focuses on the client's definitions of problems and goals is also indicated.

Effective models of practice, according to Trotter, include the following.

a) Ecological systems theory: *this emphasises the interrelatedness of people and events and the impact that intervening in one system might have on another system. The theory also recognises the importance of roles that individuals adopt.*

b) Behavioural and cognitive-behavioural theory: *these theories acknowledge the influence of the actions of others, modelling and the importance of thoughts and feelings in the production of behaviours and responses.*

c) Feminist casework: *this focuses on the way in which patriarchy disadvantages women through sex role stereotyping and the devaluing of women's experiences.*

d) Radical casework: *this acknowledges the importance of structural factors influencing the client's situation.*

e) Task-centred casework: *this uses a problem-solving focus.*

f) Solution-focused approaches: *these focus on client strengths and solutions rather than problem areas.*

Evidence-based approaches have been adapted from scientific disciplines and medicine. They propose that only those models which can be shown to work and do what they claim they can do should be learned and applied by social work students. While the latter approach may appear self-evident, it is clear that social workers do operate in complex and ever-changing situations. The two approaches rely on different ways of understanding social work and social life. These different understandings are important because they influence policy developments, which in turn affect what is done in practice and therefore what outcomes occur. However, the two approaches may not be as sharply polarised as seems at first glance. It is unlikely that a practitioner who favours an approach that takes change and uncertainty into account would not wish their intervention to work! It is equally unlikely to think that a practitioner using evidence-based approaches would believe that situations do not change and that a range of factors – such as motivation, physical and mental health, prior experiences, family situation and cultural heritage – would not influence the methods used.

A further important factor complicating the use of social work methods comes from our understanding of social work. The question 'What is social work?' is often asked and qualified practitioners, student social workers and academics have consistently failed to decide what it is. These questions are debated in Horner (2012). While teachers teach, nurses nurse, managers manage and police officers police, agreement on what social workers do is lacking. We are not certain that social work can be understood as a discrete profession globally in a similar way, perhaps, to medicine. Social work necessarily relies on local interpretations often at the level of agency practice.

There are some common elements of social work in the UK, however. It is clear that social workers work with vulnerable people who are in some way marginalised or excluded from full participation in society. They also work with the context in which people live, including other people around an individual, the physical environment and with other services working with that person. Social workers work to improve the life chances of people in their living environment. This is something not undertaken by other professions. In order to work effectively, social workers need to equip themselves with a range of methods for practice that work to reduce social exclusion and increase life chances and opportunities, and to demonstrate that effectiveness in practice.

A further issue is raised by the wide range of possible models and methods available and a lack of clarity or obscuring of the theories underlying these models. See for instance the 14 models identified by Watson and West (2006, pp53–54). Whichever model is used, however, it is clear that service users appreciate an approach that is empathic, appears genuine and displays warmth. Service users also want social workers to be honest and up-front. They do not want to be faced with hidden agendas and unexpected consequences.

The intention in this chapter is to introduce a range of models that may assist social workers in achieving desired and agreed outcomes for service users. These models will be framed by the understanding that social workers operate at many different levels in society – with individuals, families, groups and communities – and therefore an overall approach is needed that understands the ways in which the various elements of social life interact and interconnect. We will briefly introduce a *systems* a[illegible] to social life. It is also acknowledged that certain basic helping skills are c[illegible]eployment of methods and models for practice, whether these c[illegible]erson-centred approach or an evidence-based perspective.

A systems approach

In Chapter 2 you examined the first principles of the systems approach in relation to ecomaps (see page 47). While systems thinking came originally from biology and has been developed in increasingly complex ways, it is important to note that in social work systems thinking has emphasised the interactive context of social life. Individuals are not seen as isolated, unconnected beings but social and affected by and influencing others around them, the organisations with which they have contact and, indeed, wider society (Payne, 2005; Sheldon and Macdonald, 2009).

This acknowledgement is important because it recognises that a child in need or an older person with failing health affects those around them and that the response of those around them affects their well-being or otherwise. It goes wider than this, however, and links to social workers' commitment to anti-oppressive practice that understands oppression to be multi-directional and not simply personal prejudice directed by one person towards another (Dominelli, 2002; Thompson, 2006). A systems approach considers the impact that social structures, the kinds of help and support provided and access to them have on the ways in which individuals, families, groups and communities respond. It is important to reiterate that social workers operate at the edges of society, assisting those who are in some way disenfranchised from participating in society. This means, therefore, that social workers need to keep the many levels and directions of interaction in mind when intervening. Systems thinking does not offer an explanation of the reasons why things happen and does not really provide a model of intervention.

Core helping skills

Research conducted concerning service user satisfaction and the ways in which people wish to be treated by social work professionals consistently highlights some of the core interpersonal communication and helping skills (Koprowska, 2010).

Those core helping skills were first articulated by Carl Rogers (1951; 1961), a humanist psychologist, and, despite being refined and added to, remain central today. The basic qualities of helping relationships are well known and comprise:

- empathy;
- warmth;
- genuineness.

Carkhuff (1987) adds three more essential conditions to the helping relationship:

- concreteness;
- immediacy;
- confrontation.

A brief overview of these qualities is given below.

Core qualities for helping relationships

Empathy represents the ability to experience the world of another person as if it was one's own without actually losing the 'as if' quality. An important way of beginning to demonstrate empathy is to reflect the content of what is said and adjust your understanding accordingly. However, it is not content alone that you are seeking to understand but the whole experience of the person. Therefore, social workers also need to reflect feelings, the aim being to check the congruence of feelings expressed with the content of what is said: whether feelings and content match each other.

Warmth, also known as unconditional positive regard or acceptance, is shown by respecting people for what they are as unique individuals and creating a safe and trusting environment in which service users can express themselves. Showing acceptance for people in all situations can be difficult but is central to effective helping.

Genuineness relates to directness and openness in the social worker's communication. The social worker does not have hidden agendas or concealed thoughts, and does not pretend but encourages direct and open communication.

Concreteness refers to specificity. The practitioner ensures that the person they are helping is specific about the particular meanings they attach to their ideas, images, thoughts, feelings and descriptions. It adds clarity to the communication and facilitates the practitioner checking their understanding of the person in need.

Immediacy suggests that it is important not to spend too much time in talk about the past and past behaviours but to focus on the immediate and central problem or issue of concern.

Confrontation concerns the pointing out of discrepancies and disconfirmatory evidence between the social worker's view and the service user's. Common discrepancies include differences between the real and ideal view of the self, differences between the person's thinking and feelings and what they actually do in practice, and differences between the real world as seen by the practitioner and the fantasy world as seen by the person in need.

These qualities are important, but are conveyed using learned interpersonal or helping skills. When engaging in a social work relationship with a service user, social workers should be mindful of the needs of service users. Egan (2001) identifies some of the important interpersonal skills necessary for effective helping:

- attending;
- listening;
- probing;
- effective challenging.

These skills build on the qualities listed above.

A social worker being present at an important point in another person's life can make a big difference. Effective attending lets service users know that you were there and were prepared to listen. Being attentive, however, involves becoming aware of how you sit, how the room is positioned, how much eye contact you make and your own level of comfort in the situation. It also demands that you attend to the ways in which you use your body language and the messages being communicated to you by the service user's body language. What is important is that you do not become so wrapped up in interpreting body language that you miss the overt messages. The key is to be natural and relaxed as far as possible but to practise recognition of your use of body language in a safe environment. You will soon be able to apply the skills learned in a natural way. It is important to remember that you speak with colleagues every day. The skills used are similar to those applied in social work situations.

Listening is a far more complex skill than simply hearing what it is that the other person is saying. It involves being attentive to the feelings expressed when speaking: the gaps, silences, hesitations and pauses. According to Egan (2001), listening involves the following.

- Observing and reading the service user's non-verbal behaviour – this involves being mindful of our own non-verbal behaviour and recognising that there are different cultural norms and that assumptions should not be made. Check your understanding.

- Listening to and understanding the service user's verbal messages. This again demands summarising, checking and amending your understanding as appropriate.
- Listening to the whole person in the context of the social settings of their life. People develop understanding on the basis of their experiences, environment, culture and personalities. As a social worker, it is important to acknowledge the range of influences on people.
- Tough-minded listening. Social workers can help people effectively only if they are prepared to confront discrepancies and demonstrate their honest and clear approach.

These interpersonal skills are important whatever methods of intervention are used, and the deployment and use of them should begin at the outset of your relationship with service users.

RESEARCH SUMMARY

Hancock et al.'s (2012) study on dietetics offers insights for social workers into developing high quality listening skills as a means of remaining centred on those who use social work services. Their study looked at the perceptions that 17 dietetic patients had of consultations and findings centred on information, listening skills and practical administrative considerations. Respondents did agree, however, that good communication, being non-judgemental and establishing a rapport were significant in how they rated the experience.

ACTIVITY 4.1

It is important to become more aware of how you present to other people and what messages you might convey. Choose a colleague or friend and ask if they would help you to begin examining your communication skills.

Spend about 20 minutes talking together about a topic of general interest to you both. Then note down your body language, voice, pauses, questions used and consider how the use of your interpersonal skills assisted or hindered the conversation.

COMMENT

This activity is not easy and may feel a little contrived. Do not worry if you found it hard or were constrained because you were concentrating on your skills and the way you presented. It is important to begin this process of awareness-raising in a safe context before you work with service users.

Let us briefly set Rebecca, Melissa and Irene in the context of systems thinking and the use of interpersonal skills.

CASE STUDY

In simple terms we can see that the three people involved – Rebecca, Melissa and Irene – interact together and influence each other. They are also sub-systems or elements of a wider family system that interacts with social workers, health visitors, Melissa's boyfriend and no doubt with other families. The importance of this way of thinking is to recognise that Rebecca's care is not the concern of just her immediate family and that there is a range of influences on a person's life.

In undertaking the initial assessment and negotiating the plan, Mandy, Rebecca's social worker, used her skills to set everyone at ease, to listen to Melissa, Irene and others, to summarise, check and reproduce what was said. This took time and depended on developing a relationship that had clear boundaries: Mandy explained the purpose of the work, what could be confidential and what could not be. She then negotiated with the family a plan to meet Rebecca's needs. This negotiation needed to be joint and allow everyone involved to contribute in their own way. Any assessment, plan, intervention or review will be influenced by the quality of the social worker's interpersonal skills.

Empirical intervention models

As we have seen throughout this book, there is an ongoing debate concerning our interpretation of social work as either an 'art' or a 'science'. There are many crossover points between the two arguments. In this section you will be introduced to models that are empirically based, that is, the outcomes and effects can be observed and measured and an inference made as to their impact on situations. However, these models require skill and artistry to be effective and, as we shall see, they acknowledge the fluidity and dynamic aspects of service user situations. While you will be introduced to these models using a children and families perspective, the interventions can be transferred to other social work situations and service user groups. Indeed, it may be useful to spend time thinking how you might use these models with adult service users and carers.

Task-centred practice

In working directly with Melissa, Mandy used a task-centred approach to achieving the goals that were made clear by the plan. The task-centred approach is an extremely practical model for social work. It suggests that beneficial and desired changes can be achieved by working in partnership with service users to resolve other areas of concern. While partnership is stressed, task-centred practice can be used with people who do not wish to work with you and those whose capacity to make agreements is limited, because it centres on goals that are negotiated and agreed between service users and social workers. It is, therefore, a useful model to employ as part of wider social work intervention. The emphasis is upon small, achievable targets and goals and can involve individuals, whole families or wider groups in the selection, prioritising and working towards the achievement of these. It is helpful to view task-centred practice as a set of building blocks (Marsh and Doel, 2005) or as a series of steps climbed by agreement between the social worker and service users as seen in Figure 4.1.

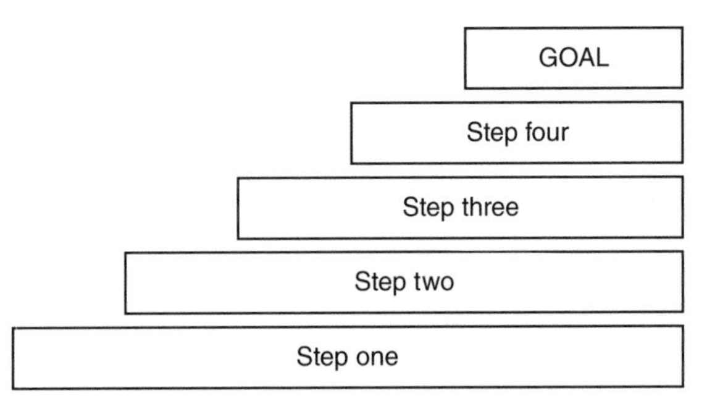

Figure 4.1 A step approach to achieving goals

Although the originators of the approach suggested that task-centred work was simply a pragmatic way of working that was not based on any underlying theory, this is not the case (Reid and Epstein, 1972; Reid, 1978). Task-centred work is associated with problem-solving and behavioural approaches to social work (Doel, 2009; Gambrill, 1994; Marsh, 2008). The successful accomplishment of tasks rewards people and motivates them to try to act in other areas of their lives. Whatever the theory underlying, task-centred practice, however, is about purposeful actions. The work undertaken is time limited, structured and problem focused. It represents an active collaboration between practitioner and service user.

Task-centred practice has been adopted by many social workers and by agencies. Its simple sequencing of steps building to agreed goals fits with the tasks demanded by policies and procedures associated with contemporary social work. Its popularity also owes a great deal to the positive features which characterise it.

- The aims and purpose are clear and specific.
- A contractual agreement is negotiated between workers and service users.
- Task-centred practice concentrates upon achievable goals.
- It is time limited.
- It is task oriented, structured and sequential.
- It is effective and measurable.

RESEARCH SUMMARY

Development of the task-centred model

The model first developed in North America in the 1960s as a response to growing dissatisfaction with open-ended psychodynamic approaches to social work and an increasing emphasis on the participation of service users. Alongside this, there was a search for effective and economically efficient models of social work intervention.

(Continued)

(Continued)

In 1969, Reid and Shyne conducted an experiment that marked the development of the specific interventive technique of task-centred practice. The relative merits of short-term and extended social work practice were compared. The idea of brief practice was a novel concept for most social workers at this time and therefore a particular intervention strategy was developed, consisting of four stages:

1. *focus on the key aspect of the problem, issue or area of concern;*
2. *open, honest and explicit collaboration;*
3. *a review of the progress made towards achieving goals and objectives;*
4. *an emphasis on generalising learning for the future.*

The findings of this research indicated that short-term focused interventions led to more progress during the intervention and that accrued benefits were just as durable six months after the intervention as longer-term approaches.

Developing from this work, Reid and Epstein (1972) developed task-centred practice. From their research they presented a seven-point typology of problems for which task-centred work may be effective:

- *interpersonal conflict;*
- *dissatisfaction in social relations;*
- *relations with formal organisations;*
- *role performance;*
- *social transition;*
- *reactive emotional distress;*
- *inadequate resources.*

In a later work, however, Reid (1978) extended this typology to include the catch-all of any other psychological or behavioural problem not specified in the original typology but fitting the general principles of task-centred practice.

There has been little contemporary research in task-centred social work practice, the main work being contributed by Reid until his death in 2003, including works on education supervision with Caspi (Caspi and Reid, 2002) and on gerontological social work with Naleppa (Naleppa and Reid, 2004 – posthumously published in the UK).

Recently, task-centred practice's contribution to developing social work methodologies has been noted in an edited work (Rzepnicki, McCracken, and Briggs, 2011). Also, Rzepnicki (2012) offers an up-to-date bibliography of some of the most useful texts on task-centred work.

A model for practice

There is a general agreement on the stages and processes involved in task-centred work. Marsh and Doel (2005) break down task-centred practice into 13 elements:

- mandate;
- problems and goals;
- goals;
- exploring problems;
- focusing problems;
- refining goals;
- time limits;
- the recorded agreement;
- tasks and the task role;
- task development;
- review;
- ending and evaluating;
- continuing.

These are more often conflated within core stages such as within the following five-stage approach:

- entry;
- developing a focus on the problem;
- reaching agreement: goals and contracts;
- developing goals into manageable tasks;
- ending and reviewing the work.

Problem-solving is central to the requirements of the qualifying degree and explicitly mentioned in the subject benchmarks. This makes task-centred practice a particularly valuable model for practice. The exploration, identification, specification and prioritisation of a problem to work upon are fundamental to the model. All models debate at some point the formulation of an agreement between service users and practitioners. There is considerable debate, however, about whether this agreement should be written or remain verbal. Although written agreements may be preferred (Doel, 2009), they may exclude those with literacy problems and people using English as a second language, and may reflect the power differentials between social workers and the people with whom they work (see Dominelli, 1996). The action focus is central to the model and process. This includes planning and agreeing tasks, specifying roles and responsibilities, completing agreed tasks, reviewing achievements and modifying planning. Although an element of review is included at each stage, the final session is devoted to an overall review of the accomplishments of the service user. We shall now explore this model in greater detail, applying it to the case of Rebecca and Melissa.

Developing a focus on the problem

The initial assessment focuses on the reasons for social work involvement and the wants and wishes of the service users and begins to create a sharper focus to the work. We have seen in Chapter 1 that assessments often take a funnel-like approach to problem specification, the problem gradually becoming more specific and focused. The use of the term 'problem' may be seen as controversial. Stress on the strengths of service users is recognised as increasingly important and talking about 'problems' may be construed as negative and to some extent 'pathological'. However, it is important to remember that service users will often describe elements of their lives and situations as problematic and we must listen to these perceptions. It would be arrogant to suggest their problems are simply 'solution opportunities'! It is also the case that by working with you as a social worker on identifying areas of life for change, service users are demonstrating strengths and capacity for change.

In task-centred practice, the identification of problems is a joint venture in which service users are encouraged to describe problems or issues as they see them. These are then placed in some kind of rank order. Social workers check their understanding and construct an initial problem profile with service users and others to gain corroborative information. At this stage agreement can be reached on the priority area to be worked upon.

Once the range of problems has been prioritised, a target problem can be chosen and described in detail. The process is collaborative at all stages and encourages the active involvement of service users.

In the assessment of Melissa, Rebecca and Irene you will recall that three issues were highlighted for work. These consisted of a break from caring, joining a young mums' group and work on Melissa and Irene's relationship. Two of these were seen as problems that Melissa wanted to overcome, while attending the young mums' group was something she wanted to try.

In the assessment process and in constructing a plan the social worker was working with Melissa to prioritise problems and to identify targets for change.

Reaching agreement: goals and contracts

The second stage of task-centred work concerns reaching an agreement about goals and working together to achieve them. The selection of goals is the next stage after the ranking in priority order of problems and issues to change. The key issue in reaching agreement about goals is to ensure that the service user leads the process. The task of the social worker is to keep the service user on track and to ensure that goals identified are achievable and realistic. Doel (2009) identifies three important factors that need to be considered when you are working with service users to define and agree upon goals. These are:

- checking that the goal is really what the person wants to achieve, as this will increase motivation to work towards it;
- making sure that goals are feasible and achievable;
- determining whether the goal is acceptable to agency policy and values.

Once a goal is identified and agreed, it is important to agree on a course of action to achieve it. An important way of recording this is to negotiate a written agreement specifying exactly what will be done, who will do what, and when and how they will do it. There is a debate as to whether the agreement between service users and practitioners should be written or should remain oral. While oral agreements can be less frightening and imposing, and are necessary where a person cannot read, a written contract or agreement adds to specificity, and can be referred to at a later date if a dispute over tasks or responsibilities arises. They can be extremely useful in establishing clear parameters for work where remembering is difficult or where there are many people involved.

The agreement reached with Melissa identified an overall goal or objective of giving *the best possible start in life for Rebecca*. This was not specific and needed to be discussed further to identify what would help achieve this broad objective in Melissa's view. The written agreement and plan added a degree of clarity to the process. While Melissa and her mother were quite literate, it is important to consider difficulties with understanding written documents and to ensure that alternative formats are available where appropriate. For instance, the use of recorded agreements may help where people have difficulty reading or an interpreter may help where English is not spoken or is a second language.

Developing goals into manageable tasks

Planned tasks must be explicit, practicable for service users to undertake outside of formal sessions and mutually agreed. Payne (1997) identifies two basic types of task in the first edition of *Modern Social Work Theory*:

- general tasks which set out the agency's intervention and work policy;
- operational tasks which define exactly what will be done to achieve the goals that are set.

Tasks may involve a single action or a set of smaller actions that join together. They may be set for the service user to complete alone, or the service user may complete one task while the social worker or another involved person does something else. Tasks may also be shared. However, it is important to note that tasks are individual to the specific situation in which they have been developed. At this point a more specific and task-focused agreement can be negotiated. An example is shown in respect of Melissa.

The general tasks for Melissa were detailed in the plan. However, Mandy worked with Melissa to consider a more detailed set of steps to integrate her into the young mums' group. To begin the process, Mandy arranged a meeting between June Bridge, the health visitor, Melissa and herself. This meeting was convened to consider the process needed to ease Melissa into the group.

Melissa had become keen to attend because of the support she would gain. She was, however, nervous about joining and meeting new people. She also found it more difficult to get up in the morning as Rebecca was not sleeping well in the night. Melissa agreed to:

- purchase an alarm clock;
- meet June Bridge on Thursday at 9.00 a.m.;
- be taken by June to the group and to stay for one hour.

This would be reviewed by June, Melissa and Mandy on the Monday following the session. It was also agreed that if this plan had worked well Melissa would meet June at the group on the following Thursday and stay for the morning. Subsequently, Melissa would attend the group on Tuesdays and Thursdays. This would be reviewed weekly for four weeks by Mandy and Melissa.

It is important to highlight again the need for clarity, specificity and simplicity when constructing the tasks. It can be helpful to think, 'If I were to be abducted by aliens and could not get to work, would my colleagues understand the tasks in the same way as I do?' It is crucial for the service user to have the same understanding as you yourself and this makes great demands on how you use and develop your interpersonal skills.

The social work role is now directed towards facilitating the achievement of the agreed tasks by the service user. As the intervention process proceeds, the tasks may be revised and made more specific and clear if this becomes necessary. This allows progress to be measured and the intervention to be altered to achieve maximum gain for the service user. The social work role, your 'tasks' and the intensity of involvement depend upon the agreement, and the strengths and capacity of the service user and others who may help with the programme. This flexibility allows the model to be used with a wide range of people in many situations.

At each session the social worker and service user should review the achievements made. This provides a useful starting point for each session and looks at strengths and obstacles or barriers to be overcome. Doel (2009) points out that service users' motivation may wane over time and, as a result, tasks may remain unaccomplished. If social workers identify this they may be able to renegotiate with service users and, if necessary, modify the goals. It was important for Mandy to support and encourage Melissa's attendance when she was getting up and going to the group on her own. It must be remembered that sometimes the goals negotiated are either not the ones the service user really wants to achieve or they are not realistic and achievable. Progress may be diverted off course, however, by a range of other factors affecting the lives of service users. There needs to be a degree of flexibility to adapt the process where necessary. It is sometimes helpful to involve carers and other involved people to assist in goal achievement. This may encourage perseverance and, if the contract is written, can help to keep a focus on the agreed tasks and the goals sought.

Ending and reviewing the work

It is important that the time-limited nature of the intervention is mentioned at the outset of the intervention and that a planned end to the work is emphasised. This clear focus can keep service users 'on track' and encourage motivation to achieve agreed goals. The ending phase is part of the agreement to work together and is therefore undertaken collaboratively between client and worker. In respect of Melissa, social work support was continuing but the specific agreement to introduce her to the young mums' group was time limited. She was eased into the group, at which point the health visitor withdrew. The social work involvement continued while she became established and after four weeks the focus of this work shifted to the other objectives identified in the plan.

It may happen, however, that no matter how carefully planned the intervention has been, the service user does not wish to end contact even if goals have been achieved. This may sometimes highlight a new and different need for work and this can be discussed as and when appropriate. When the agreed goal has not been achieved by the end of the planned sessions, more time may be negotiated if it is felt this will help service users to reach the goals (Doel, 2009). It may also be the case that the task-centred work is part of a wider involvement between social worker and service user. In this case the negotiated and planned ending of a piece of work may represent a staging post or milestone in gaining skills and assist closure of the case in the future. The process is flexible and made individual to the situation in which the work takes place.

Throughout the key stages involved in task-centred practice it is important to be both systematic in what is undertaken and flexible in response to changing needs. Being systematic keeps the service user focused on the task in hand, but you need to be flexible enough to acknowledge other concerns and factors in the service user's life. This model of intervention fits the practical emphasis of the new degree, the problem-solving focus and the need to demonstrate effectiveness. It also fits many agency approaches. We will now turn to a more complex model that is also grounded in effectiveness.

Cognitive-behavioural approaches to practice

Cognitive-behavioural approaches to practice have occasionally had a negative press over the years. This is partly due to a misunderstanding of the methods and processes involved. It has been suggested that giving rewards for good behaviour is tantamount to bribery, that feelings are ignored, that past experiences are not taken into account and that cognitive-behavioural approaches reduce human actions to component parts in a way that fails to acknowledge the whole person. By far the most common criticism of cognitive-behavioural approaches comes from those practitioners who base their views on misguided bad practice and programmes that use unethical techniques such as punishments and aversive methods. More recent criticisms stem from some of the ways in which government departments have promoted such approaches on economic grounds. While we cannot, in times of austerity, ignore the importance of how interventions and services are financed, approaches that take this as the primary purpose tend to create cynicism among practitioners and certainly do not help those who use services.

However, we all engage in behaviour. Behaviours are observable and behavioural actions represent a response to, within, on, or as part of the wider social environment in which we live. The first use of behavioural approaches considered only observable behaviours. However, recently it was recognised that behaviours are closely linked with thoughts about how we ought to act in particular situations and under particular circumstances. Thoughts often relate to our prior experiences and result from our daily 'experiments' or interactions with the world around us. Behaviour is now acknowledged to have a thinking or cognitive element to it. As a result, the term 'cognitive behavioural' has been adopted as an umbrella term for behavioural and cognitive approaches to practice.

In simple terms, cognitive-behavioural approaches involve the systematic alteration of behaviours or thoughts by increasing, decreasing or maintaining them. A cognitive-behavioural intervention involves altering the setting in which the behaviour occurs, or its triggers, cues and prompts and its consequences. Increasing the occurrence of behaviours that are agreed by social workers and service users or carers to be constructive and positive for that person, and reducing the occurrence of behaviours that are agreed to be unhelpful or negative represent the primary aims of cognitive-behavioural programmes. This objective of changing behaviours has sparked criticism that such interventions are directive, manipulative and simply uphold socially acceptable patterns of behaviour. If this were the case, it would clearly come into conflict with the range of different ways of behaving across cultures, social groups and within families and would be liable to ignore the needs of individuals.

Fortunately, this criticism is not valid as cognitive-behavioural intervention is subject to the same values and ethics of any other intervention programme in social work and, to be effective, must have the active agreement and involvement of service users.

Cognitive-behavioural approaches are based on the idea that if behaviour is learned then it can be unlearned, or new behaviours can be learned to replace less useful ones. It is the concern of people using these approaches to widen the range of possible responses that an individual can make to their environment and to be able to change it, and not to limit, direct and determine people's actions. In this sense it is a highly ethical approach that accords with the codes of ethics of social care professional bodies (British Association of Social Workers, 2002; General Social Care Council, 2002b).

A number of key theories explaining the ways in which we learn to behave have been developed. Four of these models are commonly used in social work practice:

- respondent or classical conditioning;
- operant or instrumental conditioning;
- modelling, imitative or vicarious learning;
- cognitive-behavioural theories.

Respondent and operant conditioning models are concerned with what can be seen; modelling concerns a person's interpretation of what another person does; and cognitive-behavioural approaches are related to the ways in which thoughts lead to certain consequences or actions. In this section of the chapter we will concentrate on the first two models since they are well known and acknowledged to be useful within important areas of social work practice. These models will be explored in respect of Rebecca and Melissa, although they can be applied with equal effectiveness in adult social work. As you develop your knowledge and skills, you may wish to increase your understanding of the other models. (A good place to start would be to consult Cigno, 2009; Cigno and Bourn, 1998; Parker and Randall, 1997; Sheldon, 1995; Sheldon and Macdonald, 2009.) An outline of respondent and operant conditioning models follows.

Respondent or classical conditioning

In this theory, behaviours are prompted or triggered by association with a certain event or stimulus. For instance, being asked to give an oral presentation for your course work may lead to your palms sweating, a dry throat and nausea. The same response may also occur when the initial prompt, being asked to give an oral presentation, is associated or paired with a second event or stimulus. Let us say that in this instance the oral presentation is to be assessed. When next asked to complete a piece of assessed casework, but no oral presentation, the same response occurs. This is known as 'respondent conditioning' because the behaviour is considered to be a response to the stimulus eliciting it.

Social workers using a respondent conditioning approach might attempt to replace the anxiety response by pairing the stimulus with something that would trigger more comfortable and positive reactions, perhaps associating with being asked to give an oral presentation lying on a sun-soaked beach with just enough of a breeze to keep you cool. The responses – positive and negative – would then compete and hopefully the positive response would begin to replace the negative one. Social workers might also look at adapting the response. They may teach you to relax your muscles and to breathe slowly and deeply. After learning these skills you may be gradually introduced by the social worker to the idea of undertaking an oral presentation, and you may be able to bring up the relaxed response when presented with the request to give an oral presentation. These two responses compete and, hopefully, being able to relax when faced with an initially anxiety provoking stimulus will help you to adapt the response and cope much better with this situation.

Operant or instrumental conditioning

Respondent conditioning theory is quite a simple way of describing the ways in which we learn. Another theory of learning that is similar to respondent conditioning is operant learning theory. Rather than a response or behaviour being triggered or prompted by a situation or event, this theory states that behaviours are learned and repeated because of the consequences immediately following their expression. The strength, frequency and type of these consequences greatly influence any future expression of the preceding behaviour.

Asked to give oral presentation (unconditioned stimulus)	Sweaty palms, dry throat, nausea (unconditioned response)
Asked to give oral presentation that will be assessed (unconditioned stimulus and conditioned stimulus)	Sweaty palms, dry throat, nausea (unconditioned and conditioned response)
Asked to complete an assessment (conditioned stimulus)	Sweaty palms, dry throat, nausea (conditioned response)

Figure 4.2 A respondent conditioning model

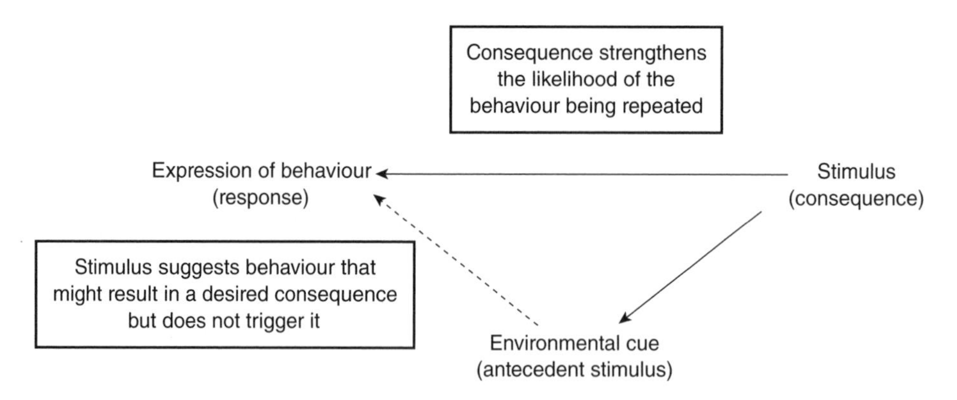

Figure 4.3 Operant learning theory

Specific settings or behaviours do not automatically elicit operant behaviour, but they are important as they provide cues for the kind of behaviour that is likely to result in gaining the reward or consequence that is desired. These cues are known as antecedent stimuli. If a social worker learns what signals or cues precede behaviour, intervention can be directed at altering them. However, social workers are also likely to want to help service users change the consequences that make the behaviour that is targeted for change likely to happen again.

Using theories of learning

Let us return to the case of Rebecca and Melissa three years forward in time to see how these models of learning can help in social work practice. In order to begin to alter behaviour, social workers will work alongside service users and carers to identify patterns that trigger or reinforce the behaviour by rewarding it. This demands a more focused and specific assessment relating directly to an identified and agreed target behaviour. This might come from the wider assessment process and the negotiations that take place. The important point to note is that the target behaviour is more likely to be changed if it is identified and agreed by the service user and social worker. This is important not only in meeting the ethical demands of social work, but also in achieving success in the intervention. The target of the intervention must be clearly and explicitly specified. This is not easy to achieve and you will benefit from practice in describing behaviours in clear, specific and commonly understandable ways.

A cognitive-behavioural assessment concerns who does what, where, when, how often and with whom. Sticking to these questions creates focus, clarity and specificity.

CASE STUDY

Rebecca is nearly four years old. Melissa is a single parent again following the break-up of her relationship two years ago. Recently, Melissa has been referred to the social work team because of 'shouting and screaming' at her daughter. Melissa was pleased with the prospect of support because of her previous involvement with social services but embarrassed and defensive because of the nature of the referral.

She told David, the social worker, that Rebecca was 'too much of a handful and will never do as she's told'. Melissa agreed that she was finding it difficult to control Rebecca and was shouting a lot. This gave David some information but it remained broad and non-specific. He used a series of 'who, what, where, when and how' questions to create focus, explaining to Melissa that they could work together to create a clear understanding of the situation and then seek alternatives.

The main times that Melissa became cross was at Rebecca's bedtime. Rebecca was very active and wanted to play games, have drinks and be read stories continually. The usual pattern was that after eating at about 5.30 pm Melissa would wash the dishes until she gave in to Rebecca's requests for a story – her favourite at the moment being The Tiger Who Came to Tea. *After the story, Rebecca would ask to play a game – generally 'snap' or 'pairs'. This would, Melissa said, continue until bedtime and then Rebecca would ask for a drink or a biscuit. On further exploration, David was told that, although Melissa tried to take some time out, the 'constant nagging' led to her giving in and responding to Rebecca's requests. When Melissa felt that Rebecca was delaying her bedtime she would 'snap' and shout.*

David had more information to work with now and asked 'What is it that you would most like to change?' Melissa brought up two things: she would like Rebecca to give her some free time in the evening and she would like to be able to stop shouting at Rebecca. A target of 30 minutes' free time divided into two 15-minute slots was agreed.

David needed to work with Melissa and Rebecca to record the frequency of these behaviours and to identify any patterns that might be amenable to change. In order to do this he needed to be very precise about what the behaviours or targets were. They decided on 'shouting at Rebecca' and 'sitting down with a cup of tea' as this characterised her attempts at free time. David explained carefully the information to be recorded and checked with Melissa that she was able to undertake this. It can be the case that insufficient attention is paid to this part of the process and service users either do not complete the recording or record something different from what the social worker expected. Feeling confident that she was able to record the situation, David suggested that she keep two questions in mind:

1. *What happens when you shout at Rebecca?*
2. *What happens when you take time away from Rebecca in the evening?*

Melissa was asked to complete two charts detailing exactly what happened before the targeted behaviour, when, where, in what ways, and with whom, and what happened immediately following the behaviour. He asked Melissa to collect this information over the course of the week and to do so as soon after the event as possible so it was not lost or 'reinterpreted'. Typical examples of the recordings follow:

(Continued)

(Continued)

Table 4.1 'ABC' charts for Rebecca and Melissa

	Antecedent	**Behaviour (agreed behaviour: shouting at Rebecca)**	**Consequence**
Date/time	Called Rebecca for bed, she asked me to play one more game with her, agreed if she would come to bed immediately after. Rebecca then asked for a drink.	Shouted at Rebecca.	I felt guilty and gave her a drink and a cuddle.
	Antecedent/situation	**Behaviour**	**Consequence**
Date/time	Sat down to drink a cup of tea.	Rebecca asked me to play snap five times.	Played snap while drinking tea.

David was able to explore with Melissa how the problems were likely to be maintained. It appeared over the course of the week that Melissa shouted at Rebecca when she 'stalled for time' in going to bed, and that while this acted as a trigger to Melissa, she was inadvertently making Rebecca's delaying tactics more likely by often doing what she had asked for in the first place. It seemed also to be the case that Melissa reinforced Rebecca's requests for her to play by eventually agreeing to play with her. It is important when looking at patterns like these not to be accusatory or to blame people for 'causing' problems. This needs to be handled sensitively and explaining the social ways in which we learn may help. David set out in visual form the pattern of occurrences.

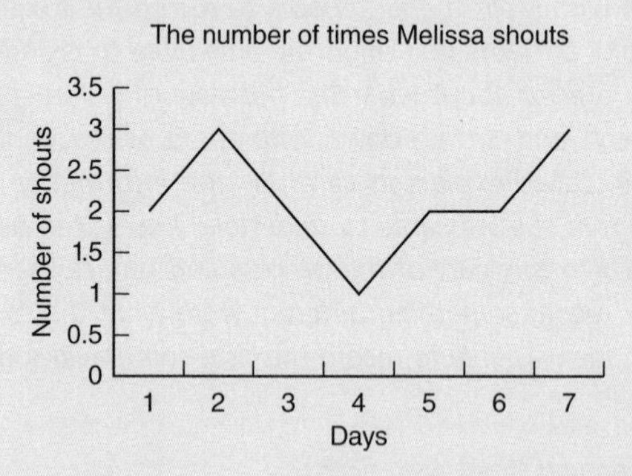

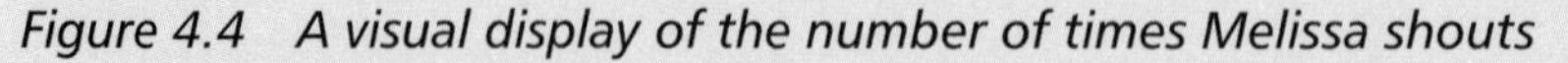
Figure 4.4 A visual display of the number of times Melissa shouts

They discussed what they might do to change the situation and David asked Melissa to bring Rebecca into this discussion, then she would be aware of the plans. It is important to involve all people who may be affected by the programme. It is courteous and shows respect, taking into account age and understanding. They agreed to plan into the evenings two 15-minute breaks during which Melissa would not play with Rebecca but after which Rebecca would be given the choice of what to do. It was also agreed to help Melissa to

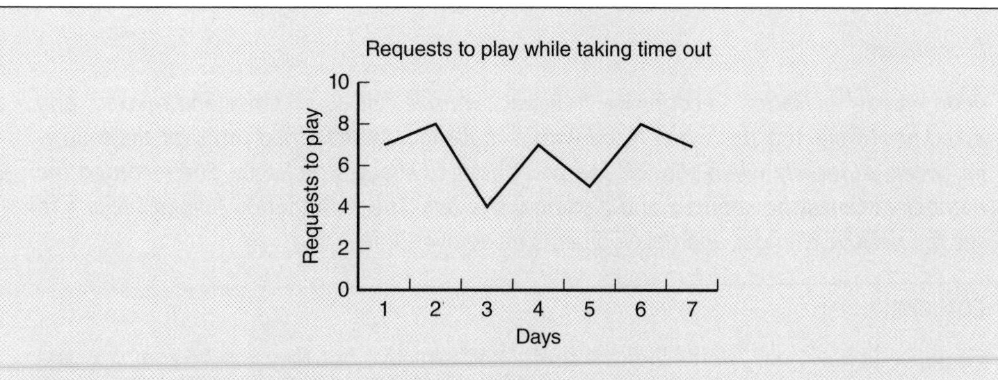

Figure 4.5 Requests to play with Rebecca

learn to relax and to use these techniques when feeling fraught. These plans drew on operant and respondent conditioning and considered manipulating triggers and consequences that seemed to be maintaining these situations.

Melissa would tell Rebecca five minutes before her break that it would be happening. Then she would mention it again as she went to spend time on her own. Rebecca agreed to play on her own and would be able to choose the next game if she did not disturb Melissa during this time. Melissa agreed to explain firmly and calmly that she was having a break if Rebecca asked her for something. She was not to give in. Importantly, David explained to Melissa that often behaviour that you wish to change gets worse for a time before gradually reducing, and that this can be a difficult time but she would succeed if she persevered. They agreed to monitor and record this situation for a week using the same forms as before, and David again prepared a visual display of the changes.

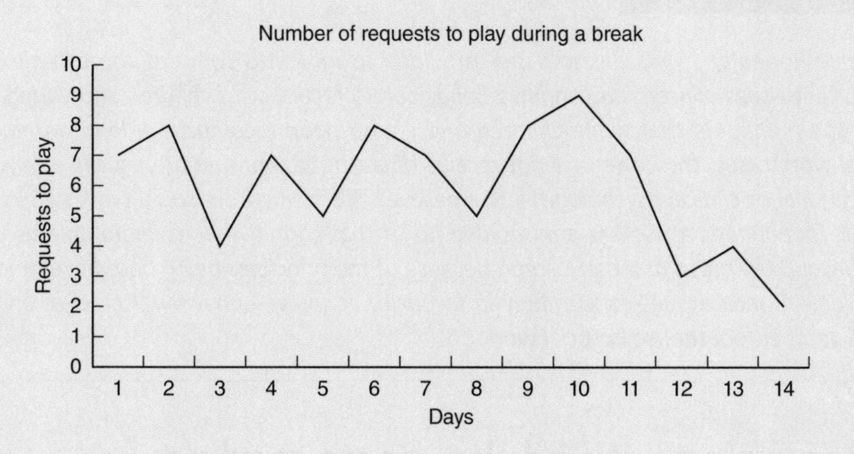

Figure 4.6 Requests to play over time

Melissa was heartened to see this working and said she felt much calmer. However, she was still concerned about shouting at Rebecca, although she was not giving in to her requests at bedtime. David encouraged her to keep a firm approach and also taught her

(Continued)

(Continued)

deep muscle relaxation, recognising how each muscle felt when tense and relaxed, and asked her to practise this when faced with a challenge. Melissa tried this over the following week, especially when she felt she was about to shout at Rebecca. She recorded the number of times she shouted and also how she felt. This information helped Melissa to see the positive changes and developments made over time.

COMMENT

Cognitive-behavioural approaches are useful and effective but they can be complex, and care must be taken over each part of the process, especially in respect of including service users in the planning and implementation of the work. It must also be remembered that if a behaviour is to change by replacing the consequence with a different one, this must be recognised by the individual as important and stronger than the consequence they already gain from behaving in the way you and they wish to change. Choosing something to reinforce a new behaviour is an activity that is complex and open to failure if it is not done in full participation with service users. Imagine a situation in which a friend wanted to help you alter one of your behaviours but this behaviour made you very popular with other friends. If your friend chose to replace the popularity you gained from behaving in this way with a chance to see a football match, but you did not enjoy football, it would be unlikely to alter your behaviour!

RESEARCH SUMMARY

Tammie Ronen's (1994) classic paper provided insight into some of the complex and important issues concerning cognitive-behavioural practice with children and young people. She highlights that while children and young people comprise a large number of social work cases, they often do not receive direct treatment and are usually referred to educational or clinical psychologists. She believes this stems from social work's psychodynamic foundations as well as a misguided belief that cognitive-behavioural interventions are beyond the grasp of most children because of the principles being based in empiricism and logic. Ronen argues convincingly in favour of cognitive-behavioural practice and this adds another tool for use in social work.

Intervening with adults: some models

Cognitive-behavioural programmes can be used with adults as well as with children and families. However, we turn now to consider interventions that can be usefully applied when working with older people within care management and personal support systems for adults. Particularly we refer to crisis intervention drawing on some psychodynamic theories and also networking skills, advocacy and volunteering skills. Older people do not have a monopoly on these interventions, and indeed they are equally appropriate for other service user groups. Nonetheless, we describe them here in order to build your knowledge and understanding so that, when we look at the developing case of Denise Lockwood, you are familiar with the interventions. Indeed, we hope that you will be able to extrapolate from the information provided in order to work out how you think the care manager, Amanda Thorpe, should have worked with Denise Lockwood in the early phases of their encounter.

Crisis theory and crisis intervention

First we look at the development of crisis theory and crisis intervention and also at the practical application of crisis intervention in social work situations. We shall then go on to consider this intervention in relation to the case of Denise Lockwood. This is an appropriate approach to use with Denise, given the way she felt when she first started to learn that her symptoms were likely to lead to a diagnosis of dementia and that her life was likely to change dramatically. For a fuller explanation of crisis intervention we suggest you read Parker's (2007b) paper on crisis intervention and people with dementia.

Let us consider some definitions which may help to unpack the concept. Crises are described as time-limited periods of psychological distress that people need to overcome but cannot do so using tried and tested methods of coping (Caplan, 1961; Roberts, 1991; Wilson et al., 2008).

Definitions of what constitutes a crisis situation are to some extent in the perception of the beholder. Further, we need to conceptualise crisis in a fluid and dynamic sense. Its interpretation does not rest upon a particular event or situation or even a particular response. Rather the individual's perception of, for example, powerlessness, lack of control and psychological distress located within a particular contextual environment, provides meaning. Whatever the event or situation triggering the crisis, it seems that there are certain key features involved in the experience of crises. Parry (1990, p15) suggests that these comprise:

- a precipitating event or the result of long-term stress;
- individually experienced distress;
- a sense of loss, danger to the self or humiliation;
- feelings of being out of control of the situation;
- events which may be unexpected;
- disruption in usual patterns and routines;
- an uncertain future; and
- continuing distress over time, although this is limited.

Crises can be *accidental* – a reaction to unexpected traumatic events – or *developmental* – a reaction to a life transition. Both types are potentially important when considering reactions to bereavement and when dealing with degenerative conditions, such as that experienced by Denise Lockwood. The idea of crisis representing a turning point that presents problems for the individual that they cannot solve without external support is helpful (Aguilera and Messick, 1974; 1982). We shall return to these ideas when illustrating our complex case.

A particular crisis event is likely to influence a particular social system in a unique way, which in turn influences and is influenced by its environment and by participating sub-systems. The use of systems theory may allow a social worker/care manager to conceptualise the wider conflicting processes impinging upon a particular crisis situation. In the case of Denise Lockwood we see how her immediate support system and networks are affected **as a result of her personal and health crises.**

RESEARCH SUMMARY

The development of crisis theory

Crisis theory and crisis intervention have a long history of development. Roberts (1991) draws on thinking from 400BC when referring to Hippocrates' understanding of the importance of crises in medicine and health. Current understanding is informed predominantly by American psychiatry. The conceptual and theoretical origins have arisen from varied sources, but primarily from psychoanalytic thinking and the principle of causality that holds that present behaviour needs to be understood in terms of life history and past experiences. Put simply, people normally cope better with crises if they have dealt effectively with other crises in their lives; conversely they cope less well if they have unresolved past problems. The theoretical base has developed in sophistication, especially following Lindemann's (1944) study of grief reactions of survivors and relatives after a night-club fire in Coconut Grove, Boston. Lindemann and colleagues found that many individuals experiencing acute grief shared five related reactions as follows:

1. *somatic distress (physical sensations such as stomach complaints or headaches);*
2. *preoccupation with the image of the deceased;*
3. *guilt;*
4. *hostile reactions;*
5. *loss of patterns of conduct.*

Also, they found that the duration of the reaction appeared to be dependent upon the success of the grief work. Lindemann found that people needed encouragement to mourn and to adjust to the changed environment.

The development of crisis theory is underpinned by a range of different and complex theories which we will not explore in detail here. They include the following.

- *Erikson's (1950) developmental psychology, and Hartmann's (1958) ego psychology: within this framework, personal development is seen as the result of a series of crises through which we move that result from adapting to attachment and loss within normal human growth and development.*

- *Drawing on Parkes' (1972) work, Payne (2005) explains that when a person has a significant loss, they may* regress to childhood experiences of stress due to loss *(p77). Similarly, Pincus' (1976) work illustrates the point that in their reaction to death, family members may reveal hidden and high levels of unresolved feelings about former relationships.*
- *Person-centred approaches (Rogers, 1961) and gestalt therapy (Perls, Hefferline and Goodman, 1973) have also influenced the development of crisis intervention. These therapies focus on the 'here and now' and on the personal growth opportunities that crisis work creates (see Parker, 2007b).*

Crisis intervention – a time of opportunity

A crisis presents an opportunity for social workers to influence positively the coping capacities of others. Conversely, crisis intervention, if handled inappropriately, may also distort reality and lead to maladaptive coping strategies. It is at this time when a person's defences are lowered and they are more likely to be motivated and willing to change, that practical application of crisis theory is effective (see work by Rapoport, 1970; Golan, 1978; Baldwin, 1979; Aguilera and Messick, 1982; Olsen, 1984; Gilbar, 1991; O'Hagan, 1991; Edlis, 1993; Parker, 2007b; Wilson et al., 2008). Given our understanding of crises as time-limited and potentially constructive periods of opportunity, it is important to determine with the service user what constitutes a successful resolution to them and to work towards clearly defined goals. This represents a fundamental aspect of crisis intervention and one that demands an approach that is negotiated, agreed and mandated by the service user.

The multiple applications of crisis theory and intervention

Crisis intervention has been used with positive results in many settings and with many different service user groups, not only with people who are bereaved or diagnosed with a degenerative illness, such as that experienced by Denise Lockwood. These include suicide, mental health issues (Roberts, 1995), domestic violence, rape crisis (Edlis, 1993), and children and families (O'Hagan, 1991).

Crisis intervention and social work

Most referrals to social workers are made at points of crisis. The initial assessment and intervention, including the provision of practical help, support and reassurance, advice and further referral when appropriate, can, as seen in the context of crisis theory, influence the outcome of that situation for good or ill. All social work skills must be employed towards achieving a constructive resolution of the crisis. For example, skills such as advocacy, bargaining, negotiation, use of empathy and appropriate challenging are drawn on. Service users are generally part of larger living systems, and changes effected within the group of family and friends with whom they live, or who are close and significant, may in some ways resolve a crisis situation. It is important to decide who is in crisis. The following checklist sets out some of the questions that are useful to ask when working with crises.

CHECKLIST

Crisis intervention flow diagram (source Parker, 2007b, p123)

1. *Determine whether the referral situation constitutes a crisis.*
2. *Identify for whom this is a crisis.*
3. *Agree the wants, wishes and needs of the significant participants.*
4. *Check:*
   i. *legal and statutory obligations;*
   ii. *availability of local resources and services;*
   iii. *values – personal, professional, service user.*
5. *Negotiate an initial working agreement.*
6. *Co-ordinate services and implement initial plan of care.*
7. *Review, renegotiate and formulate care plan.*

Crisis intervention provides a unique opportunity to work towards constructive change, to intervene in order to optimise social functioning and enable choice and participation, and to provide appropriate services. Given the possibilities for change, intervening in crises offers the practitioner a chance to build trust and rapport, and work in partnership with service users to honour the values common to social work and within the legislation – that individual choice should be respected and maximised and that people should be enabled to live as independent a life as possible. Crisis intervention is a directive approach, but it has the potential to educate people who use services in developing new skills and knowledge that is ultimately empowering. Learning new ways of coping that can be transferred to other areas of service users' lives represents a clear and ethical goal of any intervention.

CASE STUDY

Denise Lockwood and crisis intervention

John Hughes arranged to see Denise Lockwood at home three days after she had spoken to Amanda Thorpe, the care manager, following the incident in the community. It was 10 a.m. and Denise said she had not slept and had been waiting for him to arrive for hours. She looked unkempt and anxious. John tentatively 'felt his way' into what was at first a stilted conversation. She was wary but gradually he was able to put her at her ease. After a short while, he sought her permission to describe what had happened recently and how she felt. She responded at first in a flat monotone voice saying she had difficulty remembering recent events. But then she began, with some pauses and sighs, to respond to John's gentle prompting and reinforcing comments. She described how she had been frightened by the local youths and how this had given rise to much turmoil concerning her current life and past experiences. She did not know why, but the trauma of it had brought up other difficult times. She had felt once again the deep sadness on leaving the children and the family home. It had also made her think about the disappointing end to her career and having to adjust to retirement alone with nothing much to do.

At one point Denise broke down and demanded in quite a hostile manner to know why it always happened to her. Why did she still feel guilty about leaving the children? Why did things never work out? Why did she feel so alone? At that point she cried and John encouraged her to show her feelings.

She said she had thought she would cope with a life apart from the family, a new start, a new beginning, but it had never felt right and now she had left it too late to make amends. The job in Westfield, away from it all, was supposed to be the new start, an opportunity to build a new career, a new life, but she was never happy at work. She felt flat, humourless and unable to reach out to colleagues. She never seemed to make new friends and her retirement just emphasised her loneliness. The menacing incident with the local youths had brought home to her how lonely she felt, since there was no one close to turn to. She was also worried about her health, saying that her head did not feel normal and that her memory was shot. Since retiring she admitted she had 'let herself go'.

Once he had 'heard her out' and when she seemed less agitated, John tentatively said he thought she was in a state of shock and crisis and that was a normal reaction to such events. Before he left she had agreed that they would work together to 'talk about her problems and take some action'.

Five days later

Five days later John and Denise met again. This time she was less apprehensive and more ready to talk about the feelings that her trauma had triggered. She said she could not stop herself going over all the past hurts and loss in her life. She kept thinking of her mother. They had been very close, but in the last few months of her life the relationship had soured when Denise left her marriage. Her mother knew that her husband Brian was 'not right for her', but when her grandchildren took their father's side and wanted nothing to do with her, she was distraught. She blamed Denise for 'causing all this upset'. Denise's father was more censorious. He was of the old school and said she had 'made her bed and must lie on it'. When her mother died unexpectedly of a heart attack aged 72 he blamed Denise, and she has carried this guilt ever since. She never said goodbye, nor told her mother heartfelt and important things. She feels she has never got over the sudden death and continues to grieve. Denise wanted to know why this was troubling her now and why her life seemed to overwhelm her.

Although John knew a great deal about crisis intervention he was sensitive not to resort to 'jargon' or too much theory. He explained that it was common for feelings of loss and trauma in one area to trigger similar feelings in another that remained unresolved. Denise

(Continued)

(Continued)

responded to this point and said that it helped her heavy heart just to talk. John said there were no miracle cures and that Denise's crisis could go one of two ways: she could continue to be overwhelmed by it and this was a danger, or alternatively, she could take the opportunity to learn new ways of coping in both her internal emotional life and her external life. John emphasised that the power was with her; it was her choice to decide what she now wanted from life. He said that he had make no assumptions or judgements about the outcome other than that they both had to be clear what they were aiming for and what a successful resolution would look like. He also commented that it was not entirely up to Denise; other people whom she valued in the community had a part to play, as did the health and social care services. In this way John began to negotiate and construct an initial agreement.

Denise said that she wanted her life back, but not the old life. Not the passive life when she stayed alone at home watching TV and ordering takeaway meals. She recognised that she was 'frittering away' her time and that life was short. She said she felt self-conscious about her weight and ill at ease about the negative life style she had drifted into. She had been humbled by the support and kindness shown by her neighbour, Susan Brown, for whom she had had little time in the past. She was surprised and delighted that her daughter had moved into the area and seemed to want to know her again. She agreed with John that this may be an opportunity to make amends and, when the time was right, to be open and honest about past family history and her present situation. While recognising that she had health problems, Denise firmly wanted to be more involved in her neighbourhood: by joining a choir, attending a keep fit class, perhaps putting something back into the community now that she was work free and time rich. But above all she wanted to have better relationships with those people whom she had kept 'at arm's length'.

By the end of this second interview Denise was beginning to accept that life can be hard living alone and that she needed more support and events that took her out of the house. She could see that she had been avoiding facing up to her less than fulfilling life. She was now more determined to live in the present, become involved socially and see the positives in her life, such as her daughter and grandchildren now living in the same town.

ACTIVITY 4.2

What do you think is achievable and could be written into a working agreement which will help Denise to overcome this crisis?

Keep the plan simple, feasible and 'do-able'. Stay with Denise's informal life and the known links. (The support plan that involves daily living needs is dealt with in other chapters, although her wishes as expressed here will become part of that plan.)

Sometimes in crisis work it can be helpful to compose a letter to a person with whom there are unresolved issues, and often when that person is deceased. Do you think it would be helpful to Denise to compose such a letter to her deceased mother?

What do you think she would write in the letter?

We suggest you draft such a letter.

COMMENT

In constructing a 'working agreement' with Denise Lockwood to help her through her crisis, we hope that you will have drawn on her informal network and agreed tasks to enable her to recapture and strengthen that network, since it is an aspect of her life which she recognised was important to her and one which she had neglected. Your agreement may have involved her talking to her neighbour, Susan Brown, and establishing the common ground between them and the type of mutual activities they may enjoy together. It is likely that you will have set Denise the task of talking more openly with her daughter about what happened in the past and why, and hopefully rekindling areas of mutual interest and affection. Similarly you may have encouraged Denise to agree to talk more freely to those parents of the boys who were menacing to her, since they too are her neighbours and normally they seem kind and courteous towards her. This leads us to a discussion on networking, networking skills and opportunities for volunteering in the local community.

Networking skills

Networking skills in social work have increased in importance, particularly at the formal level between agencies, as government agendas (Department of Health, 1998) promote 'joined up thinking' between linked organisations, such as those in health and social care. Effective networking from an ASS perspective is not new. Professional networking and liaison between agencies draws on conventional social work interpersonal and communication skills. This does not stop at practitioner level; Coulshed's (1990) early work on management in social services indicated that female managers are particularly skilled in this area.

The emphasis in this section, however, is on the skills on which social workers draw in harnessing, supporting and understanding the informal network, such as the one where Denise Lockwood lives. Approaching service users as, first and foremost, people at the centre of their own informal networks in terms of family, friends and neighbours, and finding ways to harness these community resources was a key aspect of the Barclay Report (1982), a seminal report in terms of the development of aspects of professional social work. The role of the informal support systems and their contribution to care in the community was recognised in the White Paper *Caring for People* (Department of Health, 1989) as the following statement indicates: *The Government acknowledges that the great bulk of community care is provided by friends, family and neighbours* (para 1.9). Guidance to practitioners (Social Services Inspectorate and Department of Health, 1991a) emphasised the importance of the social network and support systems and stressed that, as part of the comprehensive assessment, service users' needs were to be understood *in their social context, which extends beyond the contribution of direct carers to a wider set of social relations* (p59). Building on and harnessing the strengths and resources of the informal network continues to be an important social work skill (Coulshed and Orme, 2006) and one which Smale and Tuson (1993) developed. They stressed the importance of working in partnership with people and service users in local communities (p40) and put forward models for care managers to work effectively from this baseline. Their 'exchange model' starts with the premise that people are *expert in their own problems* and will know more about themselves, their resources and networks than would the practitioner. The latter will bring expertise in terms of knowledge of the welfare systems and will have skills in problem-solving and developing packages of care. The key problem-solving skill of the practitioner/care manager within this model is to work with the informal and formal networks which surround and engage with the service user, and work out a compromise community care-based solution which draws on the strengths and interests of all the key participants. This process is described as follows:

> *This involves negotiating with a range of people – from the dependent person, their immediate carers and other people in the community, to service providers from different agencies and professions. Instead of the worker making 'an assessment' and organising care and support for people, which carries the implicit assumption of control, the worker negotiates to get agreement about who should do what for whom.*
>
> (Smale and Tuson, 1993, p40)

McDonald (2006) sees theoretical links between community networking skills and those of radical social work, since they both have the capacity to emphasise the importance of collective action and draw out the perception that individual problems are linked to political issues. Payne (2005, p155) makes the theoretical links between networks and networking and systems theories. Citing Walton's work (1986), he emphasises the importance of *analysing networking within social support systems* both at the formal and informal level, in order to monitor and help those members of the local community who are in need.

Networking skills continue to be an important element of care management and support systems since the social and care networks of the service user are an important aspect of the assessment. Developing networking skills can require great sensitivity and insight. Some practitioners find that drawing family trees and friendship diagrams and networks, that service users help to create, is a useful road map. However, assessing a person's informal friendship or kinship network may not be a straightforward matter. Regularity of contact may say little about the quality and elasticity of the relationship. Payne (1995) reflects that *very close relationships may involve only occasional contacts, and supportive people may live at considerable distance but offer emotional security because they exist and are prepared to help out* (p101). In a similar vein he comments that assessors of networks must be careful not to make assumptions about the transferability of relationships from one setting to another; for example, relationships based on friendship and social activities may not transfer into those based on caring (Payne, 1995, p113).

ACTIVITY 4.3

First, thinking about your own networks, construct an ecomap (see Chapter 2) which reflects the friends, relatives and acquaintances in your network. Indicate the ways in which these relationships are important to you and how often you are likely to be in contact on a monthly basis.

Secondly, if you were involved in a serious road traffic accident, whose support would you draw on from your network and why?

The learning point here is that people with whom you spend social time may not be the ones you would wish to have a 'hands on' care relationship with, and perhaps neither would they be willing or able to take on this role.

A linked point is that this personal knowledge of your own network is likely to affect how you approach engaging with the informal network of service users when developing care plans (see Chapter 3).

Advocacy

The same premise which we applied to understanding informal networking applies to the concept of advocacy, that is, to quote Smale and Tuson, *people are, and always will be the expert on themselves* (1993, p13). Within a social work context, it is the service users who should define their own needs and dictate wherever possible how their needs should be met. Early practice guidance (Social Services Inspectorate and Department of Health, 1991a) was intent on promoting service user participation in the assessment process but recognised that not all service users are in the same position:

> *Some users will have a clear understanding of their needs; others will have a more ill defined view of them or the cause of their difficulties; yet others will require the support of representatives to express their feelings.*
>
> (para 3.30, p50)

The guidance goes on to explain the types of service users who are not able to express their views and may benefit from independent representation, such as people from minority ethnic groups, people with severe learning disabilities, or people who have dementia (para 3.27, p51). The vehicle for achieving this is the introduction of advocacy schemes to ensure that care managers work closely with independent representatives. The guidance noted that:

> *This will mean ensuring that representatives have access to the necessary information, are able to consult appropriate persons to establish the best interests of the individual and have a safe-guarded role in contributing to the decision-making process.*
>
> (para 3.28, p52)

Interpreting this role into the social work/care management process, it would seem that this is not the right role for such professionals given the extensive agency and professional brief which they have to fulfil. Payne (1995) argues that care managers may think that they act in the best interests of the service user, but their roles are proscribed and they are unlikely to be in the best position to promote the preferred wishes of the service user (p193). He states unequivocally that advocates and advocacy groups need to be completely separate from the agency providing the service, in order to be able to take an independent stance (p193). Similarly, Goble (2008 in Mantell, 2009), points to the dangers of attempting a role of professional advocacy from a person-centred perspective, arguing that a service user's interests may be better served by a person who is independent from the professional organisation and professional interests (see pp43–46 for a helpful exposition of advocacy).

Strategies that promote advocacy, which are also linked to concepts of user empowerment, draw on theories of radical social work and anti-discriminatory practice. The focus is on power sharing with the service user. Payne (2005) refers to the use of advocacy as part of the movement to discharge people from long-stay hospitals and as an integral part of welfare rights initiatives (see his chapter (14) on Empowerment and Advocacy, pp295–315, for a fuller exposition of these ideas).

The position of an advocate in social work is of increasing importance. This facet of the social work perspective is not, however, without tension. As Payne (1995, p192) states, *The essential difference between advocacy and, say, negotiating on a client's behalf is that advocacy occurs in a situation in which there is opposition*.

Although advocacy has been an important part of the social work process for a considerable time, it remains ill defined and there is little evaluation of the procedure (Brandon and Brandon, 2001). Earlier evaluation (Harding and Beresford, 1996) indicated that service users and carers value the process and the service. We draw on Brandon and Brandon's stages of advocacy to help give you a steer on the process.

Stages of advocacy

- *explain the advocacy process;*
- *listen to the client's situation;*
- *explain the relevant systems – complaints procedures, appeals machinery, outline relevant legislation;*
- *take instructions;*
- *seek additional information;*
- *feed back to the client, exploring together the perceived consequences of possible decisions;*
- *take revised instructions;*
- *with permission, negotiate with influential person;*
- *feed back further to client and together explore the consequences;*

- *prepare for any possible litigation, for example ombudsman;*
- *evaluate the whole process to learn necessary lessons.*

(Brandon and Brandon, 2001, p68)

Brandon and Brandon (2001) emphasise the fact that it may not be necessary to follow all the stages indicated. The sequels and the outcome of the process will depend on the degree of difficulty of the case. They reinforce the point that in order to empower the service user the skilled advocate needs to draw on expert communication skills, particularly those of listening accurately to the service user's perspective and needs. It is then not a question of putting these needs and wants through a professional filter, neither is it the role of the advocate at the outset to broker compromise solutions. Rather they are required to pay close attention to the expressed wish as the following quotation illustrates:

> *The advocate should take instructions. This sounds reasonably simple but it isn't. He or she is being 'instructed' by the client to undertake certain agreed actions. That means that there has been an exploration and explanation by the advocate and professional in which the client is perceived as the 'dominant' partner. It is their grievance and their life.*

(Brandon and Brandon, 2001, p71)

At every turn the advocate needs to feed back to the service user the results of their enquiries, involving and including them in person wherever possible. If initial instructions have to be modified, negotiations entered into and compromises reached, it is at the behest of the service user. Brandon and Brandon stress the importance of carefully evaluating and learning from the end result from a user perspective and that these processes should be linked to annual independent reviewing procedures (p74).

The PA within a system of DP is likely to be in a strong position to take on aspects of the advocacy role, should those services be required by the service user. The latter is normally responsible for setting up, with help, the working agreement and would decide on this aspect of the contract (see discussion in Chapter 3).

The Big Society, volunteering and community initiatives

Harnessing the positive resources and activities in local communities to enable them to be more sustainable and supportive is not new and it has been given an added impetus by the Coalition Government's 'Big Society' initiative. Drawing on the work of Conservative MP Jesse Norman (2010) the Big Society was the flagship policy of the Conservative Party's election campaign. Norman holds that the state is too big and its government too prescriptive, centralist and 'top down'. He has proposed that one of the ways to bring about much needed change is through the notion of the 'Big Society' that will help reinvigorate, by social enterprise and voluntary initiatives, the concept of localism and a sense of community.

Rajan (2010) is sceptical of Norman's work since he argues that he barely acknowledges the antecedents of these ideas that are as much the thinking of the reformist Left as they are of the philanthropic Conservative Right. Indeed, Rajan states that Norman fails to attribute the common language of the 'Big Society' with recent ideas of the Left. He gives examples such as Blunkett's Scarman lecture (2003), Labour's 'Together we can' action plan (2005) and Blears 'Active Citizens' speech (2006).

Cunningham and Cunningham (2012) similarly raise concerns about the notion of the 'Big Society'. They describe it as creating an *ideological smokescreen* of *a mythical 'golden age'* of *individualism and self improvement* when people looked after themselves and their families. Such myths, they argue, enable neo-liberal sympathisers to attack the welfare state and its principles (p76). Given the direction of travel to promote philanthropy and voluntarism, they note the apparent perversity of the government in not giving encouragement to resource the initiative. Indeed the opposite appears to have happened. According to Toynbee (Toynbee, 2011 in Cunningham and Cunningham, 2012), in the initial phase of this big idea, £5.1 billion (40 per cent) of government funding has been withdrawn from charities, leading to the loss of key jobs and closure of valued initiatives. Two years later there appears to have been no let up. Writing for *The Guardian*, Bubb (2013) states that 50 per cent of local authorities have had to make disproportionate cuts to charity funding in their areas.

It may be that the 'Big Society' was too much of a 'top down' enterprise from the start, and became part of the problem rather than the solution. The global financial meltdown of 2008 and the resulting extensive public sector cuts are likely to have had an impact on 'Big Society' initiatives. A more cynical view is that it was always a ruse to camouflage the cuts. Cunningham and Cunningham (2012, p76) cite a survey in the *Times* in 2011 that suggests that the majority of the public see it in this way.

Whatever the pitfalls or accolades (and there are a few according to Bubb) concerning the 'Big Society', the concept of volunteering and the activity of voluntary agencies continue to play a key role in adult social care. We introduced a link to Age UK and also the notion of food banks when describing the case of Denise Lockwood. In this concluding section we shall look at both these enterprises.

Age UK

Age UK both offers a service to people over the age of 55 and also encourages those who approach it with social needs to actively engage as volunteers. In other words by helping others and by contributing to one's own community, a person is likely to feel a sense of achievement from purposeful activity. Age UK (formerly Age Concern) has an extensive number of Age UK partners throughout the country that run a wide variety of projects and services for older people, from day centres to helping with gardening. The organisation requires an ever-changing group of volunteers to help with its activities. The following information is taken from its website: www.ageuk.co.uk.

Examples from the current list of the type of voluntary workers required include:

- an activity buddy (helping a person become more physically active);
- day centre helper (tasks from serving meals to giving manicures);

- befriender (visiting a person who lives alone);
- driver;
- fund raiser;
- gardener;
- information and advice person;
- IT coach;
- trustee.

There is no upper age barrier to volunteering, neither is there a minimum or maximum amount of time each week one may volunteer. All reasonable expenses are paid, such as travel costs. State benefits may be claimed while volunteering. Most roles for volunteers do not require training, but for those roles that do, it is available. An informal interview usually takes place, with questions posed such as 'why do you want to become a volunteer?' and 'how many hours per week are you able to offer?' There may be formal interviews for roles that require more responsibility and knowledge, such as that of a trustee for the organisation. Volunteers are supervised and insured. Experience gained from working with, for example, vulnerable people attached to Age UK, will count as relevant when applying for social work training.

ACTIVITY 4.4

Are there volunteer tasks on the above list that Denise Lockwood could do? Explain your reasoning.

Are there any Age UK activities that she may benefit from? Explain your reasoning.

Food banks

The profile of food banks has risen in the UK, and the most likely trigger has been the global recession of 2008 and its aftermath, as described in earlier chapters. One of the best-known organisations for supporting and running food banks throughout the UK is the Trussell Trust. The following information has been adapted from its website: www.trusselltrust.co.uk.

The Trust claims that in 2012/13 over a third of a million people in the UK received crisis help from food banks, and of these at least a third were children. The Trust provides emergency food to last a minimum of three days to people in crisis. Crises normally occur when people are without food as a result of unemployment, an unexpected bill, rising food and fuel costs or changes to benefits. Food is mainly donated by the public and sorted by volunteers. People in crisis are identified by care professionals such as social workers and doctors and vouchers are issued. The person in crisis then exchanges the voucher for a box of non-perishable, nutritious food, such as tins of vegetables, rice and pasta. When collecting the food there is also time to talk and to link in to other helpful agencies.

The Trust is run on Christian principles of compassion, integrity and care of all people, regardless of background or belief. It aims to help build capacity within local communities to combat poverty and exclusion. It operates by developing partnerships with local churches and communities, and to date has developed 400 food banks in the UK. It is currently seeking funding to roll out a programme, 'Eat Well, Spend Less', which helps teach people how to cook and eat nutritiously on a low budget.

A Trussell Trust campaign that ran on two days in July 2013 resulted in an overwhelming amount of food being donated by the British public at outlets of one of the largest UK supermarkets. The pledge from the supermarket was to increase the amount donated by a third, and the net result was 26,000 trolley loads of food for distribution to local food banks. It is not surprising therefore that the Trust has been named 'Britain's Most Admired Charity' at a recent award ceremony run by Third Sector.

Volunteering at the Trussell Trust

The Trust is accommodating in the way in which people may volunteer, whether it is a few hours at a food collecting event or a full five-day week. Voluntary work specifically focusing on the food bank would include:

- sorting donated food in preparation for distribution;
- work in a food bank centre, giving out food and meeting people in need;
- helping at a food bank supermarket collection.

Other voluntary work concerns the Trust's work in Bulgaria such as the youth summer camp, in community enterprise activities such as sorting donations at a recycling centre, or in general activity to help run the Trust such as involvement in talks and publicity.

ACTIVITY 4.5

In Chapter 3 we learned that Denise Lockwood is planning to be a volunteer for a local food bank. Given her capabilities, which tasks do you think she would be able to do with assistance and which would she feel confident in accomplishing without such support?

Explain your reasoning.

Why do you think and feel that it may be a good idea for her to be more engaged with the local community and with those who are likely to be less well off than herself?

RESEARCH SUMMARY

In this summary we describe some quantitative research by Nazroo and Matthews (2012) that was commissioned by the Women's Royal Voluntary Society (WRVS) to consider if there is a relationship between volunteering in later life and the concept of well-being.

The writers contextualise the research by referring to current policy debates, such as the Big Society ideas, that concern the potential contribution to society of people who are post child rearing and post work. In a review of the literature they indicate that there are few quantitative studies on volunteering and links with positive health. Those that exist are mainly US based. The researchers hold that we can but speculate why volunteering may be linked to health and well-being. Possibilities include the link between volunteering and employability, creating a socially meaningful role and purpose in life, and, given its altruistic nature, its potential to enhance identity and social esteem. They conclude the literature search by suggesting that the positive effects from volunteering are likely to be linked to the extent to which a person has control over their volunteering activity and feels appreciated. They cite an extensive Europe-wide study by McMunn et al. (2009) on this aspect.

The researchers drew on data from the English Longitudinal Study of Ageing (ELSA). This is a national representative survey that is undertaken every two years and the research in focus accessed reports published between 2006 and 2010 (Banks et al., 2006; 2008; 2010 in Nazroo and Matthews, 2012). Data drawn from the studies focused on both those who volunteered and non-volunteers. Both groups were in the post-state pension age bracket, that is women aged 60 and over and men aged 65 and over. There was a total of 3,632 respondents. The definition of volunteering was limited to activities within formal organisations that are self-governing, not for profit and independent of government, such as the Trussell Trust, and did not include informal volunteering such as offering unpaid help to a neighbour. Data from these studies was also linked to four indicators of quality of life: symptoms of depression, quality of life, satisfaction and social isolation.

Just over a quarter of the respondents from the studies on ageing reported that they volunteered in the last year and of these four-fifths did so at least monthly. On average those who volunteered were healthier and wealthier than non-volunteers. They were also more likely to be younger and in paid employment. Considering changes in well-being, looking at each of the four indicators over a two-year period, the findings indicate that volunteers had an improved sense of well-being compared with non-volunteers. These outcomes were found to be statistically significant in each of the categories, except for social isolation. The authors illustrated how this causal interpretation was strengthened when they drew on further statistical analysis.

However, the researchers add notes of caution about their findings. For example, they raise a concern regarding the adequacy of the questions posed in the ELSA study regarding volunteering, since the results from studies that are primarily focusing on the subject, such as the National Survey of Volunteering, indicate a higher overall involvement in the activity. Nonetheless, they conclude that the study has strengths such as the detailed measurement of well-being and of relevant characteristics of respondents, thus allowing control for differences in the characteristics of volunteers and non-volunteers together with the longitudinal design and the representative nature of the sample (p28).

ACTIVITY **4.6**

Reflective journal

In your journal consider the extent to which you think and feel that volunteering may add social value and capital to the community in which you work and/or study. Perhaps also consider the extent to which you as a trained social worker should be working alongside and actively encouraging volunteers and voluntary groups to enhance your activities and social work outcomes.

CHAPTER SUMMARY

In this chapter you have been introduced to a range of interventions that can be used effectively in social work. We have illustrated these by way of our two developing case studies. Before continuing to Chapter 5 where you will consider the importance of reviewing and evaluating what you have done as a social worker, it would be useful to spend a few minutes reflecting on the ways in which task-centred practice, cognitive-behavioural work, crisis intervention, networking and advocacy approaches can be adapted to other situations and service user groups. You may also wish to consider the changing social worlds of practice that affect the level of involvement in grassroots activities, food banks and advocacy as opposed to mainstream approaches to safeguarding and so on.

Adams, R (2003) *Social work and empowerment.* 3rd edition. Basingstoke: Palgrave.

This is an overview of the concept of empowerment and its importance to social work practice.

Marsh, P and Doel, M (2005) *The task-centred book.* London: Routledge.

This is a very practical and accessible book that puts centre stage the voices of people who use and those who deliver services.

O'Hagan, K (1986) *Crisis intervention in social services.* Basingstoke: Macmillan.

While this book may seem a little dated, it offers a thorough view of crisis intervention, its history, development and theory, and grounds this in social work practice in the UK.

Payne, M (2005) *Modern social work theory.* 3rd edition. Basingstoke: Palgrave Macmillan.

The definitive book to describe, explain and critique social work theory in a comprehensive way, this title will benefit students throughout their studies.

Sheldon, B (1995) *Cognitive-behavioural therapy.* London: Routledge.

This is not an easy book for students at the beginning of a social work programme but it is worth persevering with. Sheldon covers all aspects of behavioural and cognitive-behavioural work from assessment, planning, and intervention to review.

Chapter 5
Reviews and the evaluation of practice

ACHIEVING A SOCIAL WORK DEGREE

This chapter will help you to develop the following capabilities, to the appropriate level, from the PCF.

- **Professionalism**
  Representing and being accountable to the profession.
- **Values and ethics**
  Apply social work ethical principles and values to guide professional practice.
- **Knowledge**
  Apply knowledge of social sciences, law and social work practice theory.
- **Critical reflection and analysis**
  Apply critical reflection and analysis to inform and provide a rationale for professional decision-making.
- **Contexts and organisations**
  Engage with, inform and adapt to changing practice contexts and operate effectively within own organisational frameworks and within multi-agency and inter-professional settings.
- **Professional leadership**
  Take responsibility for the professional learning and development of others through supervision, mentoring, assessing, research, teaching, leadership and management.

It will also introduce you to the following academic standards as set out in the social work subject benchmark statement.

5.1.4 Social work theory.
5.1.5 The nature of social work practice.
5.5 Problem-solving skills.
5.5.4 Intervention and evaluation.

Introduction

In this chapter the importance of the review meeting and case review will be examined. What is the role of the social worker in a review and how does it link with the processes of assessment, planning and intervention? Under what circumstances are reviews undertaken and who should or could be involved? This chapter will look at the ways in which social workers can assist service users to give their views to reviews and will consider the importance of communication skills and rights of service users and carers. Again, we draw attention to social work's multifaceted worlds and hope you are able to transfer good practice from each setting and across groups of people with whom you may be working.

You will explore ways of reviewing and evaluating social work practice and be asked to consider the potential effects of working with other professions and with informal carers and service users in carrying out reviews and evaluations of work undertaken. Student social workers, and experienced practitioners, often have many anxieties about reviewing and evaluating their work in a systematic way. In an effective review and evaluation of work undertaken, practice is subject to scrutiny and outcomes and objectives are measured and reflected upon. While this can be a somewhat daunting process, it emphasises accountability and allows practitioners to develop experience, knowledge and skills in determining what works in which circumstances. In these days of increased accountability and audit it is essential that social workers evaluate their practice. This can have the added bonus of ensuring that practice is amended to achieve agreed goals and that social work is promoted as effective to other professions and the wider public.

In this chapter you will be invited to consider how to evaluate an intervention plan in child and family work and social work with adults. Current guidance, research and advice on effective review will be provided and activities will help you to make links between knowledge and practice throughout this chapter. A particular focus will concern the recording of assessments, plans and interventions and how effective, clear recording can assist in the review and evaluation of work done. The importance of simple recording schedules and accessibility of written style will be considered. Service user involvement in the intervention process will be emphasised through student-centred activities.

You will be asked to question the purpose and use of review and evaluation, especially in respect of care and control issues, bureaucracy and management. You will also be encouraged to consider ways in which they might develop processes for evaluating your own practice and development as beginning professionals.

In the first part of the chapter you will consider why we need to evaluate and review the practice of social work. You will look at some of the external and internal pressures for evaluation and matters relating to 'effectiveness'. This will be followed by an examination of a number of evaluative strategies and methods for use within social work practice and how you might begin to use them.

Why evaluate social work practice?

Social work is complex and diverse, and the roles and tasks allotted to it are equally varied. This has been recognised for some time as fundamentally important for qualifying education. It has been acknowledged by previous professional bodies for social work – the Central Council for Education and Training in Social Work (1995) and the General Social Care Council (GSCC) (2002a) in their Code of Practice for Employees in precept six which says that social care workers should:

> *Be accountable for the quality of their work and take responsibility for maintaining and improving their knowledge and skills.*

The HCPC continues this emphasis in their SoPS, for instance, SoP 11 is to *be able to reflect on and review practice* and to reflect critically and systematically. The concern for evaluation and review is enhanced further by the twelfth SoP concerning the assurance of quality of one's own practice, focusing also on service evaluation. These standards are reflected within the PCF and its accent on critical reflection and analysis, the use of research to inform practice and contributing to service development by improving proficiency in evaluation.

The tasks and responsibilities that social workers carry range from assessment and planning to intervention and the provision of services. Social workers work with children and families, offenders within the community, adults with physical disabilities, learning disabilities and mental health problems, as well as older people within the community and within institutional care. There is also a range of ways in which social workers attempt to make a difference, as indicated in the British Association of Social Workers' Code of Ethics (2002):

> *(Social workers) work with, on behalf of, or in the interests of people to enable them to deal with personal and social difficulties and obtain essential resources and services.*
>
> *Their work may include, but is not limited to, interpersonal practice, groupwork, community work, social development, social action, policy development, research, social work education and supervisory and managerial functions in these fields.*
>
> (pp1–2)

The very range of social work practice demands some understanding of the relative effectiveness of each task undertaken. The importance of working effectively to protect vulnerable people is stressed in the requirements for the degree:

> *Social workers deal with some of the most vulnerable people in our society at times of greatest stress. There can be tragic consequences if things go wrong. Social workers often get a bad press. What they do not get is day to day coverage of the work they do to protect and provide for some of the most vulnerable people in our society.*
>
> (Department of Health, 2002a, pi)

It is important, therefore, that all social workers are educated in ways of reviewing their work and reflecting on outcomes so that practice can be continually improved, which enhances personal development and contributes to securing the best outcomes for people using social work services.

ACTIVITY 5.1

Think of some of the reasons why social work should be evaluated and reviewed. Compile a list of some of these and prioritise the reasons. Undertaking this activity may also give you insight into some of the ways you understand social work.

You may have stressed the accountability side or the necessity of providing cost-effective services. You may have included on your list ethical reasons. There are many reasons why social work practice is reviewed and evaluated and many justifications for it. To a large extent, these are determined by the agency you are working in, your own personal value base and your knowledge. There are concerns that research and evaluation have not been highlighted sufficiently in the qualifying and post-qualifying education frameworks for social work, and an increasing worry that research and evaluation skills, necessary to developing and enhancing the services provided by social workers, are being neglected. The Social Work Task Force (2009) report acknowledges this debate in respect of keeping informed and up to date. It is hoped that adequate attention is paid to the importance of evaluation in any changes to be made to social work education. The following discussion will provide a number of reasons why social work should be evaluated.

Cheetham et al. (1992) describe two continuing pressures that impinge upon social workers to evaluate the effectiveness of their work. These comprise external pressures and internal pressures. These pressures exert an influence on all aspects of social work.

External pressures

There is a continuing demand for resources to be better targeted and value for money to be achieved. This connects with the concept of effectiveness and evidence-based practice (see below). Often, public bodies scrutinise the ends, means and costs of these services within the public welfare sector. The *Best Value* initiative arising from Part I of the Local Government Act 1999 promoted economy and efficiency within social work practice and health care. There is also an increasing demand for information about the effectiveness of services and also the possibility and implications of different choices of service provision. There has been a growth in the voice of the consumer and a corresponding concern for economic efficiency and accountability where public spending is an issue. It is unfortunate, as Cheetham et al. (1992) point out, that the more positive accounts of social work practice appear to have been ignored while many studies emphasise the difficulties and problems arising from practice. This is still the case as demonstrated by the news report in *Professional Social Work* (2010) celebrating the reduction in child deaths.

Internal pressures for evaluation

External pressures may be seen by some as representing a greater degree of managerial control over social work and social care. For some it may be a way of defending social work against attack and ensuring social work's continued existence. Internal pressures for evaluation, however, arise from a general ethical and professional obligation on social workers to do their best for service users and carers and to offer the kind of help and support that is most likely to be effective in each particular case.

Such considerations are also included in the *Code of ethics for social work* produced by the British Association of Social Workers (BASW) (2002). Social workers should *maintain and expand their competence in order to provide quality service and accountable practice* (3.5.2b) and *aim for the best possible standards of service provision and be accountable for their practice* (4.3b). These principles cover the need for social workers to justify work according to agency policy and procedure and also to provide effective intervention to service users.

The GSCC *Code of practice for social care workers* (2002b) adds to the need for skills in reviewing, evaluating and improving practice as we have seen. An approach that builds on prior experience and reflection will help to protect and promote the rights of service users and carers, develop a greater degree of public trust in social work and be instrumental in social workers being accountable for the quality of their work and taking responsibility for maintaining and improving their knowledge and skills.

Effectiveness

The concept of effectiveness warrants some exploration. Different ideas about effectiveness derive from particular ways of thinking about the way the world operates which we all develop according to our personalities, experiences and reflection on them (Kelly, 1955). Different people with different roles in the social care system have different expectations, roles and responsibilities. Therefore, different people have different interpretations of what effectiveness might mean for them. What is success for one may not be so for another. Users of social services may want to know what they are getting out of the work being done. A manager of a social services team may want to know how their money is being spent and whether it is meeting agency and policy guidelines. An individual social worker might be concerned to give a young person the skills and capacity to make choices, while a local neighbourhood might want to be assured of protection from that same young person!

Sheldon and Macdonald posit a useful definition of evidence-based practice that refers to the *conscientious, explicit and judicious* (2009, p68) application of the best current available evidence for making decisions in social work. In this context, being *conscientious* concerns a continual striving for understanding of social issues and the research concerning what works to effect change. An *explicit* approach requires an open, negotiating style of working and one which privileges research evidence rather than theoretical preferences. Finally, being *judicious* refers to making a *considered, prudent judgement* (Sheldon and Macdonald, 2009, p71) based on robust research evidence. They also suggest that we need to ask 'why' and 'how' questions alongside a more quantitative approach that asks 'how many', 'by when' and 'because of what'. This definition provides an important conceptual approach to review and evaluation in social work practice.

While there are many different forms of evidence that need to be taken into account when considering social work practice (Humphries, 2008), attention remains focused on what works to make practice effective. Understanding evidence in this way includes the impact of social policies and structural factors on the lives of people who use social work services and is therefore more appropriately inclusive.

ACTIVITY 5.2

Write down what you think effectiveness means in relation to social work practice and intervention. Think of possible ways you might review this.

COMMENT

The activity above may draw a number of different responses. If you have some experience of working in a health or social care environment, you may have related your thoughts back to reviews and performance indicators set by your agency for your appraisal or wider agency remit. You may, on the other hand, consider effectiveness to relate to user satisfaction rather than agency outcomes. It is likely that whatever you thought of has some relevance to our understanding of effectiveness and how it might be reviewed. The important point to note is that how we measure effectiveness and how we review our work depends on the position we start from and there are other valid approaches to be taken into account. This is especially important in social work because of the range of stakeholder groups (interested parties) involved, and the complexity and 'messiness' of human life with which social workers engage. Evaluation research is hard work but requires commitment if we are to improve practice (see Macdonald and Popay, 2010).

Reviewing work in children and families social work

In childcare, review and evaluation are noted as central to good practice. At the top level, joint area reviews have been conducted for integrated children's services by OFSTED. These reviews consider outcomes for children's services, and social workers contribute to these by data gathering and performance reporting.

Reviews take place when a child or young person is looked after by the local authority. These reviews are statutory and form part of the expected work of social workers when planning and revising plans for children and young people. There are child protection reviews to determine the level of support and protection a child, young person and family need. When events go wrong there is a system of serious case review to determine what lessons can be learned and how practice can be changed in the future. We will explore these different types of review below and illustrate how you might begin to review your casework by references to the developing case study of Melissa and Rebecca. It is also important that social workers review their practice with individual cases and evaluate what they are doing and how effective their practice is in achieving agreed goals. We have seen this in respect of task-centred work and behavioural work with Rebecca and Melissa and will review the evaluation of casework towards the end of this section.

Reviews in childcare

Reviews are wider than individual cases. For instance, the duty of a local authority to review day care and related services in consultation with health professionals, voluntary agencies and other interested parties is clearly stated in the guidance accompanying the Children Act 1989 (Department of Health, 1991a) and guidance to safeguard and promote the welfare of children (HM Government, 2005a). As part of the process of joint planning and commissioning, monitoring and reviewing the outcomes of services are set in the context of annual performance assessments, Joint Area Reviews and also self-monitoring, which is intended to develop an improvement culture within services. However, it is usually individual cases that we consider when thinking about reviews.

Statutory childcare reviews

Local authorities are empowered under the Children Act 1989 s.26 and by the Review of Children's Cases Regulations 1991, as amended by the Review of Children's Cases (Amendment) (England) Regulations 2004, to make provision for reviews of childcare cases where the child is looked after by the local authority. The amended guidance includes voluntary organisations and registered homes that also accommodate children, demonstrating the iterative and fluid nature of practice over time that demands social workers be 'fleet of foot' in negotiating these areas. An independent reviewing officer (IRO) is appointed to ensure that reviews are completed and outcomes of those reviews monitored appropriately. The IRO must be informed when plans and outcomes are not met. The early guidance relating to family placements gave a clear definition of reviews which illustrated their importance as a key element of social work practice.

> *Reviews form part of a continuous planning process – reviewing decisions to date and planning future work. The purpose of the review is to ensure that the child's welfare is safeguarded and promoted in the most effective way throughout the period he is looked after or accommodated. Progress in safeguarding and providing for the child's welfare should be examined and monitored at every review and the plan for the child amended as necessary to reflect any significant change.*
>
> (Department of Health, 1991b, 8.1, p80)

Review is seen, therefore, as a continuous process that considers what has been achieved from the planning stage and revises or refines plans accordingly, similar to an action-planning or action-research cycle. This requires the social worker to develop a number of skills:

- planning;
- negotiation and consultation;
- information gathering;
- discussion and analysis;
- replanning.

The guidance offers an outline of the process that should be followed including a broad agenda for the review meeting, which should deal with three core elements: the progress made in achieving the plan, any need for change and the possible reallocation of tasks or change in the child or young person's status. The last item for consideration relates to the possibility of discharging any order existing in respect of the child or young person (see Johns, 2009, for a greater explanation of the law relating to children). The guidance is clear that children, young people and parents should be as fully involved as possible in the decision-making process, that plans should be structured and that the process should itself be subject to a system of checks. Good practice is promoted in accounting for communication and language difficulties, ensuring that written information and an agenda are sent to all participants prior to the review meeting, and that records are kept. The review is there to make plans that continue to safeguard the child.

The timing and minimum frequency of reviews are specified. A first review must be held four weeks after a child or young person begins to be looked after by the local authority and again three months after this. Following the second review, further reviews should be carried out at least every six months. This is designed to ensure the process is continuous and that changes in the child or young person's circumstances are taken into account.

Child protection reviews

The child protection conference represents the key forum in which professionals and families discuss concerns, analyse risks and make recommendations to safeguard children and young people. They happen after a child or young person has been the subject of an investigation under section 47 of the Children Act 1989. The core group process, while not always fully adhered to in practice, forms a useful forum for social workers to co-ordinate social work plans and intervention and monitor progress that can add valuable information to the child protection review.

Any child protection plan needs to be regularly reviewed if it is to remain effective in promoting the welfare of and protecting the child. The original document *Working Together* (Department of Health, 1991c) was updated in 1999, again in 2006 and most recently in 2013. The guidance originally specified that child protection reviews should be called three months after the first conference and every six months thereafter as long as the child is subject to a child protection plan. Continued review of the guidance is intended to keep up the momentum and focus on safeguarding and promoting the welfare of the child or young person and ensuring that needs are met, but we must not lose sight of the ideological reasons for reviewing such guidance and ensure that, as social workers, we maintain a critical eye on the impact any changes may make. In 2006, the purposes of a child protection review were set out clearly:

> *The purposes of the child protection review are to:*
>
> - *review the safety, health and development of the child against planned outcomes set out in the child protection plan;*
> - *ensure that the child continues to be safeguarded from harm;*
> - *consider whether the child protection plan should continue in place or should be changed.*
>
> (HM Government, 2006, p136)

The 2013 guidance builds on this, stating the purpose is:

> *To review whether the child is continuing to suffer, or is likely to suffer, significant harm, and review developmental progress against child protection plan outcomes.To consider whether the child protection plan should continue or should be changed.*
>
> (HM Government, 2013a, p43)

The review can decide to take a child or young person off the register and then make recommendations for their continued protection. The importance of the child protection review is that it is a multidisciplinary meeting involving all those who have an interest in the well-being of the child or young person, including the parents and children where possible. Child protection reviews highlight the importance of the process of social work by moving back through assessment and plans made to determine whether changes have taken place and whether risks have been reduced or mitigated. Social workers are central to the review in leading discussion, sharing information and formulating decisions. Given the highly charged emotions likely to be invested in such matters, it is important that social workers take a reflexive and critical stance in relation to reviews and do not simply engage in unquestioning compliance but consider all eventualities and opinions.

Serious case reviews

Local Children's Safeguarding Boards have a clear role in promoting the role of reviews in establishing learning and good practice in social work with children and young people. Serious case reviews were previously known as *Part 8 reviews*. These are convened whenever an incident that led to the death of a child occurred, although a child death review is also conducted, or when *a child is seriously harmed and there are concerns about how organisations or professionals worked together to safeguard the child* (HM Government, 2013a, p66).

The serious case review checklist sets out the role of the Local Safeguarding Children Board (LSCB) in conducting the review, outlining that the final report should:

> - *provide a sound analysis of what happened in the case, and why, and what needs to happen in order to reduce the risk of recurrence;*
> - *be written in plain English and in a way that can be easily understood by professionals and the public alike; and*
> - *be suitable for publication without needing to be amended or redacted.*
>
> (HM Government, 2013a, p71)

As part of the learning focus, and building on the Munro report (Munro, 2011), research has been undertaken to pilot and evaluate the Social Care Institute for Excellence (SCIE) 'Learning Together' systems approach which focuses on those lessons that can be learned and applied to improve practice (Munro and Lushey, 2013). Findings are as yet somewhat equivocal.

Reviews in childcare

The review called in respect of Rebecca, the subject of our case study was not a statutory childcare review; she was not 'looked after' by the local authority. Nor was it a child protection review or serious case review. However, the importance of the review process should not be lessened as a result. The Climbié Report identified the continued monitoring of performance as being central to good practice.

> *Monitoring performance plays a vital role in delivering good outcomes for children and their families. Robust systems that monitor what is actually taking place and its effectiveness is critical [sic].*
>
> (Laming, 2003, 17.64, p357)

The report goes on to take issue with past performance monitoring that concentrates on measurable inputs and quantity-related outcomes rather than the quality of social work practice. There is also a suggestion that monitoring processes should be undertaken across services working to protect children.

Monitoring, review and evaluation of social work with children and families have often been marginalised. Children and families, once they are receiving a service, may drift along without change being considered. This may happen because of the pressures on staff in other areas, or indeed may result from not wanting to change and adapt if things are seen to be working adequately for fear of being blamed if things go wrong. However, we know that children grow and develop, that families adapt and respond to new situations and, if we are to respond appropriately to meet the needs of children and families, we must review and evaluate our practice. Brandon et al. (2009) found in their analysis of serious case reviews that the recording skills of social workers were somewhat lacking. The Looked-after Children forms have been helpful in promoting a continuous process of review and replanning in respect of children looked after by local authorities (Ward, 1995; Bailey et al., 2002). The seven dimensions of well-being have been integrated into the *Framework for Assessment* (Department of Health, Department for Education and Employment, Home Office, 2000), and gradually the process of an integrated review system is being rolled out to all children receiving a statutory service. Using such a process of review is good practice even when there is no statutory involvement. Let us return to the case of Rebecca and Melissa and see how the review process worked for them.

CASE STUDY

In the original plan for Rebecca set out in Chapter 3, it was noted that a review of the social work plan and what had been achieved would take place following the four sessions involving Irene and Melissa. The purpose of this review was to consider what had taken place and to decide whether anything more needed to be done or the plan revised. Throughout the task-centred work, Mandy and Melissa regularly reviewed each session and tasks completed between sessions. This was also reviewed after four weeks to check how she was managing at the young mums' group. However, the casework review undertaken after the four sessions concerned all three aims agreed in the initial plan:

- *Is Irene looking after Rebecca twice a week as agreed to give Rebecca a break?*
- *Has Melissa joined the support group?*
- *How has the work to improve Irene and Melissa's relationship progressed?*

Mandy began to prepare for this review at the outset of her involvement with Melissa and Rebecca by introducing the structured approach to the work they would undertake and by stating clearly that a review would take place within the plan. However, preparations for the review began in earnest during the final two weeks prior to the review. Mandy telephoned June, the health visitor, the child support worker who looked after Rebecca at the family support centre, and Irene and spoke directly with Melissa to arrange a convenient date and time for the review. It was not possible to speak with Rebecca because of her age but her daily routines and patterns were taken into account so that she would not be disrupted by the review. It is important to be sensitive to the needs of all people involved and not to assume that because a person cannot voice their opinions they are not affected by decisions taken.

After having agreed a date and time, Mandy began to collect information for the review. She returned to the assessment and care plan for Rebecca and asked each person involved for their views about the work that had been undertaken. She explained that she would be writing a short report about the work to discuss further at the review and agreed to send it to each person with a formal invitation confirming date and time. She also said that any disagreements with the report or work could be taken up at the review or noted prior to it. To ensure that she reflected the views of those involved as accurately as possible, however, she summarised her understanding of what they had said after gathering their views.

Mandy asked her team leader, Geoff, to act as chairperson for the review. It is important to have a chair who is slightly removed from the day-to-day aspects of the case. This helps in keeping a focus and ensuring that issues not seen by those directly involved can be picked up. It must be remembered also that review meetings are daunting affairs – for some professionals as well as service users and carers – and the more formal the meeting, the greater the potential anxiety. It is the social worker co-ordinating the review and the chair who are responsible for creating a relaxed and welcoming atmosphere so as to encourage service users and carers to put their points of view forward. Sometimes it is appropriate for a friend or other supportive person to be allowed to accompany service users and carers. Both Melissa and Irene were comfortable with the process, however, having met Geoff before and because of his welcome and clear explanation of the review meeting, what it was there to achieve and how it would be run.

Geoff welcomed everyone to the meeting, stating that they were there to review the care plan made in respect of Rebecca. He then asked everyone to introduce themselves and say a little about the ways in which they were involved with Rebecca. Those present were called on to give their views about the plan, and how it had worked. This began with Mandy being asked to speak about her report and was followed by opportunities

(Continued)

(Continued)

for the others to add to, clarify or question the report. Geoff summarised what was said at frequent intervals to check understanding and to keep the meeting focused. He made sure that everyone was given an opportunity to contribute and when the three points had been covered, and views of what had been achieved had been expressed, he moved the review to consider what should be done next.

Irene had begun to offer Melissa breaks from Rebecca of one afternoon and one evening each week. Irene was enjoying the contact with her granddaughter and Melissa said that she was able to get time out with friends and felt she had 'a breathing space'. Both of them agreed that this was helped by the open discussions they had together at the family support team office and that airing views frankly had helped them see each other's perspective. The family support worker who looked after Rebecca during these sessions reported that Rebecca was a happy and inquisitive baby who seemed to enjoy the company of Irene and Melissa. The health visitor agreed and said that she believed Melissa had been helped by the support she had received from the other mothers at the support group. Melissa agreed and said she did not want to lose that support.

At the review meeting it was agreed that the plans had had positive results. There did not seem to be a need for any further family sessions or indeed for further social work involvement. However, it was suggested that a revised agreement be made so that Irene continues to offer a break to Melissa and that Melissa is able to continue to attend the young mums' group.

ACTIVITY 5.3

Imagine that you are the social worker involved with Rebecca and Melissa. After the review you have been asked to write a letter explaining what the outcomes and agreements made were. Have a go at writing this letter and think of the importance of how issues are worded and phrased.

COMMENT

Rather than providing you with an example letter to check against for the activity above, it is more important for you to examine what you have written as though you were the person receiving the letter. Is the letter clearly written? Do you set out the reasons why the letter is being written and what it relates to, and do you carefully spell out the outcomes that were agreed? Can any part of the letter be understood in a different way from the one you intended? If so, rewrite that part of the letter until you are sure it will say exactly what you want it to say.

Remember also to check that it is simply written, that jargon is avoided and that sentences are short and to the point. It is possible to write a clear and simple letter conveying all the information you want to get across without being patronising!

Reviewing and monitoring in adult social services

We will now turn to consider how case review and monitoring apply in care management and also personal support services within ASS, and make links to the case of Denise Lockwood. In both approaches monitoring and reviewing are important for adults who have long-term needs, degenerative diseases and chronic illness and who may be vulnerable. These aspects of adult care were neglected prior to the NHS and Community Care Act 1990 (Social Services Inspectorate and Department of Health, 1991a; 1991b). What happened prior to the Act was that services were arranged and rarely altered unless there was a major incident. As Payne (1995, p213) commented, *...crises were often reached unnecessarily. The lack of periodic review in many adults' cases meant that they drifted with very little strategic thought about 'what next?* Prior to 1991, monitoring was often a passive activity.

Monitoring and reviewing are stages in the care management process that are often linked, since one informs the other. The function of care management was to promote the objectives of the care plan and provide evidence on which refinement and review of it could be based. Signs of difficulties were to trigger early reviews. Close monitoring, coupled with systematic recording, also provided managers with the framework in which manager/practitioner accountability could be scrutinised (Social Services Inspectorate and Department of Health, 1991a). This reinforces points made in Chapter 3 about local authority governance and 'top down' bureaucracies.

In terms of reviewing, early guidance (Social Services Inspectorate and Department of Health, 1991a) had described it as *the mechanism by which changing needs are identified and services adapted accordingly* (p83). The process was to take account of the preferences and needs of the service user and carer. They were to be kept informed of its purpose and given the choice to have a representative present, and the venue was to be chosen with their needs in mind. A large-scale review with its tendency to be dominated by professionals was not envisaged, unless a crisis point required new and complex arrangements. Ideally the chair should be independent, particularly if there were contentious and conflicting issues. Practitioners were to inform service users and their carers of their rights to complain and they were to be kept at the centre of the process. A review record within care management is likely to include the following.

- Review the achievements of the care plan objectives.
- Learn from and examine the reasons for the success or failure of the plan.
- Question whether current services have been cost effective/of the right quality.
- Reassess the current needs of the service user and carer.
- Consider whether the eligibility level remains the same – extend, reduce or withdraw services as appropriate and provide a full explanation to the service user and/or their representative.

- Re-evaluate and revise as appropriate the original care plan objectives – setting new short-term objectives for service provider(s), bearing in mind the wishes of the user and carer.
- Re-define and renegotiate service contracts as necessary.
- Re-calculate the cost and revise the budget, subject to management approval, for the period leading to the next review.
- Identify areas where quality of service is deficient.
- Set a date for the next review.
- Record and share a copy of the review report with the user and, subject to confidentiality constraints, other contributors to the review.

(Adapted from Social Services Inspectorate and Department of Health, 1991a, pp85–6)

Twelve years later a revised, redefined and more succinct purpose of the review was published in the FACS guidance on eligibility (Department of Health, 2003a) as follows.

- Establish how far the support and treatment have achieved the outcomes set out on the care plan.
- Reassess the needs and issues of individual service users.
- Help determine users' continued eligibility for support and treatment.
- Confirm or amend the current care plan, or lead to closure.
- Comment on how individuals are managing DP, where appropriate.

Note the reference to DP, indicating that by this point it had become part of mainstream work in ASS.

Monitoring and reviewing: room for improvement

Monitoring and reviewing are not uncontentious areas. Lymbery (2005, p181) cites the fact that practice guidance linked to FACS (Department of Health, 2003b) included an imperative to improve the quality of the review processes *that testifies to the fact that these had been neglected*. Similarly, McDonald (2006, pp61–70) draws on research to illustrate that the two tasks were not viewed as distinctive and were seen as of secondary importance to that of assessment. She notes that within the reviewing process the emphasis was on accountable practice rather than good practice, which demonstrates, she argues, the predominance of the procedural nature of the task.

Staff shortages and staff changes in social care provision create problems that can be unsettling for service users and early guidance had warned against the wishes of users and carers being subordinate to those of service providers (Social Services Inspectorate and Department of Health, 1991a). Similar concerns have been reported by the ombudsman (McDonald, 2006). In a study on how older people defined a quality service (Joseph Rowntree Foundation, 2000) it was found that service users rated highly factors such as staff reliability, continuity of care, continuity of staff, and the kindness and understanding of care workers. Inconsistency of carers and uncertainty about which formal carer will be walking down the path continues to be a criticism levelled at services provided by the local authority (Leece, 2010).

Flexibility to respond to changing needs and requirements was another key finding of the Rowntree study. The capacity among health and social care professionals to respond creatively and flexibly as the situation changes sends a message to service users which is both empowering and anti-oppressive. Similarly, the reverse effect may be created by the tendency within care management structures to wait until the review occurs before adjustments are made. Tensions may occur, particularly in the current financial climate, concerning which services should be available to older people in need. McDonald (2006, p20) reminds us that local authorities cannot overlook their statutory duty, under Schedule 8 of the NHS Act 1977, to provide a home help service for older people that is appropriate to the needs of the area. She notes, nonetheless, that an increasing trend in ASS when delivering personal care to vulnerable people is to see domestic cleaning very much as a secondary role, and only for those with high-level needs.

Negotiating the professional territory between health and social services is similarly not new (Bradley and Manthorpe, 2000). The Health Act 1999 created the framework for pooling joint budgets and delivering joint services between health and social care. These initiatives were consolidated when care trusts were established and integrated working became of greater importance (Quinney, 2006). Effective inter-professional working has long been at the heart of government's 'joined up' agenda (Department of Health, 2002b). While colleagues from different disciplines recognise the importance of working together effectively, their training and professional views may lead to different assessments of a case such as that of Denise Lockwood. For example, social work training is more likely to lead practitioners to take a holistic view of service users and see them in their broader social context, recognising the ethical dilemmas associated with balancing risks against a service user's rights and desires. Health-trained professionals are more likely to focus on physical and health constraints in their assessments. Research (Ramon, 2002) suggests that these inter-professional boundaries are not easy to resolve.

CASE STUDY SEQUEL

The financial assessment of Denise Lockwood

Two weeks before the date of the review of the personal support plan, Denise Lockwood was informed that the RAS had decided that she was eligible for personal support that would amount to 14 hours a week of a PA's time. Amanda was pleased with the decision since she had feared that the RAS may not have accepted the 'substantial' category of eligibility in which she and Denise had agreed she should be banded. In light of this she left the financial assessment forms for Denise and her daughter to complete (see discussion in Chapter 3 on financial assessment). When she picked up the form some days later she was concerned, although not too surprised, to learn that Denise's financial position was

(Continued)

(Continued)

precarious. That day Denise's recall was muddled but she confirmed she had had a large credit card debt and suggested Amanda speak with her daughter Alice about it.

When Amanda spoke to Alice she was worried and felt that her mother was much less able to handle her affairs than she had thought. 'Where is it all going to end?' she asked. She told Amanda that she was distressed when she realised the scale of her mother's financial problems. She had been shocked by the size of the credit card debt and also by the knowledge that her mother had not completed the paperwork that would have released a small private pension that was due when she retired. Had this been sorted, her mother would likely be solvent, given that she had been in receipt of her state pension since she was 60. Alice has acted swiftly to pay most of the important outstanding bills, to place the utility bills onto direct debit and to help her mother open a bank account with a bank in walking distance of her home. This was relatively straightforward, since four weeks prior she had obtained legal powers of control over her mother's finances. Her mother's GP, Dr Dyson, had signed the medical form indicating that Denise had the mental capacity to understand the implications of, and agreed to, her daughter having Lasting Power of Attorney over her finances. Amanda knew about this development. At the time she thought Alice was acting 'hastily', but in light of what has been uncovered, she is now relieved.

On walking away from the house Amanda reflected that, given the personal debt, absence of savings and a house in negative equity (following the recession and falling house prices in the North), it would be highly unlikely that Denise would be required to make a financial contribution towards the cost of her social care.

Review of the personal support plan

In 2010 SCIE published details of what a review of a personal support plan should include and the following information is taken from this document (see section 3.5 Implications for practice). Readers will recognise that it builds on much of the good practice established in reviews within a care management system. The revised review within a support plan is to cover key aspects of the person's circumstances and details of the way the plan is working. This is to include changes to outcomes, needs, risks, requirements, finances and co-ordination arrangements, and scope for widening the contributions the individual is making to family/community life.

Staff undertaking reviews must:

- *ensure the review process is open and transparent, promotes the participation of individuals and carers, is correctly recorded and conforms to relevant council procedures and inter-agency agreements;*
- *meet any additional needs for support to participate in reviews, including those arising from a person's limited capacity or communication difficulties;*
- *recognise signs and symptoms of deterioration because of physical, mental or emotional difficulties;*

- *ensure the record of the review is in an accessible format and language and is compliant with council and inter-agency agreements;*
- *ensure that individuals, and where appropriate their support networks, have copies of the review, know how to raise any queries or concerns and know when the next review will take place.*
- *promote positive relationships with adults with low and moderate needs to ensure they are able to renew contact before problems reach a crisis.*

(SCIE, 2010, section 3.5)

ACTIVITY 5.4

What do you think are the main differences between reviewing within a care management system and within a personal support plan?

Explain and write in your journal why you think these changes have been made.

CASE STUDY

Amanda Thorpe's reflections on the reviewing process

Amanda Thorpe is thinking how she should manage a review within a personal support plan and how it will differ from that of a care management review. The latter, after many years of being a care manager in a busy ASS team, has become 'ingrained'. She is good at setting up a review and working with an independent chair. Now the line within her ASS is that a personal support plan review is likely to be smaller in size, less formal and less bureaucratic, and has to take place within three months of help being provided to a new service user and be outcome based (Department of Health, 2010b). She knows she will approach it with the same attention to detail and sensitivity to the expressed wishes and needs of Denise. She will also be explicit about decisions agreed and back these up with a written record for all who attend.

She is uncertain about the event since things have not quite gone to plan. There was an incident the previous Wednesday when Denise went to choir for the first time without Susan. Amanda visited her the following day and they talked through the details and agreed that it would need to be discussed at the review. Denise seemed philosophical about it but she knows that Alice, her daughter, has not taken it well. This is coupled with the fact that Dr Dyson has now said that he and the consultant neurosurgeon are of the view that she has dementia-type symptoms. With Denise's permission, Amanda has also spoken on the phone to Alice, but was not able to allay her anxieties. It is now two weeks since the DP money was made available and Susan Brown and Rachel Armitage have been appointed Denise's PAs. This new arrangement is 'bedding in' and will need to be discussed. Amanda and Denise go over the planning for the review. Amanda is anxious since she knows that Denise's capacity fluctuates and meetings such as these may put too much pressure on her.

ACTIVITY 5.5

Denise Lockwood: review of the personal support plan

You are preparing for Denise Lockwood's support plan review. The plan was finally put together by Denise and Amanda and linked closely to the decisions made at the last meeting. Think back over these decisions and the weekly plan that you drafted and consider what is likely to have gone well and less well within the first eight weeks of implementation.

Keep your notes and refer to them as we recount the review process.

CASE STUDY

Eight weeks on: the personal support plan review meeting in Denise Lockwood's home

***Present**: Denise Lockwood, Amanda Thorpe, Alice Richards, daughter, Susan Brown, neighbour and PA, Rachel Armitage, Advocate and PA, and David Hobson OT.*

Amanda opened the review by introducing Rachel and David to everyone, saying that they are now more directly involved with Denise's support and she wishes them to be present. She confirmed the purpose of the meeting and the RAS decision and welcomed Susan and Rachel as Denise's new PAs. Amanda said she will write a minute of decisions agreed and circulate this once Denise has confirmed them.

Amanda told the meeting that Denise wished to share with them what happened last Wednesday when she became completely lost on her way to choir, and how she has reflected on it. Hesitantly Denise explained that it was the first time in seven weeks that Susan had not walked to choir with her. She was in two minds whether to go, but then at the last minute decided to. By this time she was running late and rushed out of the house. She knew it was a ten-minute walk from home but she had never paid much attention to the route, since Susan knew the way. However, once she started walking it seemed as if all the terraced streets were identical, or maybe it was her poor memory. Whatever the reason, within a short time she felt completely lost. She realised that she had left her mobile phone on the kitchen table and she had no contact numbers with her. She began to panic. A kind, middle-aged woman noticed her distress and tried to calm her. Eventually she was able to tell her what had happened and also the name of her GP. The woman knew him and that the surgery was only a few streets away. She took her there and the receptionist contacted Alice who later collected her.

There was a pause in the meeting. It was clear that Alice was not comfortable and then she spoke. She said her mother was not safe to be left, particularly since it was now certain that she has dementia. She suggested she would be better in sheltered housing.

Amanda was respectful of Alice's view. She then turned to Denise and asked what she felt and thought. It was clear that she did not want to go against her daughter's wishes. Nonetheless, she said she would prefer to stay at home, particularly now she had more day-to-day support from her PAs, although sometimes she felt 'in a fog and quite lost'.

Amanda said they should return to these important points once they had reviewed the full picture of the past eight weeks. It was clear from the transformed state of the house that Denise, with Alice's help, had 'decluttered' and got rid of excess stuff and general rubbish. With David's help a well-labelled transparent filing system was in place. The house was clean now that Alice had found a weekly cleaner for her mother (which she was paying for given her mother's debts). Following the weekly shop to the supermarket with Susan, the kitchen shelves and fridge were well stocked. Denise was enjoying short daily walks around the block with Lucy. The choir had been a good move and she found the work for the food bank rewarding.

Following the RAS decision and the appointment of the two PAs it had been decided that Rachel would have nine hours and Susan five hours per week to help support Denise. From their responses it was clear that they had yet to establish a system about who did what, when and how. Susan voiced her concern about not knowing when it was PA time or just good neighbourliness. Amanda would have liked to clarify this but was told that they wanted to sort it between them. She reminded them, perhaps a little too formally, that a CRB check and references were still required even though the PAs were known to Denise.

David said there were several practical things that Denise could do to help with her short-term memory lapses and help allay her anxieties. He suggested she use prompts to charge her mobile regularly, keep it with her at all times, and also carry a note with names and details of her main contacts. He also thought that now, while she was in the early stages of dementia, would be the time to think about assistive technology and attendance at a memory clinic. He described the use of electronic reminder devices, such as for medication, and voice prompts on leaving the house to remind her to take her mobile and check both doors were locked. He went on to explain how a pendant alarm would work and also tracking devices, either when Denise is inside the house or outside, and that both devices could be linked to a 24-hour care centre so that her whereabouts are known. Denise said that she could see the benefit of everything he had mentioned apart from the pendant and the tracking device, which seemed too intrusive at this point.

Amanda, in light of the confirmed diagnosis, explained that Dr Dyson was willing to prescribe a drug for early onset dementia that, while it would not cure the degenerative disease, should stop the symptoms getting more severe for a period of up to two years. She said that the funding of the drug by the NHS had recently been agreed by the government.

Amanda asked if there was anything else on which to report and Alice informed the meeting that she had Lasting Power of Attorney for her mother's finances. She also said that while some of her anxieties had been allayed, she still thought that there were long periods when her mother was completely alone, that she was often confused and she had fears for her future. Amanda did not dismiss her anxieties, recognising that Denise's capacity did fluctuate from day to day. She said that it was never an easy matter to balance risks with Denise's right to live an independent life for as long as she is able. She closed the meeting on a positive note stating that there had been much that was positive to report and confirmed plans for future monitoring and review of the support plan.

RESEARCH SUMMARY

Leece and Leece (2011) report on their research findings concerning the role social workers should play in the new personalised landscape. Their empirical research chronicles the views of disabled people, carers and elders on this subject. Using a grounded theory they gathered data by posting a thread on 18 internet forums. In this way they were able to access users who were normally 'hard to reach' and enabled people to participate who may have been put off by more traditional approaches to research.

The threads were designed in the form of accessible statements and questions about the future role of social workers. During the months of October and November 2009, 153 responses were posted by 66 individuals. Of these, most (41) were disabled people, over a quarter were carers (18) and seven were older people. Ethical approval had been gained from Manchester Metropolitan University and steps were taken to maintain the confidentiality and trust of the respondents.

Concepts of power and autonomy of social workers and social work organisations were apparent in the findings. More than half the respondents questioned whether social workers and social services were useful to them and made it clear that they valued their personal autonomy. For example, one respondent felt that his social worker was too intrusive in terms of how his personal budget should be spent. The researchers recognised in many of the responses an ongoing critique from a disability perspective. The extent to which social workers should carry out the role of support brokers was also explored. The predominant view was that such a role should be independent of statutory services, to avoid possible conflict of interest. A number of respondents thought that brokerage should be a function of user-led organisations. Leece and Leece (2011) commented that, by preferring independent brokers/advocates, respondents were expressing their desire to avoid institutional power and the impact it has over their lives (p216). When issues were raised concerning the local authorities' responsibilities to protect vulnerable adults, a few respondents (5) said social workers should have a role. Some, however, were wary of defining people in such a way, since it assumed weakness and lack of autonomy in all areas of life, not just in specific areas.

The authors caution against transferring findings from a small unrepresentative random group to the wider society. However, by interpreting and locating their findings within a framework of power and autonomy and by drawing on the broader literature, they raise real concerns about the power of social workers and their statutory agencies.

ACTIVITY 5.6

Considering the above research findings and reflecting on the way in which Amanda Thorpe chaired the Personal Support Planning Meeting do you think she was:

- *controlling;*
- *enabling;*

- *overly bureaucratic;*
- *person centred?*

Was she right to share medical information at the review?

We suggest you find evidence for your answers from the description of the review meeting above and write this up in your reflective journal.

Dementia, safeguarding and the Mental Capacity Act

In the above review it has now become clear that Denise has dementia-type symptoms. Moore and Jones (2012) inform us that dementia is not a condition in itself, but a way of describing a range of conditions and illnesses that *affect a person's brain functioning and cause them to experience a decline in their cognitive skills* (p2). This is likely to cause problems with short-term memory as well as with thinking and communication skills (p3). A diagnosis of this nature is likely to cause anxiety for families and also professionals as they project ahead and think of the possible consequences of such an illness, such as risks caused from wandering and possible abuse. In his seminal work on the person-centred approach to dementia care, Kitwood (1997 in Moore and Jones, 2012) encouraged professionals to see the unique qualities of a person and focus on these rather than on the illness. He developed a theory and a model to work with people with dementia known as the 'enriched model of dementia' that included identifying interactions to increase well-being. Positive person work was one of the ways that the personhood, as he described it, of people with dementia was upheld. For a fuller explanation we suggest you read Moore and Jones pp15–20.

Safeguarding

During the later stages of Denise Lockwood's dementia it may be the case that she begins to lose her ability to make decisions for herself, becomes a risk to herself and is vulnerable when unsupervised in her local community. As the social worker involved in her case, you would need to be informed about the concept of safeguarding and the Mental Capacity Act (MCA) 2005 (see below) when assessing the risk and reviewing her needs. The concept of safeguarding and its important agenda was triggered by the Department of Health's (2000b) report *No Secrets*. More recently the term safeguarding adults is used to cover all adults at risk (see SCIE's 2011a *Prevention in Adult Safeguarding Report*). Risk assessment and risk management have for some time been integral aspects of the process of care planning and personal support planning. McDonald reminds us that assessing risk is *a balancing process in which the application of judgement is brought to bear* (2006, p51). The process is one in which the likelihood of an event happening, its foreseeable consequences and the interests of those people affected by the consequences are balanced against the costs of taking precautions and sometimes over-robust interventions that may override the expressed wishes of the individual. So, for example, a person in a similar position to Denise Lockwood may be persuaded to move to a 'less risky' environment such as a sheltered housing complex. Risk assessment must not, however, be dismissed and should be an integral part of all assessments of vulnerable adults. It is an important tool for practitioners to monitor and be alert to a range of consequences, for example elder abuse. This concept has not been well reported and may take several forms: emotional, physical and financial. It is not limited to one age group, gender or culture and yet older people living alone may be more likely to suffer from financial abuse and neglect at the hands of others (McCreadie, 1996). Legislation in this area is not extensive but there is a considerable amount of guidance. *No Secrets* (Department of Health, 2000b) helped develop a multi-agency response to deal with the abuse of vulnerable adults. It was also the catalyst for the Association of Directors of Adult Social Services (2005) to develop policy and procedures and issue national guidance and standards for good practice in England. In 2009 the Department of Health reviewed the earlier document. Nonetheless, the criticism has been that this remains guidance and that the principles that underpin safeguarding, such as protection and accountability, are not covered by statute and therefore some authorities may take it less seriously. The legal responsibilities and duties of local authorities are being addressed in the Care Bill 2013, which at the time of writing is progressing through due process of parliament.

RESEARCH SUMMARY

This section highlights a small qualitative study by Manthorpe et al. (2009b). It is part of the evaluation by Glendinning et al. (2008) of a large pilot study commissioned by the Department of Health in 13 local authorities concerning personalised support for adults in the form of individualised budgets (IBs). The aim of the main pilot study was to enable service users to have a greater say in their social care preferences and thus enhance their quality of life. This aspect of the evaluation focuses on interviews with adult protection leads (APLs) from the pilot sites concerning their perceptions of the IB project and links with safeguarding and risk agendas. Manthorpe et al. (2009b) inform us that the IB scheme differs from DP since following self-assessment a person may be given a budget rather than receiving a number of 'hours per week' of support; services utilised may be a mixture of public, private or own arrangements; resources are 'ring fenced' and draw on a wider range of funding streams, such as housing support; and IBs can be spent on a wider range of support options such as purchasing a house (p1467).

The 13 APLs were interviewed by phone using a semi-structured interview guide that drew on the literature of personalisation and adult protection. Most APLs (10) confirmed that there were systems in place in their authorities that linked adult protection polices and self-directed support, such as identifying potential risk factors for abuse and ways in which these could be recognised in an individual's support plan. However, they were of the view that more fine tuning was needed in relation to IBs. One APL said some people might make unwise choices about the services and /or individuals they engaged (p1473). Other concerns raised included: IB may result in some people becoming socially isolated; money may be misspent resulting in the local authority needing to pay twice for services; safety checks for monitoring and review may undermine a person's independence and choice; and the collective voice regarding commissioning services may be lost. It was held that risks may be minimised if adult protection awareness training and its links with IB were raised not only with social services staff, but also with people using services, volunteers, PAs, and the new workforce linked to the IB initiative. One APL suggested that PAs working in the public sphere should be placed on the Protection of Vulnerable Adults (POVA) list.

When the research was carried out there had been no adult protection referrals linked to the IB project, but most APLs were aware of referrals in relation to DP concerning financial abuse, neglect and the quality of service provided. One APL suggested that social workers/ care managers should be encouraged to develop a competence in overseeing and 'sorting out' a person's finances, so that they are less vulnerable to exploitation.

In conclusion, the APLs recognised that whatever strategies and public assurances were put in place to enable greater personal safety within the IB system, this needed to be balanced against the freedom, choice and control over personal support.

The Mental Capacity Act 2005

The Mental Capacity Act 2005 (MCA) sets a single and clear test that helps to assess whether someone lacks capacity (HM Government, 2005). The first part of the test of capacity requires you to consider *if the person has an impairment of the mind or brain, or is there some other sort of disturbance affecting the way their mind works?* Moore and Jones (2012, p32) explain that if a person has dementia that is an impairment of the brain, then one would presume they lacked capacity. However, the second part of the test requires you to consider *if the impairment or disturbance means that the person is unable to make the decision in question at the time it needs to be made.* Thus this section requires the assessment of capacity to be specific in terms of the timing of when a decision is made. Since the effects of dementia can change from day to day, so too can the capacity of a person with this condition to make decisions. Hence on a particular day a person may well have the capacity to make a decision. This point will have been relevant when it was decided by a medical person that Denise Lockwood had, on the day, the capacity to understand the principle of Enduring Power of Attorney.

There are five principles that underpin the Act:

1. A person must be assumed to have capacity unless it is established that they lack capacity.
2. A person is not to be treated as unable to make a decision unless all practicable steps to help them to do so have been taken without success.
3. A person is not to be treated as unable to make a decision merely because they make an unwise decision.
4. An act done or decision made under this Act for or on behalf of a person who lacks capacity must be done, or made, in their best interests.

5. Before the act is done, or the decision is made, regard must be had to whether the purpose for which it is needed can be as effectively achieved in a way that is less restrictive of the person's rights and freedom of action.

(For a fuller explanation of these principles see Moore and Jones, 2012, pp33–35.)

This Act provides a statutory framework to protect and empower vulnerable people. A fundamental change is that more consideration has to be given to help the person make decisions, rather than assume capacity is lacking. Further, if a person is not able to make decisions for themself, then it clarifies who is able to make these decisions, in which circumstances and how the nominated person can go about this. Under the auspices of the MCA, local authorities or NHS trusts may appoint Independent Mental Capacity Advocates (IMCAs) to act on behalf of people who lack capacity. In this role the latter are supported by the IMCAs to help clarify their wishes and thus make decisions. Normally such people are only employed to advocate in this way when families and friends are not involved. Sometimes, however, they can be helpful when families are present, but think that they know best and are not putting the wishes of the person without capacity uppermost. This can be a complex area. Mantell and Scragg (2011) point out that a person may have the capacity to make decisions about some things, such as what to eat and what to wear, but lack the capacity to make higher-level decisions, such as where to live. Decisions that may appear unwise (and this is a fine line, given the third principle of the Act), such as going to the same place every day for an unhealthy breakfast, may be a thoughtful decision to a person beginning to lack capacity, since such a routine may provide comfort and stability. SCIE (2011b) in its recent work on safeguarding adults at risk, has drawn attention to the fact that professionals in health and social care are not always clear about the working of the MCA, particularly concerning concepts such as best interest and who should make decisions when capacity is an issue.

The Alzheimer's Society (2012) have produced helpful guidance regarding how to go about making a decision on behalf of a person believed to lack mental capacity in that person's best interests. They recommend that the decision maker must:

- not assume the decision should be based on the person's age, appearance, condition or behaviour;
- consider if the decision can be postponed until the person has sufficient mental capacity to make the decision themselves;
- involve the person who lacks mental capacity in the decision as much as possible;
- find out the person's views (current or past), if possible, and take these into account;
- consider the views of others, such as carers and people interested in the person's welfare, where appropriate, and take these into account;
- not be motivated by a wish to bring about the person's death if the decision relates to life-sustaining treatment.

Once the decision maker has considered the relevant information, they should weigh up all the points and make a decision they believe to be in the person's best interests.

The MCA also includes Deprivation of Liberty Safeguards (DOLS). Introduced in 2009 following the Bournewood trial (R v Bournewood Community and Mental Health NHS Trust ex parte L, 1998), these safeguards offer legal protection to vulnerable people and are designed to protect their interests in ways that are least restrictive. This relates to the fifth principle of the MCA concerning best interests being served in the least restrictive environment. It has a direct fit with the Human Rights Act (1998) Article 5 – the right to liberty and security. The Bournewood case concerned a man known as HL who was informally admitted to a psychiatric hospital and was prevented from seeing his carers since it was thought that he would wish to leave the institution when they departed and that this would be detrimental to his care and health. The case was taken by the carers to the European Court of Human Rights that ruled that HL's right to liberty had been breached (Mantell and Scragg, 2011).

The MCA enables the potentially vulnerable person to plan ahead for a time when they may not have the capacity to act in an informed way by taking out a Lasting Power of Attorney (LPA). The Office of the Public Guardian, acting under the remit of the MCA, helps protect people by registering such powers in order for decisions to be made over finance or health and welfare. Note, however, that LPAs can only be implemented for people who have capacity and not for those who are losing capacity. Guidance in the form of a Code of Practice is linked to the Act and refers to those working in a professional capacity, such as doctors and social workers, who have a duty to have regard for the code. In essence, the MCA requires that more consideration has to be given to support vulnerable adults to make decisions in the least restrictive ways and to move away from a position that assumes too readily that they lack capacity. As mentioned, we may assume that Denise Lockwood's GP made the decision regarding her capacity to understand the concept of LPA with these factors in mind. Further guidance and detail on the Act can be found on the Department of Health's website: www.dh.gov.uk/ (see also SCIE, 2011c, *Mental Capacity Act Resources*; SCIE, 2011b, *Safeguarding Adults at Risk of Harm: a Legal Guide*).

Self-directed support and social work with people who are losing capacity

Amanda Thorpe is moving into unchartered territory in terms of her practice experience of working with an adult with dementia in receipt of DP. She is uncertain of her social work role within self-directed support. At local level, due to financial imperatives mentioned earlier, there is pressure on qualified staff to focus their work with adults solely on safeguarding matters. Lymbery and Morley (2012), in a recent and timely article, remind us that this is not the government's intention. They cite a recent official publication regarding social work skills, to the effect that these will *continue to have a valued place across the whole continuum of need in adult services and should not be reduced to safeguarding alone* (Department of Health, 2009 p35 in Lymbery and Morley, 2012, p317). They also refer to a recent briefing from a government-linked organisation (SCIE, 2010 in Lymbery and Morley, 2012, pp317–18) that outlines five areas for social work tasks with adults within the personalisation agenda. These include working through conflict, knowing and applying legislation, and accessing personal support and services. They argue, nonetheless, that there can be dissonance and uncertainty for skilled workers operating within the new agenda. They draw on two complex cases that illustrate dilemmas concerning concepts of capacity and best interest. Within each case it is plausible to think that the capacity of the service user is greater than it really is. This, when coupled with the underlying principles of the current mental capacity legislation that requires social workers to make decisions that reflect the wishes and desires of service users, can, they argue, be *tricky to operationalise* and requires highly skilled work from practitioners. It is these highly skilled social workers, they remind us, whose jobs may be vulnerable due to local cuts in services (p324).

There may be a range of possible endings to the way the case study evolves in light of Denise's experiences of DP and her fluctuating mental capacity. In the final case sequence we give you a possible perspective of the PA that draws attention to increasing concerns about this role as highlighted in Leece's (2010) research summarised below.

CASE STUDY CONTINUED

Monitoring – Two months on from Denise Lockwood being in receipt of DP

In the intervening months Denise has absorbed little of the information concerning DP. This is mainly a result of her short-term memory lapses and she has also found the material dry and hard to take in, particularly the detail concerning managing her PAs, such as processing sickness and holiday pay and related matters. She had thought that Rachel, her PA who is familiar with these things, could sort it, but she insisted it needed someone who was 'independent'. Denise was persuaded and now for a small fee an agency working for Age UK does the work, so finally the paperwork is completed and the contracts set up.

With very little by way of preparation, and following a rather brief conversation between the three of them, Rachel and Susan commenced work for nine and five hours per week respectively. There has been no formal induction or training into their roles. Amanda has called by from time to time. She is normally short of time, working under pressure and seems relieved when things seem OK.

It has begun to dawn on Susan that as the neighbour she is always the first point of contact when Denise needs something. Even though her number of paid hours is limited, Denise now seems to think that she can phone at virtually all hours. The boundaries between good neighbour and paid PA have never been properly drawn. Her husband is beginning to feel annoyed since Denise always seems to phone when they are having a meal. He tells his wife that she spends her five hours a week taking Denise to the supermarket, the choir and the food bank. 'Why does she need to do more?' he asks. She knows this to be true, and each of these events requires skill and tact. There have been moments when she feels out of her depth and not certain whom to turn to for support and advice. Last week, when they were doing the weekly shop, she tried to encourage Denise to stick to her healthy diet, but Denise told her in no uncertain terms to back off. She has also been quite dismissive when she suggested they both cleared up the mess in the house. What used to be enjoyable events, such as packing the bags for the food bank, have now become more of a duty since all the time she is discreetly checking if Denise is doing it 'well enough'. She is not certain whether the changes in their relationship are a consequence of the dementia or the contractual arrangement between them.

Sometime she feels she is being taken advantage of. In contrast, Rachel is more precise about hours worked since she has to drop off and collect children at specific times, and she seems much happier with the work. Amanda keeps asking all of them how things are working out. Susan feels she would be being disloyal to Denise if she were to say something and so far she has said nothing.

The following outline of a small piece of empirical research will help you to understand the power dimension between a DP user and his/her PA, compared with the relationship between a service user and a person employed by a local authority to deliver home care.

RESEARCH SUMMARY

Leece (2010) describes her qualitative research based on empirical evidence concerning the type of relationship between a PA and his/her DP user. She informs us that most research in this area has focused on the perspective of the DP user. The relatively small amount of research that considers the PA normally points to the problems and danger of such work. The overall omission has been the lack of comparison between direct employment of PAs and non-direct employment as found in the delivery of home care within a local authority.

The research design was aided by three disabled researchers who acted as a panel of experts. A grounded theory approach was used and interviews were held with DP users, PAs, homecare users and homecare workers. In each of the four groups there were eight participants making a total of 32. All were based in the same local authority. DP users and homecare users were matched so that they had similar gender, ethnicity and age profiles, for example they had an average of 52 and 52.8 years respectively.

The in-depth interviews covered concepts such as independence and autonomy, power, reciprocity, interdependence, boundaries, stress and job satisfaction. Leece (2010) found that elements of power were evident throughout the data and DP users had more of it compared with non-direct employers. The former had the power to choose their worker; determine the boundaries of the relationship; set the agenda and be reciprocal if they chose; make their interests take precedent; and to a lesser extent set terms and conditions of employment (p191).

All of the homecare users agreed that they had no control over the number of workers involved in their support and Leece holds that this reduces their autonomy and power. The boundaries between the two types of relationship were not always clear, but those receiving DP had more discretion and PAs did a much wider variety of tasks, such as decorating. Homecare workers focused mainly on personal care and worked more by rules of 'good practice' set by the local authority.

Several of the PAs were friends of the service user and this sometimes meant that it was difficult to separate non-work from work, which often resulted in working beyond their

(Continued)

(Continued)

paid hours. This was in contrast with the homecare workers who rarely worked unpaid hours.

Leece warns about making generalisations from this small study. Nonetheless, she notes that it logs a shift of power from the local authority to the user of DP. In this relationship the authority has only retained the power to assess users' needs. She notes that PAs generally enjoyed the close personal relationship with their employer but that there is a downside. The PAs are paid less. The work is also less secure with poorer working conditions, involving more unpaid work that may encroach on personal life. She makes the point that being part of the family as a PA may be a double-edged sword – making it more worthwhile but harder to leave (2010, p202).

She suggests that it may be beneficial to redress the imbalance for PAs by encouraging them to join, for their protection, a trade union, to form support networks and to register with the social work validating body. Looked at more broadly, she argues that if local authorities were lobbied to pay higher DP rates then the overall terms of employment for PAs would be improved.

Final reflections on the case of Denise Lockwood

We leave you with the reflection that complex cases such as that of Denise Lockwood, that straddle health and social care divides and that include a progressive disease such as dementia, do not lend themselves to short-term resolutions.

In presenting and building the case stage by stage, we hope we have gone some way to explain the evolving process within the new agenda of self-directed support for adult social care. Throughout we have reinforced the importance of listening carefully to the service user and keeping her expressed needs and wishes at the heart of the matter.

As practitioners we need to consider whether we have a tendency to be over-protective, ageist and discriminatory towards service users of a particular age. Are people such as Denise Lockwood allowed to take the same level of risk as other adults in society? Do we treat older people as part of a homogenous group and fail to challenge society's stereotypes? We should like to think that Denise as a 'young older person' will continue to have the rights to a life of independence and dignity for as long as she is able.

ACTIVITY 5.7

Reflective journal

We have not dealt with the detail of how the case of Denise Lockwood fully unfolded. We leave it unfinished so that you can write a range of endings in different and creative ways.

We hope, in this final phase of writing your journal, that you raise issues and dilemmas that remain unresolved and challenging to you, and that you go back to them as your practice wisdom and knowledge evolve.

Casework evaluation

Social workers do not simply operate as bureaucrats following explicitly laid-out agency procedures. There is an emphasis in social work on developing professional judgement and critical thinking skills, and reflecting on the ways in which social work progresses. There are professional, developmental and ethical reasons for reviewing and evaluating individual casework, as Alston and Bowles (2003) state:

> *Workers in the welfare field must be accountable for the service they provide, the resources they expend and the outcomes they achieve. Accountability is expected by governments, clients and taxpayers. Evaluation and accountability have always been important concepts for social workers. Handled effectively program evaluation gives us the means to develop techniques for ensuring our practice is enhanced and effective and allows us to incorporate accountability and transparency into our practice. Program evaluation techniques allow us to be more effective and efficient workers, which can only enhance our work with clients and the communities we serve.*
>
> (p140)

It is essential to gain an understanding of the importance of the ways research can inform practice and you will be encouraged as a social worker to develop *research mindedness*. This means you will be able to recognise that research is important, read it with a degree of understanding, but also be able to undertake your own research concerning your practice with the intention of improving and updating it (see Hardwick and Worsley, 2010).

It is not possible in this chapter to give a detailed account of practitioner research but it is important to note that attention to ways in which you might evaluate your practice is part of the process of developing good and effective social work practice. By reference to Rebecca and Melissa, we will introduce a visual way of considering whether an intervention is making a difference. Note the importance of user satisfaction and of reflection and *practice wisdom*, or developing an appreciation of the art involved in improving social work practice.

In Chapter 4 you were introduced to a graphic display of targets for your intervention with Melissa and Rebecca the second time they had contact with social workers.

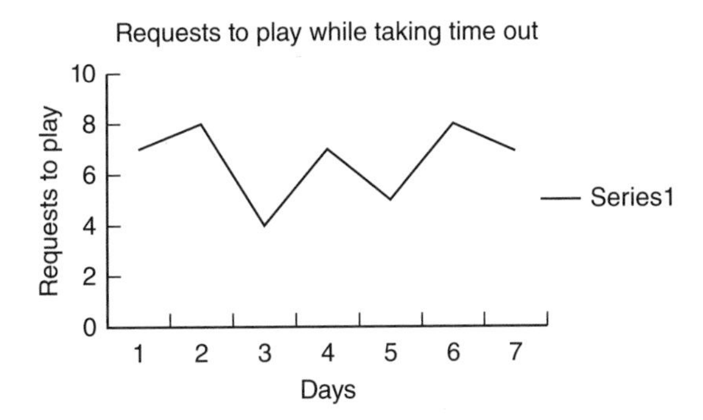

Figure 5.1 Requests to play

The number of times that Rebecca asked Melissa to play when she was having a rest in the evening was noted. This formed a 'baseline' period or a display of how things looked before the intervention.

By continuing the monitoring of the situation and recording the number of times Rebecca asked Melissa to play during the intervention period, changes could be clearly shown in Figure 5.2.

While this does not 'prove' that the intervention was successful, it provides a visual display of what happened and an indication that change occurred during the intervention period. There are more complex ways of assessing whether or not your intervention was responsible for the change but it is best to start with simple methods. Further and more detailed information can be found in Sheldon (1995).

The advantage of tracking changes like this is that they help to show service users that there is a difference in the situation but also help you to judge whether or not your practice needs adapting. However, interventions cannot be judged solely from the perspective of the social worker.

User perspectives

Since the seminal work undertaken by Mayer and Timms (1970) the service user perspective has grown in importance in social work. However, asking service users and carers what they think about services received or how satisfied they are is fraught with difficulties. This stems partly from the different ways in which we might understand 'satisfaction' and partly from the likelihood that service users may feel unable to give a true opinion because they do not want to upset the social worker or, indeed, they would like to upset the social worker, or because people may fear having services withdrawn if they express dissatisfaction. Despite these concerns it is important to give service users and carers an opportunity to present their views and encouragement to do so in an honest and open way.

Social workers may also find they are required to undertake studies from the perspective of service users to fulfil the Quality Assurance demands of their teams and employing agencies.

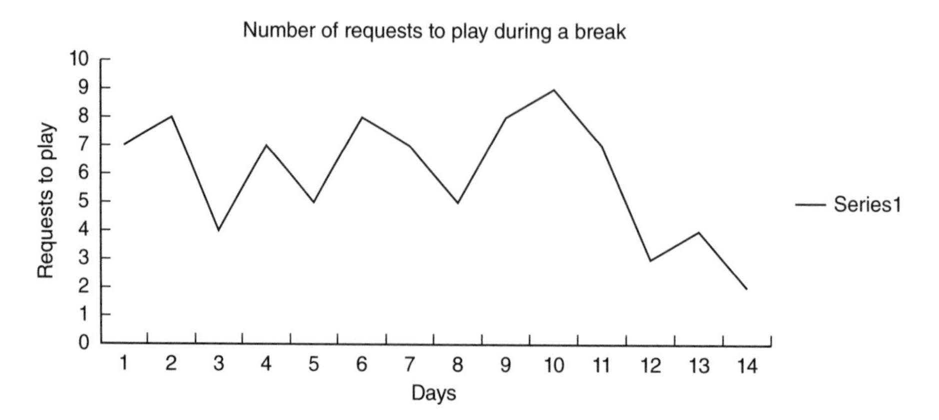

Figure 5.2 Requests to play over time

Practice wisdom

Notions of reflexivity, which require practitioners to reflect on and in their actions in practice (Schön, 1987), and praxis, which encourages an active approach to interpreting the world, seeking alternatives and challenging received knowledge (Friere, 1972), are also important in developing a critical perspective on evaluation in respect of one's own practices. Developing an explicit approach to identifying and drawing on knowledge that develops in a tacit way from your experiences can enhance your capacity to evaluate and review individual casework practice. Practice wisdom refers to the collated experiences and interpretations that develop over time from engaging with, reflecting on and testing out hypotheses and methods of practising. These are important in social work, which deals with complex and messy human situations and cannot be bounded neatly into rigid frameworks. However, when a systematic, theory-driven approach is melded with practice wisdom, it can have a positive impact on developing a thoughtful, knowledgeable and flexible approach to each case evaluation undertaken, hopefully assisting you in improving your practice as a social worker.

Pluralistic evaluation

Traditional ways of evaluating intervention or social work projects tend to look at the views of only one party involved, perhaps those of the social worker, the service user or the carer. They often do not include the views of other professions. Pluralistic evaluation (Smith and Cantley, 1985) acknowledges that there are many, and sometimes conflicting, opinions and the ways of judging success may differ according to whether you are a service user, service provider, carer, practitioner or manager. In practical terms, pluralistic evaluation involves collecting the views and opinions, including the different notions of success, of all those involved. While you may not use such an approach in your casework, it is important to be aware of the many different ways an outcome can be assessed.

CHAPTER SUMMARY

This chapter has covered two areas of social work practice that are often relegated to last place in the minds of many social workers. While this may be understandable in some respects – people have busy case loads and pressure to take on new cases – it is not defendable. The situations in which service users and carers find themselves are ever-changing and need regular review to ensure that services provided are the ones that are most likely to be effective in producing change. Also, it is important that social workers continually strive to improve their practice and are able to demonstrate to service users, carers and their employers that what they are doing is working. Attention to a regular system of review and monitoring of casework is part of good practice. Developing a research-minded approach to one's practice and development can assist the overall process that we have begun to describe throughout this book.

Department of Health (1991a) *The Children Act guidance and regulations. Volume 2. Family support, day care and educational provision for young children.* London: HMSO.

Department of Health (1991b) *The Children Act guidance and regulations. Volume 3. Family placements.* London: HMSO.

These two volumes form part of a comprehensive range of early guidance issued in respect of the Children Act 1989. They are useful in providing basic information and an understanding of the Children Act in practice.

HM Government (2013) *Working Together to Safeguard Children: A guide to inter-agency working to safeguard and promote the welfare of children.* Available at: http://media.education.gov.uk/assets/files/pdf/w/working%20together.pdf (accessed 13.1.14).

This volume updates earlier guidance and provides information designed to enhance good practice and prevent communication difficulties that have beleaguered helping professions.

Laming, H (2003) *The Victoria Climbié inquiry report.* Cm 5730. London: The Stationery Office.

Lymbery, M and Morley, K (2012) Self-Directed Support and Social Work Practice. *Social Work in Action,* 24(5): 315–17.

Lymbery and Morley consider the place for qualified social workers within the context of self-directed support and personalisation. They caution against cutting posts of skilled workers with adults, particularly those who work with service users who lead chaotic and potentially dangerous lives.

McDonald, G and Popay, J (2010) Evidence and practice: The knowledge challenge for social work, in Shaw, I, Briar-Lawson, K, Orme, J and Ruckdeschel, R (eds) *The Sage handbook of social work research.* London: Sage.

Macdonald and Popay explore the 'effects' of social work practice rather than 'effectiveness', describing the importance of taking data from a wide range of sources to ensure we know as much as possible about what works, what the practice means for those receiving it, what it costs and what might go wrong. The chapter provides a useful balance between fluid, uncertain practices and those based on inflexible approaches to evidence-based practice. The concepts explored are important when evaluating social work practice.

Moore, D and Jones, K (2012) *Social Work and Dementia.* London: Sage/Learning Matters.

This is a timely and helpful textbook that provides evidence and thoughtful direction for social workers to work effectively with people with dementia and enable them to live as full a life as possible. We recommend you read Chapter 2, 'Legislation, guidance and dementia'.

Conclusion

This book has outlined key elements of social work practice in a range of settings in the UK. Although much of the legislation, policy and guidance that we have discussed in the book relates specifically to England, it is the practice that lies behind this that is important and transferable. The text does not seek to be comprehensive – an impossible task given the breadth of social work practice in the UK let alone throughout the world! – but to prepare you for future and continued study, something that is particularly important as a professional social worker (Keen et al., 2013; Higham, 2013). There is a danger that the parts we have described may be taken apart from the process that makes up social work practice; indeed, we have seen that happen in some circumstances and this reduces social work into instrumental and rigid practices that have little to do with the interpersonal practice that is social work. The sum is greater than the parts! We have stressed throughout the book that assessment is *part* of the process of intervention in another person's life and that planning begins before the assessment starts. Plans for the review are made at the outset of the work. What we have attempted to avoid is a piecemeal approach and to see the elements that we have included as linking with each other, forming part of a much wider whole: social work practice (see Parker, 2008; 2013). It is our belief, hopefully portrayed in the book, that social work is a complex, non-linear process that weaves a tapestry moving back and forth across and between the processes that it involves.

Of course, in practice you may be asked to concentrate on one aspect of social work as opposed to others depending on where you practise, but the process is still there. While we need to see the process of practice integrated with its component parts, similarly we must not lose sight of the bigger picture of social work within which critical and emancipatory or transformative practice is placed. It is a central concern and challenge to social welfare and social justice in many modern and developing states and countries. A potential problem in UK social work is the demarcation of boundaries suggesting that assessment is a discrete task that can be seen apart from others. We would like to challenge that way of conceptualising social work and to promote it as an holistic activity.

The building blocks of practice and the developing themes and stages set out in this book are likely to remain central within the ever-changing panoplies of social work education and training. However, while the guiding principles underlying these aspects of practice may remain relatively constant, the procedural details and guidelines are likely to be refined in response to the changing needs and perspectives of service users and carers, and the changing professional, cultural and political tides. Such is the speed of change in social work that many of the procedures and much of the guidance provided by government are likely to change several times throughout your education and certainly when working as a qualified social worker. We have made an assumption throughout the book that you will be increasingly aware of this factor and that you are embarking on a future professional role in which learning and professional development are lifelong. We hope that, as a consequence of reading the book and participating in the activities, we have further encouraged you down this path, and that your development as a beginning practitioner is based on a commitment to this process of exploration. We hope that you will be in a position to be able to, and motivated to want to, access professional and academic journals and websites to help keep you well briefed and current in your thinking and practice, and motivated to continue to refine your thinking and find new ways to link practice to the best theories around. Indeed your future registration requirements demand it! It is our intention that you will be in a position to transfer learning from this work to your first job as a social worker and that it will inform your induction and beyond. We also would like to think that we have started the process of enabling you to become a critical and effective practitioner: that is, a social worker who is able and willing to 'think out of the box'; one who sees further than the local practice guidance and procedures; one who makes the links between debates in parliament today and social work practice tomorrow and can see the value of engaging with those debates.

Social work does not stand still, and neither is it bound by geography and territory, or indeed by rigid definitions of what it might entail or be. Indeed, questions about the possible decline and fragmentation of social work methods, central components of the social work process, have been debated elsewhere (Parker and Doel, 2013), raising worrying issues. These concerns relate to ongoing and iterative debates about the nature of social work in context, and whether or not it has a distinctive theory and knowledge base from which to practise. These are important issues but if separated from the political they lose some of their immediacy, focusing more on abstracts than pressing human concerns. The processes of social work outlined in this book need to be grounded in the living contexts and environments of social work practice to make them come alive. In practice learning and employed practice post-qualification you will be able to reflect on the components of practice in collaboration with those requesting and using your services, and delineate a course to follow, negotiating the problems of living in our late modern society. Critical practice when held up to the light should be more than the sum of its parts, just like the social work process we have described throughout this book. It should also reflect the commitment of both social work as a profession and individual social workers to peaceful co-existence and social justice for all.

Appendix 1

Professional capabilities framework

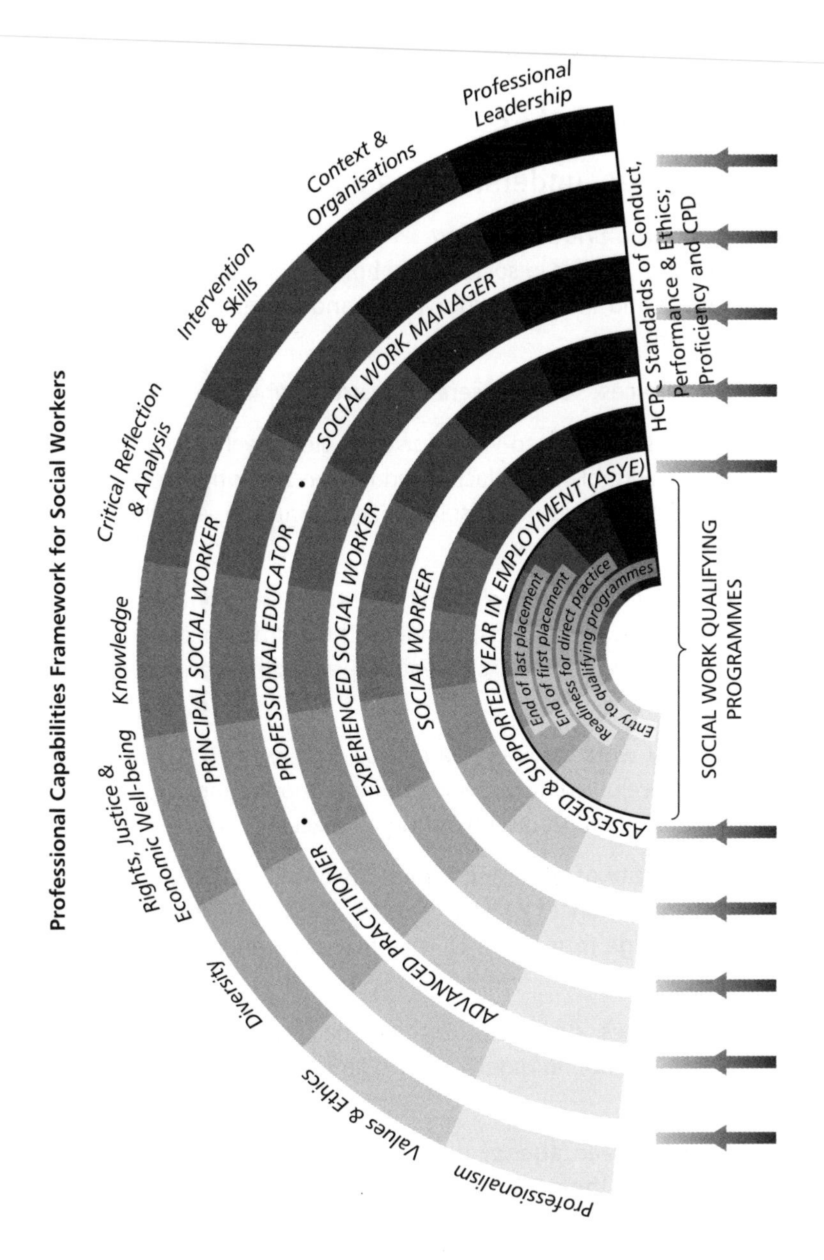

Appendix 2
Subject benchmark for social work

4 Defining principles

5 Subject knowledge, understanding and skills

Subject knowledge and understanding

5.1 During their degree studies in social work, honours graduates should acquire, critically evaluate, apply and integrate knowledge and understanding in the following five core areas of study.

5.1.1 **Social work services, service users and carers**, which include:

- the social processes (associated with, for example, poverty, migration, unemployment, poor health, disablement, lack of education and other sources of disadvantage) that lead to marginalisation, isolation and exclusion, and their impact on the demand for social work services
- explanations of the links between definitional processes contributing to social differences (for example, social class, gender, ethnic differences, age, sexuality and religious belief) to the problems of inequality and differential need faced by service users
- the nature of social work services in a diverse society (with particular reference to concepts such as prejudice, interpersonal, institutional and structural discrimination, empowerment and anti-discriminatory practices)
- the nature and validity of different definitions of, and explanations for, the characteristics and circumstances of service users and the services required by them, drawing on knowledge from research, practice experience, and from service users and carers
- the focus on outcomes, such as promoting the well-being of young people and their families, and promoting dignity, choice and independence for adults receiving services
- the relationship between agency policies, legal requirements and professional boundaries in shaping the nature of services provided in interdisciplinary contexts and the issues associated with working across professional boundaries and within different disciplinary groups.

5.1.2 **The service delivery context**, which includes:

- the location of contemporary social work within historical, comparative and global perspectives, including European and international contexts
- the changing demography and cultures of communities in which social workers will be practising
- the complex relationships between public, social and political philosophies, policies and priorities and the organisation and practice of social work, including the contested nature of these
- the issues and trends in modern public and social policy and their relationship to contemporary practice and service delivery in social work
- the significance of legislative and legal frameworks and service delivery standards (including the nature of legal authority, the application of legislation in practice, statutory accountability and tensions between statute, policy and practice)
- the current range and appropriateness of statutory, voluntary and private agencies providing community-based, day-care, residential and other services and the organisational systems inherent within these
- the significance of interrelationships with other related services, including housing, health, income maintenance and criminal justice (where not an integral social service)
- the contribution of different approaches to management, leadership and quality in public and independent human services
- the development of personalised services, individual budgets and direct payments
- the implications of modern information and communications technology (ICT) for both the provision and receipt of services.

5.1.3 **Values and ethics**, which include:

- the nature, historical evolution and application of social work values
- the moral concepts of rights, responsibility, freedom, authority and power inherent in the practice of social workers as moral and statutory agents
- the complex relationships between justice, care and control in social welfare and the practical and ethical implications of these, including roles as statutory agents and in upholding the law in respect of discrimination
- aspects of philosophical ethics relevant to the understanding and resolution of value dilemmas and conflicts in both interpersonal and professional contexts
- the conceptual links between codes defining ethical practice, the regulation of professional conduct and the management of potential conflicts generated by the codes held by different professional groups.

5.1.4 **Social work theory**, which includes:

- research-based concepts and critical explanations from social work theory and other disciplines that contribute to the knowledge base of social work, including their distinctive epistemological status and application to practice
- the relevance of sociological perspectives to understanding societal and structural influences on human behaviour at individual, group and community levels
- the relevance of psychological, physical and physiological perspectives to understanding personal and social development and functioning
- social science theories explaining group and organisational behaviour, adaptation and change
- models and methods of assessment, including factors underpinning the selection and testing of relevant information, the nature of professional judgement and the processes of risk assessment and decision-making
- approaches and methods of intervention in a range of settings, including factors guiding the choice and evaluation of these
- user-led perspectives
- knowledge and critical appraisal of relevant social research and evaluation methodologies, and the evidence base for social work.

5.1.5 **The nature of social work practice**, which includes:

- the characteristics of practice in a range of community-based and organisational settings within statutory, voluntary and private sectors, and the factors influencing changes and developments in practice within these contexts
- the nature and characteristics of skills associated with effective practice, both direct and indirect, with a range of service users and in a variety of settings
- the processes that facilitate and support service user choice and independence
- the factors and processes that facilitate effective interdisciplinary, interprofessional and interagency collaboration and partnership
- the place of theoretical perspectives and evidence from international research in assessment and decision-making processes in social work practice
- the integration of theoretical perspectives and evidence from international research into the design and implementation of effective social work intervention, with a wide range of service users, carers and others
- the processes of reflection and evaluation, including familiarity with the range of approaches for evaluating service and welfare outcomes, and their significance for the development of practice and the practitioner.

Subject-specific skills and other skills

5.2 As an applied subject at honours degree level, social work necessarily involves the development of skills that may be of value in many situations (for example, analytical thinking, building relationships, working as a member of an organisation, intervention, evaluation and reflection). Some of these skills are specific to social work but many are also widely transferable. What helps to define the specific nature of these skills in a social work context are:

- the context in which they are applied and assessed (e.g. communication skills in practice with people with sensory impairments or assessment skills in an interprofessional setting)
- the relative weighting given to such skills within social work practice (e.g. the central importance of problem-solving skills within complex human situations)
- the specific purpose of skill development (e.g. the acquisition of research skills in order to build a repertoire of research-based practice)
- a requirement to integrate a range of skills (i.e. not simply to demonstrate these in an isolated and incremental manner).

5.3 All social work honours graduates should show the ability to reflect on and learn from the exercise of their skills. They should understand the significance of the concepts of continuing professional development and lifelong learning, and accept responsibility for their own continuing development.

5.4 Social work honours graduates should acquire and integrate skills in the following five core areas.

Problem-solving skills

5.5 These are sub-divided into four areas.

5.5.1 **Managing problem-solving activities:** honours graduates in social work should be able to plan problem-solving activities, i.e. to:

- think logically, systematically, critically and reflectively
- apply ethical principles and practices critically in planning problem-solving activities
- plan a sequence of actions to achieve specified objectives, making use of research, theory and other forms of evidence
- manage processes of change, drawing on research, theory and other forms of evidence.

5.5.2 **Gathering information:** honours graduates in social work should be able to:

- gather information from a wide range of sources and by a variety of methods, for a range of purposes. These methods should include electronic searches, reviews of relevant literature, policy and procedures, face-to-face interviews, written and telephone contact with individuals and groups

- take into account differences of viewpoint in gathering information and critically assess the reliability and relevance of the information gathered
- assimilate and disseminate relevant information in reports and case records.

5.5.3 **Analysis and synthesis:** honours graduates in social work should be able to analyse and synthesise knowledge gathered for problem-solving purposes, i.e. to:

- assess human situations, taking into account a variety of factors (including the views of participants, theoretical concepts, research evidence, legislation and organisational policies and procedures)
- analyse information gathered, weighing competing evidence and modifying their viewpoint in light of new information, then relate this information to a particular task, situation or problem
- consider specific factors relevant to social work practice (such as risk, rights, cultural differences and linguistic sensitivities, responsibilities to protect vulnerable individuals and legal obligations)
- assess the merits of contrasting theories, explanations, research, policies and procedures
- synthesise knowledge and sustain reasoned argument
- employ a critical understanding of human agency at the macro (societal), mezzo (organisational and community) and micro (inter and intrapersonal) levels
- critically analyse and take account of the impact of inequality and discrimination in work with people in particular contexts and problem situations.

5.5.4 **Intervention and evaluation:** honours graduates in social work should be able to use their knowledge of a range of interventions and evaluation processes selectively to:

- build and sustain purposeful relationships with people and organisations in community-based and interprofessional contexts
- make decisions, set goals and construct specific plans to achieve these, taking into account relevant factors including ethical guidelines
- negotiate goals and plans with others, analysing and addressing in a creative manner human, organisational and structural impediments to change
- implement plans through a variety of systematic processes that include working in partnership
- undertake practice in a manner that promotes the well-being and protects the safety of all parties
- engage effectively in conflict resolution

- support service users to take decisions and access services, with the social worker as navigator, advocate and supporter
- manage the complex dynamics of dependency and, in some settings, provide direct care and personal support in everyday living situations
- meet deadlines and comply with external definitions of a task
- plan, implement and critically review processes and outcomes
- bring work to an effective conclusion, taking into account the implications for all involved
- monitor situations, review processes and evaluate outcomes
- use and evaluate methods of intervention critically and reflectively.

Communication skills

5.6 Honours graduates in social work should be able to communicate clearly, accurately and precisely (in an appropriate medium) with individuals and groups in a range of formal and informal situations, i.e. to:

- make effective contact with individuals and organisations for a range of objectives, by verbal, paper-based and electronic means
- clarify and negotiate the purpose of such contacts and the boundaries of their involvement
- listen actively to others, engage appropriately with the life experiences of service users, understand accurately their viewpoint and overcome personal prejudices to respond appropriately to a range of complex personal and interpersonal situations
- use both verbal and non-verbal cues to guide interpretation
- identify and use opportunities for purposeful and supportive communication with service users within their everyday living situations
- follow and develop an argument and evaluate the viewpoints of, and evidence presented by, others
- write accurately and clearly in styles adapted to the audience, purpose and context of the communication
- use advocacy skills to promote others' rights, interests and needs
- present conclusions verbally and on paper, in a structured form, appropriate to the audience for which these have been prepared
- make effective preparation for, and lead meetings in a productive way
- communicate effectively across potential barriers resulting from differences (for example, in culture, language and age).

Skills in working with others

5.7 Honours graduates in social work should be able to work effectively with others, i.e. to:

- involve users of social work services in ways that increase their resources, capacity and power to influence factors affecting their lives
- consult actively with others, including service users and carers, who hold relevant information or expertise
- act cooperatively with others, liaising and negotiating across differences such as organisational and professional boundaries and differences of identity or language
- develop effective helping relationships and partnerships with other individuals, groups and organisations that facilitate change
- act with others to increase social justice by identifying and responding to prejudice, institutional discrimination and structural inequality
- act within a framework of multiple accountability (for example, to agencies, the public, service users, carers and others)
- challenge others when necessary, in ways that are most likely to produce positive outcomes.

Skills in personal and professional development

5.8 Honours graduates in social work should be able to:

- advance their own learning and understanding with a degree of independence
- reflect on and modify their behaviour in the light of experience
- identify and keep under review their own personal and professional boundaries
- manage uncertainty, change and stress in work situations
- handle inter and intrapersonal conflict constructively
- understand and manage changing situations and respond in a flexible manner
- challenge unacceptable practices in a responsible manner
- take responsibility for their own further and continuing acquisition and use of knowledge and skills
- use research critically and effectively to sustain and develop their practice.

References

Adams, R (2003) *Social work and empowerment.* 3rd edition. Basingstoke: Palgrave.

Age UK (2013) *Factsheet 41 Oct 2013.* Available at: www.ageuk.co.uk (accessed 13.1.14).

Aguilera, DC and Messick, JM (1974) *Crisis intervention. Theory and methodology.* St Louis, Missouri: CV Mosby and Co.

Aguilera, DC and Messick, JM (1982) *Crisis intervention therapy for psychological emergencies.* New York: Plume.

Alston, M and Bowles, W (2003) *Research for social workers: An introduction to methods.* 2nd edition. London: Routledge.

Alzheimer's Society (2012) *Mental Capacity Act 2005 Factsheet 460 – March 2012.* Available at: http://alzheimers.org.uk (accessed 13.1.14).

Ashencaen Crabtree, S, Husain, F and Spalek, B (2008) *Islam and social work: Debating values, transforming practice.* Bristol: Policy Press.

Association of Directors of Adult Social Services (2005) *Safeguarding adults: A national framework of standards for good practice and outcomes in adult protection work.* London: ADASS.

Association of Directors of Adult Social Services (2009a) *Making progress with putting people first: Self directed support.* London: DH/ADASS.

Association of Directors of Adult Social Services (2009b) *Common resource allocation framework* London: ADASS.

Audit Commission (1986) *Making a reality of community care.* London: HMSO.

Audit Commission (2000) *Charging with care.* London: The Stationery Office.

Bailey, S, Thoburn, J and Wakeham, H (2002) Using the 'looking after children' dimensions to collect aggregate data on well-being. *Child and Family Social Work,* 7, 3, 189–201.

Baldwin, BA (1979) Crisis intervention: An overview of theory and practice. *The Counseling Psychologist,* 8, 2, 43–52.

Banks, S (2004) *Ethics, accountability and the social professional.* Basingstoke: Palgrave MacMillan.

Barclay Report (1982) *Social workers: Their roles and tasks.* London: Bedford Square Press.

Barker, P (1986) *Basic family therapy.* Oxford: Blackwell.

Bartlett, H (1970) *The common base of social work practice.* New York: National Association of Social Workers.

Bates, N, Immins, T, Parker, J, Keen, S, Rutter, L, Brown, K and Zsigo, S (2010) 'Baptism of fire': The first year in the life of a newly qualified social worker. *Social Work Education,* 29, 2, 152–70.

Bradley, G (2003) Administrative justice and charging for long-term care. *British Journal of Social Work,* 33, 641–57.

Bradley, G (2005) Movers and stayers in care management in adult services. *British Journal of Social Work,* 35, 511–30.

Bradley, G (2007) The induction of newly qualified social workers: Some implications for social work educators. *Social Work Education,* 1–17.

Bradley, G and Manthorpe, J (1997) *Dilemmas of financial assessment.* Birmingham: Venture Press.

Bradley, G and Manthorpe, J (eds) (2000) *Working on the fault line.* Birmingham: Venture Press.

Bradley, G, Manthorpe, J, Stanley, N and Alaszewski, A (1996) Training for care management: Using research to identify new directions. *Issues in Social Work Education*, 16, 2, 26–44.

Brandon, D and Brandon, T (2001) *Advocacy in social work.* Birmingham: Venture Press.

Brandon, M, Bailey, S, Belderson, P, Gardner, R, Sidebotham, P, Dodsworth, J, Warren, C and Black, J (2009) *Understanding serious case reviews and their impact: A biennial analysis of serious case reviews 2005–07.* London: DSCF.

British Association of Social Workers (BASW) (2002) *The code of ethics for social work.* Birmingham: BASW.

Brownell, P (1997) The application of the culturagram in cross-cultural practice with elder abuse victims. *Journal of Elder Abuse and Neglect*, 9, 2, 19–33.

Bubb, S (2013) The 'big society' means little when charities are suffering. *Guardian*, 8.1.13. Available at: www.theguardian.co.uk (accessed 13.1.14).

Bubb Carkhuff, R (1987) *The art of helping.* 6th edition. Amerhurst, MA: Human Resource Development Press.

Burnham, J (1986) *Family therapy.* London: Tavistock.

Caplan, G (1961) *An approach to community mental health.* New York: Grune and Stratton.

Carmichael, A and Brown, L (2002) The future challenge of direct payments. *Disability and Society*, 17, 7, 797–808.

Caspi, J and Reid, W (2002) *Educational supervision in social work: A task-centered model for field instruction and staff development.* New York: Columbia University Press.

Central Council for Education and Training in Social Work (CCETSW) (1995) *DipSW rules and requirements for the diploma in social work.* CCETSW Paper 30. London: CCETSW.

Cheetham, J, Fuller, R, McIvor, G and Petch, A (1992) *Evaluating social work effectiveness.* Buckingham: Open University Press.

Cigno, K (2009) Cognitive-behavioural practice. In Adams, R, Dominelli, L and Payne, M (eds) *Critical practice in social work.* 2nd edition. Basingstoke: Palgrave.

Cigno, K and Bourn, D (eds) (1998) *Cognitive-behavioural social work in practice.* Aldershot: Ashgate/ Arena.

Clifford, D (1998) *Social assessment theory and practice: A multi-disciplinary framework.* Aldershot: Ashgate.

Commission on Funding of Care and Support (2011) *Fairer care funding – the report of the commission on funding of care and support.* (The Dilnot Report). London: The Stationery Office.

Community Care (2013) *Care Bill 2013.*Available at: (home page) www.communitycare.co.uk (accessed 13.1.14).

Compton, B and Galaway, B (1975) *Social work processes.* Homewood, IL: Dorsey Press.

Congress, E (1994) The use of culturagrams to assess and empower culturally diverse families. *Families in Society*, 75, 9, 531–40.

Congress, E (2004) Cultural and ethical issues in working with culturally diverse patients and their families: The use of the culturagram to promote cultural competent practice in health care settings, *Social Work in Health Care*, 39, 3/4, 249–62.

Cooper, B (2000) The measure of a competent child care social worker? *Journal of Social Work Practice*, 14, 2, 113–24.

Coulshed, V (1990) *Management in social work.* London: Macmillan.

Coulshed, V and Orme, J (2006) *Social work practice: An introduction.* 4th edition. Basingstoke: Palgrave Macmillan.

Cournoyer, B (1991) *The social work skills workbook.* Belmont, CA: Wadsworth.

Crawford, K and Walker, J (2008) *Social work with older people.* 2nd edition. Exeter: Learning Matters.

CSCI (2008) *Cutting the cake fairly: CSCI review of eligibility criteria for social care.* Newcastle: CSCI.

Cunningham, J and Cunningham, S (2012) *Social policy and social work: An Introduction.* London: Sage/Learning.

Department of Education (2013a) The CAF Process. Available at: www.education.gov.uk/childrenandyoungpeople/strategy/integratedworking/caf/a0068957/the-caf-process (accessed 13.1.14).

Department for Education (2013b) *Improving safeguarding for looked after children: Consultation on changes to the care planning, placement and case review (England) Regulations 2010.* London: Department for Education.

Department for Education and Skills/Department of Health (2004) *National service framework for children, young people and maternity services.* London: Department of Health.

Department of Health (1989) *Caring for people: Community care in the next decade and beyond* (Cm 849). London: HMSO.

Department of Health (1991a) *The Children Act guidance and regulations. Volume 2. Family support, day care and educational provision for young children.* London: HMSO.

Department of Health (1991b) *The Children Act guidance and regulations. Volume 3. Family placements.* London: HMSO.

Department of Health (1991c) *Working together under the Children Act 1989. A guide to arrangements for inter-agency co-operation for the protection of children from abuse.* London: HMSO.

Department of Health (1998) *Modernising social services: Promoting independence, improving protection, raising standards* (Cmd 4169). London: The Stationery Office.

Department of Health (1999) *Working together to safeguard children. A guide to inter-agency working to safeguard and promote the welfare of children.* London: The Stationery Office.

Department of Health (2000a) *The NHS plan: A plan for investment. A plan for reform.* London: Department of Health.

Department of Health (2000b) *No secrets: Guidance on developing multi-agency policies and procedures to protect vulnerable adults from abuse. DOH circular HSC 2000/007.* Available at: www.gov.uk/government/publications/no-secrets-guidance-on-protecting-vulnerable-adults-in-care (accessed 13.1.14).

Department of Health (2000c) *No Secrets: The development of multi-agency responses to the abuse of vulnerable adults.* London: The Stationery Office.

Department of Health (2001a) *National service framework for older people.* London: Stationery Office.

Department of Health (2001b) *Fairer charging policies for home care and other non-residential social services – Guidance for councils with social services responsibilities.* LAC (2001) 32. London: Department of Health.

Department of Health (2001c) *Valuing People: a new strategy for learning disability for the 21st century.* London: Stationery Office.

Department of Health (2002a) *Requirements for social work training.* London: Department of Health.

Department of Health (2002b) *The single assessment process guidance for local implementation and annexe.* HSC 2002/001; LAC (2002)1. London: Department of Health.

Department of Health (2002c) *Fair access to care services: Guidance on eligibility criteria for adult social care.* LAC (2002)13. London: Department of Health.

Department of Health (2002d) *Fair access to care services: Policy guidance.* London: Department of Health.

Department of Health (2003a) *Fair access to care services guidance on eligibility criteria for adult social care.* London: The Stationery Office.

Department of Health (2003b) *Fair access to care services: Practice guidance – implementation questions and answers.* London: Department of Health.

Department of Health (2004) *The community care assessment directions.* LAC (2004) 24. London: Department of Health.

Department of Health (2005) *Independence, well-being and choice: Our vision for the future of social care for adults in England.* Cm 6499. London: Department of Health.

Department of Health (2006) *Our health, our care, our say: A new direction for community services.* Cm 6737. Norwich: The Stationery Office.

Department of Health (2007) *Putting people first: A shared vision and commitment to the transformation of adult social care.* Available at: http://webarchive.nationalarchives.gov.uk/20130107105354/http:/www.dh.gov.uk/en/Publicationsandstatistics/Publications/PublicationsPolicyAndGuidance/DH_081118 (accessed 13.1.14).

Department of Health (2009) *Safeguarding adults – Report on the consultation on the review of 'No Secrets': Guidance on developing and implementing multi-agency policies and procedures to protect vulnerable adults from abuse.* London: The Stationery Office.

Department of Health (2010a) *A vision for adult social care: Capable communities and active citizens.* London: Department of Health.

Department of Health (2010b) *Prioritising need in the context of putting people first: A whole system approach to eligibility for social care – guidance on eligibility criteria for adult social care.* London: Department of Health.

Department of Health (2010c) *Fairer contribution guidance: Calculating an individual's contribution to their personal budget.* London: Department of Health.

Department of Health (2012) *Factsheet A1 Health and Social Care Act.* Available at: www.gov.uk/government/publications/health-and-social-care-act-2012-fact-sheets (accessed 13.1.14).

Department of Health and Cleaver, H (2000) *Assessment recording forms.* London: The Stationery Office.

Department of Health, Department for Education and Employment, Home Office (2000) *Framework for the assessment of children in need and their families.* London: The Stationery Office.

Department of Health, Social Services Inspectorate (1995) *The challenge of partnership in child protection: Practice guide.* London: HMSO.

Doel, M (2009) Task-centred work. In Adams, R, Dominelli, L and Payne, M (eds) *Critical practice in social work.* 2nd edition. Basingstoke: Palgrave.

Doel, M and Marsh, P (1992) *Task-centred social work.* Aldershot: Arena/Ashgate.

Dominelli, L (1996) Deprofessionalising social work: Anti-oppressive practice, competences and postmodernism. *British Journal of Social Work,* 26, 1, 153–75.

Dominelli, L (2002) *Anti-oppressive social work theory and practice.* Basingstoke: Palgrave.

Edlis, N (1993) Rape crisis: Development of a center in an Israeli hospital. *Social Work in Health Care,* 18, 3/4, 169–78.

Egan, G (2001) *The skilled helper: A problem-management and opportunity-development approach to helping.* 7th edition. Pacific Grove: Brooks/Cole Publishing.

England, H (1986) *Social work as art: Making sense for good practice.* London: Allen and Unwin.

Erikson, E (1950) *Childhood and society.* London: WW Norton.

Fook, J (2012) *Social work: A critical approach to practice.* 2nd edition. London: Sage.

Forrester, D, Kershaw, S, Moss, H and Hughes, L (2008) Communication skills in child protection: How do social workers talk to parents? *Child and Family Social Work,* 13, 1, 41–51.

Fowler, J (2003) *A practitioners' tool for child protection and the assessment of parents.* London: Jessica Kingsley.

Friere, P (1972) *The pedagogy of the oppressed.* Harmondsworth: Penguin.

Gambrill, E (1994) What's in a name? Task-centred, empirical and behavioural practice. *Social Service Review*, 68, 4, 578–99.

Gardner, A (2011) *Personalisation in social work.* London: Sage/Learning Matters.

General Social Care Council (GSCC) (2002a) *Code of practice for employees.* London: GSCC.

General Social Care Council (GSCC) (2002b) *Code of practice for social care workers.* London: GSCC.

General Social Care Council (GSCC) (2009) *Raising standards social work education 2007–2008.* London: GSCC.

Gilbar, O (1991) Model for crisis intervention through group therapy for women with breast cancer. *Clinical Social Work Journal*, 19, 3, 293–304.

Glasby, J and Littlechild, R (2002a) Independence pays? Barriers to the progress of direct payments. *Practice*, 14, 1, 55–66.

Glasby, J and Littlechild, R (2002b) *Social work and direct payments.* Bristol: Policy Press.

Glendinning, C, Arksey, H, Jones, K, Moran, N, Netten, A and Rabiee, P (2009) *The individual budgets pilot projects: Impact and outcomes for carers.* University of York: Social Policy Research Unit; University of Kent: Personal Social Services Research Unit.

Glendinning, C, Challis, D, Fernandez, J, Jacobs, S, Jones, K, Knapp, M, Manthorpe, J, Moran, N, Netten, A, Stevens, M and Wilberforce, M (2008) *Evaluation of the individual budgets pilot programme: Final report.* York: SPRU.

Golan, N (1978) *Treatment in crisis situations.* New York: Free Press.

Golightley, M (2014) *Social work and mental health.* 5th edition. London: Learning Matters/Sage.

Gotterer, R (2001) The spiritual dimension in clinical social work practice: A client perspective. *Families in Society*, 82, 2, 187–93.

Griffiths, R (1988) *Community care: Agenda for action.* (The Griffiths Report). London: HMSO.

Gustavsson, N and MacEachron, A (2013) The virtual ecomap: A diagrammatic tool for assessing the digital world of clients. *Families in Society*, 94, 4, 243–50.

Hancock, R, Bonner, G, Hollingdale, R and Madden, A (2012) 'If you listen to me properly, I feel good': A qualitative examination of patient experiences of dietetic consultations. *Journal of Human Nutrition and Dietetics*, 25, 275–84.

Harding, T and Beresford, P (1996) *The standards we expect: What service users and carers want from social services workers.* London: NISW.

Hardwick, L and Worsley, A (2010) *Doing social work research.* London: Sage.

Hartman, A (1995) Diagrammatic assessment of family relationships. *Families in Society*, 76, 2, 111–22.

Hartmann, H (1958) *Ego psychology and the problem of adaptation.* New York: International University Press.

HCPC (2012) *Standards of proficiency – social workers in England.* London: Health and Care Professions Council. Available at: www.hpc-uk.org/publications/standards/index.asp?id=569 (accessed 13.1.14).

Hepworth, D, Rooney, R, Rooney, G, Strom-Gottfried, K and Larsen, J (2009) *Direct social work practice: Theory and skills.* 8th edition. Belmont, CA: Brooks Cole.

Higham, P (2013) Understanding continuing professional development, in Parker, J and Doel, M (eds) *Professional social work.* London: Sage. pp132–51.

HM Government (2005) *Statutory guidance on making arrangements to safeguard and promote the welfare of children under section 11 of the Children Act 2004.* London: The Stationery Office.

HM Government (2005) The Mental Capacity Act 2005. Available at: www.legislation.gov.uk/ukpga/2005/9/contents (accessed 13.1.14).

HM Government (2006) *Working together to safeguard children: A guide to inter-agency working to safeguard and promote the welfare of children.* London: The Stationery Office.

HM Government (2012a) *Caring for our future: White Paper.* London: The Stationery Office.
HM Government (2012b) *Draft Care and Support Bill.* Cm 8386. London: The Stationery Office. Available at: www.official-documents.gov.uk/document/cm83/8386/8386.pdf (accessed 13.1.14).
HM Government (2013a) *Working together to safeguard children: A guide to inter-agency working to safeguard and promote the welfare of children.* Available at: http://media.education.gov.uk/assets/files/pdf/w/working%20together.pdf (accessed 13.1.14).
HM Government (2013b) *The Care Bill explained including a response to consultations, pre-legislative scrutiny on the Draft Care and Support Bill.* Cm 8627. London: The Stationery Office.
Hodge, D (2001) Spiritual assessment: A review of major qualitative methods and a new framework for assessing spirituality. *Social Work*, 46, 3, 203–14.
Hodge, D (2005) Developing a spiritual assessment toolbox: A discussion of the strengths and limitations of five different assessment methods. *Health and Social Work*, 30, 4, 314–23.
Horner, N (2012) *What is social work?* 4th edition. London: Learning Matters/Sage.
Horwath, J (2009) *The child's world: The comprehensive guide to assessing children in need*, 2nd ediiton. London: Jessica Kingsley Publishers.
House of Commons Children, Schools and Families Committee (2009) *Training of children and families social workers: Seventh report of session 2008–09.* Vols 1&2, HC 527. London: The Stationery Office.
House of Commons Children, Schools and Families Committee (2010) *Training of children and families social workers: Government response to the seventh report of session 2008–09.* HC 358. London: The Stationery Office.
Howe, D (1992) *An introduction to social work theory.* Aldershot: Arena.
Howe, D (2013) *Empathy: What it is and why it matters.* Basingstoke: Palgrave Macmillan.
Hughes, B (1995) *Older people and community care.* Buckingham: Open University Press.
Humphries, B (2008) *Social work research for social justice.* Basingstoke: Palgrave.
Humphries, R (2013) *Paying for social care beyond Dilnot.* London: The King's Fund.
International Association of Schools of Social Work and International Federation of Social Workers (2001) Joint agreed definition of social work. 27 June. Copenhagen.
Johns, R (2009) *Using the law in social work.* 4th edition. Exeter: Learning Matters.
Joseph Rowntree Foundation (2000) *Older people's definitions of quality services.* York: Joseph Rowntree Foundation.
Keen, S, Gray, I, Parker, J, Galpin, D and Brown, K (eds) (2013) *Newly-qualified social workers: A handbook for practice.* 2nd edition, London: Learning Matters/Sage.
Kelly, G (1955) *Principles of personal construct psychology.* New York: Norton.
Koprowska, J (2010) *Communication and interpersonal skills in social work.* 3rd edition. Exeter: Learning Matters.
Laird, S (2008) *Anti-oppressive social work: A guide for developing cultural competence.* London: Sage.
Laming, H (2003) *The Victoria Climbié inquiry report.* Cm 5730. London: The Stationery Office.
Laming, H (2009) *The protection of children in England: A progress report.* HC 330. London: The Stationery Office.
Leece, D (2010) Paying the piper and calling the tune: Power and the direct payment relationship. *British Journal of Social Work*, 40, 188–206.
Leece, D and Leece, J (2006) Direct payments: Creating a two-tiered system in social care? *British Journal of Social Work*, 36, 8, 1379–93.
Leece, J and Leece, D (2011) Personalisation: Perceptions of the role of social work in a world of brokers and budgets. *British Journal of Social Work*, 41, 204–23.

Lewis, J and Glennerster, H (1996) *Implementing the new community care*. Buckingham: Open University Press.

Limb, G and Hodge, D (2007) Developing spiritual lifemaps as a culture-centered pictorial instrument for spiritual assessments with native American clients. *Research on Social Work Practice*, 17, 2, 296–304.

Limb, G, Hodge, D, Leckie, R and Ward, P (2013) Utilizing spiritual lifemaps with LDS clients: Enhancing cultural competence in social work practice. *Clinical Social Work Journal*, 41, 4, 395–405.

Lindemann, E (1944) Symptomatology and management of acute grief. *American Journal of Psychiatry*, 101, 141–48.

Lloyd, M and Taylor, C (1995) From Hollis to the Orange Book: Developing a holistic model of social work assessment in the 1990s. *British Journal of Social Work*, 25, 691–710.

Lymbery, M (1998) Care management and professional autonomy: The impact of community care legislation on social work with older people. *British Journal of Social Work*, 28, 6, 863–78.

Lymbery, M (2005) *Social work with older people: Context, policy and practice*. London: Sage Publications.

Lymbery, M (2012) Social work and personalisation: Fracturing the bureau-professional compact?' *British Journal of Social Work*, 42(4), 783–92.

Lymbery, M and Morley, K (2012) Self-directed support and social work. *Practice: Social Work in Action* 24(5), 315–17.

Lymbery, M and Postle, K (2010) Social work in the context of adult social care in England and the resultant implications for social work education. *British Journal of Social Work*, 40, 2502–22.

Lyons, J (2005) A systems approach to direct payments: A response to 'Friend or Foe?' Towards a critical assessment of direct payments. *Critical Social Policy*, 25, 2, 240–52.

Macdonald, G and Popay, J (2010) Evidence and practice: The knowledge challenge for social work, in Shaw, I, Briar-Lawson, K, Orme, J and Ruckdeschel, R (eds) *The Sage handbook of social work research*. London: Sage.

McCreadie, C (1996) *Elder abuse: Update on research*. London: Age Concern Institute of Gerontology.

McDonald, A (2006) *Understanding community care: A guide for social workers*. 2nd edition. Basingstoke: Palgrave Macmillan.

McGoldrick, M, Gerson, R and Petry, S (2008) *Genograms: Assessment and intervention*. 3rd edition. New York: Norton.

McNally, D, Cornes, M and Clough, R (2003) Implementing the single assessment process: Driving change or expecting the impossible? *Journal of Integrated Care*, 11, 2 18–29.

Mandelstam, M (2007) *Betraying the NHS: Health abandoned*. London: Jessica Kingsley.

Mantell, A (2009) *Social work skills with adults*. London: Learning Matters/Sage.

Mantell, A and Scragg, T (2011) *Safeguarding adults in social work*. 2nd edition. London: Learning Matters.

Manthorpe, J, Stanley, N, Bradley, G and Alaszewski, A (1996) Working together effectively? Assessing older people for community care services. *Health Care in Later Life*, 1, 3, 143–55.

Manthorpe, J, Jacobs, J, Rapaport, J, Challis, D, Netten, A, Glendinning, C, Stevens, M, Wilberforce, M, Knapp, M and Harris, J (2009a) Training for change: Early days of individual budgets and the implications for social work and care management practice: A qualitative study of the views of trainers. *British Journal of Social Work*, 39, 7, 1291–305.

Manthorpe, J, Stevens, M, Rapaport, J, Harris, J, Jacobs, S, Challis, D, Netten, A, Knapp, M, Wilberforce, M, and Glendinning, C (2009b) Safeguarding and system change: Early perceptions of the implications for adult protection services of the English individual budgets pilots – A qualitative study. *British Journal of Social Work*, 39, 1465–80.

Marsh, P (2008) Task-centred work, in Davies, M (ed) *The Blackwell companion to social work.* 3rd edition. Oxford: Blackwell.

Marsh, P and Doel, M (2005) *The task-centred book.* London: Routledge.

Marsh, P and Triseliotis, J (1996) *Ready to practise? Social workers and probation officers: Their training and first year in work.* Aldershot: Avebury.

Mayer, J and Timms, N (1970) *The client speaks.* London: Routledge and Kegan Paul.

Middleton, L (1997) *The art of assessment.* Birmingham: Venture Press.

Milner, J and O'Byrne, P (2009) *Assessment in social work.* 3rd edition. Basingstoke: Palgrave.

Moore, D and Jones, K (2012) *Social work and dementia.* London: Sage/Learning Matters.

Munro, E (1998) *Understanding social work: An empirical approach.* Atlantic Heights, NJ: Athlone Press.

Munro, E (2011) *The Monro review of child protection: Final report, a child centred approach.* Available at: www.education.gov.uk/munroreview/downloads/8875_DfE_Munro_Report_TAGGED.pdf (accessed 13.1.14).

Munro, E and Lushey, C (2013) *Undertaking serious case reviews using the Social Care Institute for Excellence (SCIE) Learning Together systems model: Lessons from the pilots.* CWRC Working Paper No. 17. London: Institute for Education.

Murphy, D, Duggan, M and Joseph, S (2013) Relationship-based social work and its compatibility with the person-centred approach: Principled versus instrumental perspectives. *British Journal of Social Work,* 43(4), 703–92.

Naleppa, M and Reid, W (2004) *Gerontological social work: A task centered approach.* New York: Columbia University Press.

Nazroo, J and Matthews, K (2012) *The impact of volunteering on well-being in later life: A research report to WRVS.* Available at: www.royalvoluntaryservice.org.uk/our-impact/reports-and-reviews/the-impact-of-volunteering-on-well-being-in-later-life (accessed 13.1.14).

Ney, T, Stoltz, J and Maloney, M (2013) Voice, power and discourse: Experiences of participants of family group conferences in the context of child protection. *Journal of Social Work,* 13, 2, 184–202.

Norman, J (2010) *The Big Society. The anatomy of the new politics.* Buckingham: The University of Buckingham Press.

O'Hagan, K (1991) Crisis intervention in social work, in Lishman, J (ed) *Handbook of theory for practice teachers in social work.* London: Jessica Kingsley.

Oliver, M (1996) *Understanding disability: From theory to practice.* Basingstoke: Macmillan.

Olsen, MR (ed) (1984) *Social work and mental health.* London: Tavistock.

Olsen, S, Dudley-Brown, S and McMullen, P (2004) Case for blending pedigrees, genograms and ecomaps: Nursing's contribution to the 'big picture'. *Nursing and Health Sciences,* 6, 295–308.

Orme, J (2000) Equal opportunities, in Davies, M (ed) *The Blackwell encyclopaedia of social work.* Oxford: Blackwell.

Parker, J (2000) Social work with refugees and asylum seekers: A rationale for developing practice. *Practice,* 12, 3, 61–76.

Parker, J (2007a) The process of social work: Assessment, planning, intervention and review, in Lymbery, M and Postle, K (eds) *Social work: A companion for learning.* London: Sage.

Parker, J (2007b) Crisis intervention: A practice model for people who have dementia and their carers. *Practice,* 19, 2, 115–26.

Parker, J (2007c) Disadvantage, stigma and anti-oppressive practice, in Burke, P and Parker, J (eds) *Social work and disadvantage.* London: Jessica Kingsley.

Parker, J (2008) Assessment, planning, intervention and review, in Davies, M (ed) *The encyclopaedia of social work.* Oxford: Blackwell.

Parker, J (2010) *Effective practice learning in social work.* 2nd edition. Exeter: Learning Matters.

Parker, J (2013) Assessment, intervention and review, in Davies, M (ed) *The Blackwell Companion to Social Work.* 4th edition. Oxford: Blackwell. pp311–20.

Parker, J (forthcoming) Single shared assessments in social work, in Wright, JD (ed) *The international encyclopedia of social and behavioral sciences.* 2nd edition. Elsevier.

Parker, J and Doel, M (2013) Professional social work and the professional social work identity?, in Parker, J and Doel, M (eds) *Professional social work.* London: Learning Matters/Sage.

Parker, J and Penhale, B (1998) *Forgotten people: Positive approaches to dementia care.* Aldershot: Ashgate/Arena.

Parker, J and Randall, P (1997) *Using behavioural theories in social work.* Birmingham: BASW/OLF.

Parkes, CM (1972) Psycho-social transitions: A field for study. *Social Science and Medicine,* 5, 101–15.

Parry, G (1990) *Coping with crises.* London: BPS Books/Routledge.

Pawson, R, Boaz, A, Grayson, L, Long, A and Barnes, C (2003) *Types and quality of knowledge in social care. Knowledge Review 3.* London: SCIE.

Payne, M (1995) *Social work and community care.* Basingstoke: Palgrave Macmillan.

Payne, M (1997) *Modern social work theory.* Basingstoke: Macmillan.

Payne, M (2005) *Modern social work theory.* 3rd edition. Basingstoke: Palgrave Macmillan.

Perls, F, Hefferline, R and Goodman, P (1973) *Gestalt therapy: Excitement and growth in the human personality.* Harmondsworth: Penguin.

Pierson, J (2002) *Tackling social exclusion.* London: Routledge.

Pincus, A and Minahan, A (1973) *Social work practice. Model and method.* Itasca, IL: Peacock.

Pincus, L (1976) *Death and the family: The importance of mourning.* London: Faber.

Platt, D (2011) Assessments of children and families: Learning and teaching the skills of analysis. *Social Work Education,* 30, 2, 157–69.

Postle, K (2001) The social work side is disappearing. I guess it started with us being called care managers. *Practice,* 13, 1, 13–26.

Postle, K (2002) Working 'between the idea and the reality': Ambiguities and tensions in care managers' work. *British Journal of Social Work,* 32, 3, 335–52.

Preston-Shoot, M (2012) The secret curriculum. *Ethics and Social Welfare,* 6(1), 18–36.

Price, E (2011) Caring for mum and dad: Lesbian women negotiating family and navigating care. *British Journal of Social Work,* 41, 1288–1303.

Professional Social Work (2010) Major reduction in child deaths revealed. *Professional Social Work,* March, 6.

Puchalski, C (2006). Spiritual assessment in clinical practice. *Psychiatric Annals,* 36(3), 150–55.

Quality Assurance Agency (2008) *Social work 2008.* Mansfield: QAA.

Quinney, A (2006) *Collaborative social work practice.* Exeter: Learning Matters.

Quinney, A and Hafford-Letchfield, T (2013) *Collaborative social work practice.* 2nd edition. London: Learning Matters/Sage.

Rajan, A (2010) Review of 'The Big Society'. *Independent,* 21.11.10. Available at: www.independent.co.uk (accessed 13.1.14).

Ramon, S (2002) Mental wellbeing in the workplace. *Professional Social Work,* April, 14–15.

Rapoport, L (1970) Crisis intervention as a mode of brief treatment, in Roberts, RW and Nee, RH (eds) *Theories of social casework.* Chicago: Chicago University Press.

Reamer, G (1993) *The philosophical foundations of social work.* Columbia: Columbia University Press.

Reid, W (1978) *The task-centred system.* New York: Columbia University Press.

Reid, W and Epstein, L (1972) *Task-centred casework.* New York: Columbia University Press.

Reid, W and Shyne, A (1969) *Brief and extended casework.* New York: Columbia University Press.

Richmond, M (1917) *Social diagnosis.* New York: Russell Sage Foundation.

Roberts, AR (ed) (1991) *Contemporary perspectives on crisis intervention and prevention.* Englewood Cliffs, NJ: Prentice-Hall Inc.

Roberts, AR (ed) (1995) *Crisis intervention and time-limited cognitive treatment.* Thousand Oaks, CA: Sage.

Rogers, C (1951) *Client-centred therapy: Its current practice, implications and theory.* Boston: Houghton Mifflin.

Rogers, CR (1961) *On becoming a person: A therapist's view of psychotherapy.* London: Constable.

Ronen, T. (1994) Cognitive-behavioural social work with children, *British Journal of Social Work,* 24 (3): 273–85.

Royal Commission on Long Term Care (1999) *With respect to old age.* London: The Stationery Office.

Ruch, G. (2013) Understanding contemporary social work: We need to talk about relationships, in Parker, J and Doel, M (eds) *Professional Social Work.* London: Sage/Learning Matters.

Rzepnicki, T (2012) Task centered practice. Oxford Bibliographies. Available at: www.oxfordbibliographies.com/view/document/obo-9780195389678/obo-9780195389678-0150.xml (accessed 13.1.14).

Rzepnicki, T, McCracken, S and Briggs, H (eds) (2011) *From task-centered social work to evidence-based and integrative practice: Reflections on history and implementation.* Chicago: Lyceum Books Inc.

Saleebey, D (1996) The strengths perspective in social work practice: Extensions and cautions. *Social Work,* 41, 3, 296–305.

Schelly, D (2008) Problems associated with choice and quality of life for an individual with intellectual disability: A personal assistant's reflexive ethnography. *Disability and Society,* 23, 7, 719–32.

Schön, D (1987) *Educating the reflective practitioner.* San Francisco: Jossey-Bass.

SCIE (2010) *Fair access to care services (FACS) 2010 e-learning resource (text only).* Available at: www.scie.org.uk/assets/elearning/fairaccesstocareservices/facs01/resource/html/object/object1_1.htm (accessed 13.1.14).

SCIE (2011a) *Prevention in adult safeguarding. Adults' services report 41.* Available at: www.scie.org.uk/publications/reports/report41/files/report41.pdf (accessed 13.1.14).

SCIE (2011b) *Safeguarding adults at risk of harm: A legal guide for practitioners. Adults' services report 50.* Available at: www.elderabuse.org.uk/Documents/Other%20Orgs/A%20legal%20guide%20-%20mandelstam.pdf (accessed 13.1.14).

SCIE (2011c) *Mental Capacity Act resource.* Available at: www.scie.org.uk/publications/mca/about.asp (accessed 13.1.14).

Scottish Executive (2006) *Changing Lives: Report of the 21st century social work review.* Available at: www.scotland.gov.uk/Resource/Doc/91931/0021949.pdf (accessed 13.1.14).

Sheldon, B (1995) *Cognitive-behavioural therapy.* London: Routledge.

Sheldon, B and Macdonald, G (2009) *A textbook of social work.* London: Routledge.

Sheppard, M, Newstead, S, DiCaccavo, A and Ryan, K (2001) Comparative hypothesis assessment and quasi triangulation as process knowledge assessment strategies in social work practice. *British Journal of Social Work,* 31, 6, 863–85.

Smale, G and Tuson, G, with Biehal, N and Marsh, P (1993) *Empowerment, assessment, care management and the skilled worker.* London: NISW/HMSO.

Smale, G, Tuson, G and Statham, D (2000) *Social work and social problems: Working towards social inclusion and social change.* Basingstoke: Macmillan.

Smith, G and Cantley, C (1985) *Assessing health care.* Buckingham: Open University Press.

Social Services Inspectorate and Department of Health (1991a) *Care management and assessment: Practitioners' guide*. London: HMSO.

Social Services Inspectorate and Department of Health (1991b) *Care management and assessment: Managers' guide*. London: HMSO.

Social Work Task Force (2009) *Building a safe, confident future: The final report of the social work task force November 2009*. London: DCSF.

Spandler, H and Vicker, N (2005) Enabling access to direct payments: An exploration of care co-ordinators' decision-making practices. *Journal of Mental Health*, 14, 2, 145–55.

Sutton, C (1999) *Helping families with troubled children. A preventive approach*. Chichester: Wiley.

Thompson, N (2006) *Anti-discriminatory practice*. 4th edition. Basingstoke: Palgrave.

Thompson, N (2013) The emotionally competent professional, in Parker, J and Doel, M (eds) *Professional Social Work*. London: Sage/Learning Matters.

Trevithick, P (2005) *Social work skills: A practice handbook*. 2nd edition. Buckingham: Open University Press.

Trotter, C (2004) *Working with involuntary clients: A guide to practice*. London: Sage.

Turney, D, Platt, D, Selwyn, J and Farmer, E (2011) *Social work assessment of children in need: what do we know? Messages from research*. London: Department of Health.

Walton, RG (ed) (1986) Integrating formal and informal care – the utilisation of social support networks. *British Journal of Social Work*, 16 (supplement).

Ward, H (ed) (1995) *Looking after children: Research into practice*. London: HMSO.

Waterson, J (1999) Redefining community care social work: Needs or risks led? *Health and Social Care in the Community*, 7, 4, 276–79.

Watson, D and West, J (2006) *Social work process and practice: Approaches, knowledge and skills*. Basingstoke: Palgrave Macmillan.

Webb, S (2001) Some considerations on the validity of evidence-based practice in social work. *British Journal of Social Work*, 31, 1, 57–80.

Webb, SA (2006) *Social work in a risk society: Social and political perspectives*. Basingstoke: Palgrave Macmillan.

Webber, M and Robinson, K (2012) The meaningful involvement of service users and carers in advanced-level post-qualifying social work education: A qualitative study. *British Journal of Social Work*, 42, 7, 1256–74.

Whyte, S and Campbell, A (2008) The strengths and difficulties questionnaire: A useful screening tool to identify mental health strengths and needs in looked after children and inform care plans at looked after children reviews. *Child Care in Practice*, 14, 2, 193–206.

Williams, P and Evans, M (2013) *Social work with people with learning difficulties*. 3rd edition. London: Sage/Learning Matters.

Wilson, K, Ruch, G, Lymbery, M and Cooper, A (2008) *Social work: An introduction to contemporary practice*. Harlow: Pearson Education.

Wolfensberger, W (1972) *The principle of normalisation in human services*. Toronto: National Institute on Mental Retardation.

Wood, H (2011) *Assessing the feasibility of using an actuarial risk assessment tool to identify risks in child protection cases*. Unpublished PhD thesis. Bournemouth University, UK.

Yu, SWK and Tran, CTL (2011) The diversity based approach to culturally sensitive practices. *International Social Work*, 54, 1, 21–33.

Index

Added to the page number 'f' denotes a figure and 't' denotes a table.